PIMLICO

501

THE DREAMER OF THE
CALLE DE SAN SALVADOR

Roger   k-
teen ye   n
1992. H is   f
cultural a
include *Th*
of Geology
Revenge and De
Roger Osborne   es
based on *The Floating Egg* a   or of a
play based on *The Dreamer of the Calle de San Salvador*, broadcast on BBC radio.

THE DREAMER OF THE CALLE DE SAN SALVADOR

Visions of Sedition and Sacrilege in Sixteenth-Century Spain

ROGER OSBORNE

PIMLICO

Published by Pimlico 2002

2 4 6 8 10 9 7 5 3 1

Copyright © Roger Osborne 2001

Roger Osborne has asserted his right
under the Copyright, Designs and Patents Act 1988
to be identified as the author of this work

First published in Great Britain by Jonathan Cape 2001
Pimlico edition 2002

Pimlico
Random House, 20 Vauxhall Bridge Road,
London SW1V 2SA

Random House Australia (Pty) Limited
20 Alfred Street, Milsons Point, Sydney,
New South Wales 2061, Australia

Random House New Zealand Limited
18 Poland Road, Glenfield,
Auckland 10, New Zealand

Random House South Africa (Pty) Limited
Endulini, 5A Jubilee Road, Parktown 2193, South Africa

The Random House Group Limited Reg. No. 954009

A CIP catalogue record for this book
is available from the British Library

ISBN 0-7126-6497-1

Papers used by Random House Limited are natural,
recyclable products made from wood grown in sustainable forests.
The manufacturing processes conform to the environmental
regulations of the country of origin

Printed and bound in Great Britain by
Biddles Ltd, Guildford and Kings Lynn

Contents

In which Lucrecia dreams of a wagon drawn by buffaloes and carrying a great tower, of the wagon crushing the people beneath its wheels, of a person called the Ordinary Man, and of a palm for a new king.

And in which we learn of the identity of the dreamer, of her three dream-time companions, of a universal belief in the end of the world, and of the ways in which dreams might be understood rather than explained.

In which Lucrecia dreams of a man who brings justice to the world, of crows eating the heart of a lion, and of her own interpretation of her dream.

And in which we learn of the beginnings of the story of Lucrecia de Léon, of the preservation of her dreams, of Penelope's dream of Odysseus, of Doña Alda's dream of the death of Roldán and of Freud's youthful fascination with a Cervantes story which takes the form of a dream.

In which Lucrecia dreams of the sky coloured like blood, of a prophecy of the king's death, of a battle between crows and doves, and of a dark eagle that watches but does not fight.

And in which we learn of Lucrecia's parents and the growth of Madrid, of the ominous portents for the coming year, of John the Baptist and Christ, and of how God will visit the earth only to destroy it.

In which Lucrecia dreams of being taken to the highest tower in the world, of a terrifying climb down its outer walls, of the companions at the seashore and their explanation of her visions, of seeing Francis Drake in England, and of impending war.

And in which we learn of the temptation of Christ, of the story of Piedrola, the Soldier Prophet, of the Church's tolerance of doomsayers, of Lucrecia's desire to know the identity of her companions, of the execution of Mary Queen of Scots, of Elizabeth's delicate manoeuvrings, and of the embarkation of Drake from Plymouth bound for mischief on the Spanish coast.

warn the dying king, of a woman being stripped and stabbed by four men, of the same woman giving birth to a boy, and of how this boy, born of sin, is to reign in Castile.

And in which we learn of dreams within dreams, of Lucrecia's desire to warn the king, of her difficulties in appearing to remain naive and ignorant, of Philip's real, painful and ignominious death, of the Papacy in secular politics, and of the increasing power of princes.

In which Lucrecia dreams of Turkish armies in Constantinople, of the citizens of England preparing for war, of three crosses borne upon the sea, of a coffin containing the Duke of Alba, of Alba's evil deeds in Flanders, and of a basket of chickens with women's faces.

And in which we learn of revelation and apocalypse in Christian scripture and tradition, of Lucrecia's task as a prophet, of the seafarers of Genoa, of the tragic story of Prince Don Carlos, and of madness among the Habsburgs.

In which Lucrecia dreams of being told that death comes from the great tower, of a river of blood from the stables encircling the palace, of how God's terrible deeds should not be regretted, of the priests of Toledo fighting the besiegers of the city, and of how the evil that was prophesied is coming to pass.

And in which we learn of the problems of translating the dreamworld to the woken, of the oppression of Moors in Spain, of the theology of compassion, and of the preparation of Lucrecia for her role in the coming catastophe.

In which Lucrecia dreams of an army of Moors armed with arquebuses, of the king in agony, of how his bedhead becomes an artichoke which is being plucked secretly by his courtiers, and of the palace grounds turned into pastures.

And in which we learn of the chronic ill-health of the king, of the effect of health on governance, of the role of monarchs as governors and symbols, and of the disentailment of common lands which turned the poor against their king.

In which Lucrecia dreams of the treachery of Diego de Córdoba, of the poor complaining of losing their lands, of three men beating back a stream of blood at the gates of Toledo, of great armies of Turks, French and English, of a man in a damask garment being crowned king, and of a poetic ending.

And in which we learn of the economic revolution in sixteenth-century

Europe, of the destruction of prosperity by war, of the *desengaño* or disillusionment of the Spanish people, of Spain's economic wealth and woes, of dreams of a new David, and of the nature of endings.

The Mirror and the *Sopeña*

30 January 1588

In which Lucrecia dreams of looking into a mirror and seeing great armies, of being told that she is the mirror in which the people are to see themselves, of the cave or *Sopeña* where the band of Christians must hide, of Pastor Miguel leading an army out of the *Sopeña* to raise the siege of Toledo, and of being told of her own future.

And in which we learn of the legend of King Pelayo, of the rise of the Arab empire and the conquest of Spain, of the battle of Covadonga, of the conversion of the Moors, of the founding of the cult of Lucrecia, and of the promise of better things to come.

The Habsburgs and the Admiral

2 February 1588

In which Lucrecia dreams of those who are traitors in the Spanish court, of unknown books where the pages are uncut, of a palm tree with small dogs in its branches, of the end of Habsburg rule in Spain, of a plan to rescue Piedrola from prison, and of a prophecy of the death of the Marquis of Santa Cruz.

And in which we learn of messages revealed only on the Day of Judgment, of the reign of Philip and his father Charles, of the Habsburgs as usurpers in Spain, of the use of the dreams as encouragements to action, and of the life and death of Santa Cruz, Spain's greatest admiral, on the eve of the sailing of the Armada.

The Dragon and the Monastery

10 February 1588

In which Lucrecia dreams of a great dragon passing through the streets of Madrid, of some people being swept off to Heaven by the dragon's tail while others are crushed or drowned in stinking pools, of a monastery sinking into the ground, and of a warning to Don Alonso that he should keep his affairs secret.

And in which we learn of the beast in Revelations, of the Bible as the model for all books, of the question of endings, of the books known as the Apocrypha, of the prophet Esdras, and of the seductions of flattery.

The Duke of Parma

12 February 1588

In which Lucrecia dreams of being told that she must carry the cross into battle, of Drake hearing of the Armada, of the Duke of Parma's desire to inherit the throne of Spain, of a great fire roaring through Spain from Seville, and of how God will not renew the world more than three times and that this time will be the last.

And in which we learn of Santa Cruz's replacement as commander of the Armada, of the Farnese dynasty, of the briliant military exploits of the Duke of Parma, of the Spanish involvement in the Netherlands, and of the ways in which the world is renewed.

Arrest and Intimidation

In which Lucrecia dreams of being chastised by the Ordinary Man for her lack of courage, of being with the king with a naked sword in her hand, of two devils being beaten with their own shoes, of the king being stripped and fleeing to the besieged city, and of being told to go into hiding.

And in which we learn of Lucrecia's arrest and interrogation by the royal confessor, of threats made to her, of Mendoza securing her release, of her father saying that he will kill her, of the enhancement of her reputation, of her doubts about the identity of the Ordinary Man, of the difficulties of narrative development with which the dreams present us, and of the notion of imagination as a form-giving power.

'God Save Me, Who Calls My Name?'

In which Lucrecia dreams of a hooded figure entering her room, of being taken to a house that is the prison of the Inquisition, of the impostor denying that he is the Devil, of a prophet in armour on a white horse unmasking the Devil, and of the Devil's plots against her.

And in which we learn of the problems of identity, of creative confusion in the dreamworld, of Lucrecia's family and neighbourhood, of the triviality of the Devil's schemes, of the necessity of fearing God, and of the dilemma that will destroy Lucrecia.

The Vengeful Angels

In which Lucrecia dreams of being told to begin to retreat from the world, of the time when the people will come to honour her, of an angel descending from Heaven on to a hill-top, of the descent of 'the king's angel' who tells of the painful death of Philip, and of hearing of the words of God to St Peter.

And in which we learn of instructions from the dreamworld to Lucrecia's supporters, of the role of the Virgin Mary, of the assembling of fearsome creatures, of the embodiment of the sublime in terror, and of the recovery of a dream.

The Fishermen Come to Madrid

In which Lucrecia dreams of the Ordinary Man being John the Baptist, of the two companions leaving the seashore to come to her room, of a bunch of bulrushes turning from green to white, and of the two fishermen speaking in tongues.

And in which we learn of Lucrecia needing help and being suspicious of those who offer it, of her having doubts about the three companions, of the dispute between Philip and the people of Aragón, of Lucrecia's own feelings about her visions, and of a growing sense of intimidation and conflict.

The End of Mercy

7 March 1588

In which Lucrecia dreams of streets full of stone statues, of how the Armada must sail before April and of how it will fail, of three figures of Christ crucified that sweat blood, of the pope being stripped of his honours by his bishops, of lions and tigers emerging from caves to roam the earth, and of how the time is past when mercy could be shown to the world.

And in which we learn of Lucrecia's qualities as a narrator, of the progress and peculiar impossibility of the Armada and of the reasons for its failure, and of a fearsome and vengeful God.

Hours Not Months

16 March 1588

In which Lucrecia dreams of being told that catastrophe is imminent, of the king receiving news of ships from the Armada being lost, of an extraordinary conversation between Fray Lucas and the king, and of a bundle of papers that run with blood.

And in which we learn of Lucrecia's accurate predictions of the Armada's fate, of how the news of the Armada reached Spain, of her ability to move her ground, and of the strange and shifting relationship between the king and the Franciscan friar as God's judgment comes nearer.

Wine and Milk for the King

The first dream of 17 March 1588

In which Lucrecia dreams of a visit from a famous visionary, of telling her visitor to warn the king, of the king at a great banquet being given wine secretly mixed with milk, of him being drunk and awarding dukedoms to everyone there, of the arrival of the prophet, and of the Ordinary Man enraged because the visions are beyond his control.

And in which we learn of the Nun of Lisbon and her stigmata, of the torture of the flesh bringing spiritual cleansing, of how God brings trials to those who have the strength to bear them, and of Lucrecia's role as a successor to Piedrola.

The Walled Garden

The second dream of 17 March 1588

In which Lucrecia dreams of a meeting in the house of Pedro de Robles, of how these people have heard of her visions and are preparing for the conflict to come, of being in a walled garden with her mother, of being trapped in the garden, of escaping by a secret door, and of finding herself in a wide meadow by a river 'in level country'.

And in which we learn of Lucrecia taking control of her dreams, of whether she will be fighting for the king in the imminent conflict, of the hallucinatory quality of dreams, of how one scene melts into another, and of tiredness in the middle of sleep.

Lucrecia de Léon, the dreamer of these dreams, is such an enchanting subject and the ways of fiction-writers are so ingenious, that the reader may wonder whether she is a product of this author's imagination. But, although she fulfils many of the requirements of a fictional character, Lucrecia de Léon was a real person. It has not been necessary to invent Lucrecia or her dreams, simply to rediscover them.

Lucrecia de Léon was born in Madrid in 1568 and lived there until 1590. In 1587 her extraordinary dreams began to be recorded by two clergymen. On several days each week Lucrecia would sit and dictate her dreams of the previous night, while either one of these priests carefully wrote down everything that she said. This process went on for two and a half years during which more than four hundred of her dreams were transcribed. When Lucrecia was arrested by the Inquisition in May 1590 the transcripts were seized and placed in evidence at her trial. Thanks to Lucrecia's conflict with the authorities and the efficient bureaucracy of the Inquisition, these documents have been preserved and are still kept in the Archivo Histórico Nacional in Madrid.

I first came across some extracts from the dreams of Lucrecia de Léon in 1991. Immediately captivated by their strange beauty, I spent time over the next nine years reading the entire transcripts of many of the dreams and thinking about how they might be presented to a wider world. A book that simply contained translations of all of Lucrecia's dreams would be useful for specialist historians, but would be unlikely to be read by anyone else. I therefore decided to make a selection of complete dream transcripts from the hundreds that were available, and to provide some supporting information that would make the dreams more accessible to the reader.

This volume contains transcripts of thirty-five of Lucrecia's dreams, all from the first four months – the period from December 1587 to March 1588. I have chosen these particular dreams for three reasons. Firstly they contain all of the themes which recur throughout her dreams, and can therefore be fairly said to be representative.

The second reason is that these thirty-five dreams, although at first sight as full of diverse and chaotic imagery as any of the others, do reveal a progression. Within each dream there is a series of events, incidents and impressions, so that altogether the dreams contain a host of narratives. But taken as a whole these dreams also have an overarching story to tell. This is important because, as well as giving momentum to this work, this story is central to Lucrecia's view of the world. The third reason for selecting these particular dreams is that they are readily available in the original Castilian for those who wish to study them further (see Sources).

The commentaries that accompany each dream are not forays into dream interpretation but are an attempt to understand both the dreams themselves and the ways in which Lucrecia allowed her dreams to convey her sense of the world around her. Through the commentaries and dreams we look at the world through the eyes of Lucrecia de Léon. This gives the book an unusual structure and leads to an apparently fractured and disoriented picture of Lucrecia's world. Although the dreams are arranged in chronological order, Lucrecia did not neatly envision the world in any particular order. Her dreams and her mind looked at the world in a radically disordered, yet entirely normal way. Instead of seeing this seemingly chaotic diversity as a problem, I have taken it as the fundamental driving force and philosophical underpinning of this book. It has often been said that we surrendered our belief in myth and tradition only to substitute an overwhelming regard for linear history and historical continuity. When we look at the past we inevitably impose a sense of order on what we see but our desire to bring meaning readily slips into a tendency to delineate and conform. By presenting a selection of Lucrecia de Léon's dream transcripts in their entirety and by using the content of those dreams as a route into this particular piece of history, I hope I have done something to resist the perils of refinement and to preserve the exuberance and variety and vitality of the past.

Roger Osborne, Scarborough, 2001

THE DREAMER OF
THE CALLE DE SAN SALVADOR

On the first of December of the said year [1] the Ordinary Man [2] came to me. [3] He called me to the window and told me to look out into the street. I heard a great noise and asked him, 'What is this noise?' He answered, 'Soon you will see.'

Then I saw, coming from the east, a wagon drawn by two buffaloes (this is what he told me they were), and on the wagon there was a tower. By the side of the tower lay a dead lion, and on the top a dead eagle with its breast cut open exposing its heart. [4]

The wheels of the wagon were soaked in blood and as it went it crushed many people beneath its wheels. Many men and women, by their habit and dress Spanish, held on to the wagon and cried out the end of the world. [5]

I asked the Ordinary Man, 'What vision is this that I see?' and he said, 'I am unable to say' (though seemed as though he wished to tell me).

At that moment the Old Man, the fisherman, appeared. [6]

I asked, 'Why have you left the seashore and come here?'

He replied that he had come because the Ordinary Man wanted to explain the vision, but that this should not be done until the third night.

I saw that the Old Man carried in his hands a palm leaf. I asked him who it was for and he said, 'For the new king who will be so pleasing to God that it will be fitting to give him this palm. [7] For now I can say no more.'

And then I awoke.

1. *the said year.* The year is 1587. Madrid, the city where these dreams are dreamed, is the centre of the world. A barren land on the half-forgotten edge of Europe has risen in a hundred years to become its greatest power. The fulcrum has moved west. The Mediterranean is ceding its role at the centre of western civilisation and power. Spain, sitting between the old Mediterranean and the new Atlantic, her king inheritor of half the world, her galleons fetching silver and gold from Peru and Yucatán, is drawing power to itself. Spain has been bent on conquest and adventure and is beginning to excel in philosophy, painting, drama, architecture and new forms of literature. This is *El Siglo de Oro*, the Golden Age of Spain. But at its greatest hour, when its citizens should sleep soundly in their beds, safe from the violence, rebellion and anarchy that floods and ebbs across the rest of the continent, one inhabitant of Madrid meets only paranoia and foreboding in her nights.

2. *the Ordinary Man.* The constant companion of this dreamer. It is the Ordinary Man who shows her the things that he or some others wish her to see, who takes her to the places where it is necessary that she goes and who sometimes is moved or persuaded to explain to her the meaning of the things that she sees. Who is the Ordinary Man? He has, it seems, some other identity which is hinted at but not made explicit. He himself is, as we shall see, reluctant to reveal his identity to the woman who dreams of him. We assume that she calls him the Ordinary Man (*el Hombre Ordinario*) in order to contrast him with the other unnamed figures in the dreams.

3. *me.* Lucrecia de Léon – dreamer, visionary, prophet, subversive, agent of sedition, voice of God? Whatever; dreamer.

   Lucrecia; nineteen years old, unmarried, unlettered, still living with her parents and sisters and brothers, her curious night-life full of wonder and terror.

   Each morning for the past twenty days a high-ranking Franciscan cleric has made his way through the streets of the parish of San Sebastian to the small house on the Calle San Salvador. Lucrecia has told him of her dreams, which he has carefully noted down. Fray Lucas de Allende, prior of the Franciscan convent in Madrid, has been persuaded by his friend Don Alonso de Mendoza, a canon of the Cathedral of Toledo, first to become Lucrecia's confessor and then to undertake the

2

task of transcribing her dreams. Watch these clerics. They are drawn to Lucrecia by her dreams, which they believe to be of divine inspiration, but other things must follow from this.

Fray Lucas de Allende and Don Alonso de Mendoza believe in Lucrecia's dreams. But if their spiritual interest is pure, the uses to which they put the dreams are not. The two men believe that, if God has sent these dreams, they are not simply for the girl's wonder and diversion. They must be for some greater purpose.

4. *By the side of the tower lay a dead lion, and on the top a dead eagle with its breast cut open exposing its heart.* The explanation of the symbolic elements being transported into Lucrecia's mind on the back of the buffalo wagon is to be given on the fourth night of this vision. But there is something odd going on here. The Ordinary Man shows Lucrecia a vision and then she asks him for an explanation of what she is being shown. But if the meanings of the visions are to be explained, why is she not simply told the meanings directly? Why is it necessary for her to see the visions at all? Could she not just be visited by an Ordinary Man who tells her what he wishes her to know?

One answer is that, if the visions come from God, then the Ordinary Man has little choice in the matter. He is showing Lucrecia what she must be shown, and is then somehow permitted to help her to understand it. But this begs the question of why God traditionally and habitually reveals His will through visions and interpretations. We know that it is God's nature not to speak directly to His prophets but that tradition does not of itself offer us a reason.

The reason probably lies before us. Lucrecia's visions are infinitely richer and more resonant than the symbolic interpretations which are sometimes given by her dream companions. Her dreams are a demonstration of the value of experience over instruction. She is shown these things in order to be brought to an understanding that will be more profound than the information they provide.

5. *the end of the world.* For hundreds of years all Christians knew that the end of the world was imminent. Lucrecia's task was not to declare the destruction of the earth but to describe how it would happen.

6. *At that moment the Old Man, the fisherman, appeared.* Another of Lucrecia's three frequent companions. Lucrecia calls him a fisherman because

she almost always meets him at the seashore. Here he has come to restrain the Ordinary Man and there is little doubt that he is in a superior position. The characters of the companions are consistent throughout Lucrecia's dreams and the shifting relations between the four of them comprise a drama of considerable sophistication.

7. *I saw that the Old Man carried in his hands a palm leaf. I asked him who it was for and he said 'For the new king who will be so pleasing to God that it will be fitting to give him this palm.'* Is the 'new king' to be a secular replacement for King Philip or a new Messiah? Any new king would have to await the death of Philip. The death of the monarch is one of the central elements of Lucrecia's visions* since Philip is an inconvenient barrier to the coming together of the earthly and the divine. And if the new king of Lucrecia's dream is to be pleasing to God we may take it that the present one is not. Here lies Lucrecia's potency and her danger.

---

* The word 'vision' is generally used, in religious experience, to mean a holy supernatural image seen by a woken person, as opposed to a dream. I am using it in a different sense, to mean an image seen by Lucrecia within a dream.

On the 2nd of December I[1] saw the same vision as the previous night, though this time I also saw a man with an unsheathed sword in his hand. He rode with one foot on each buffalo and wore a red tunic with blue skirts. Seeing the Ordinary Man he said, 'Justice will make it right.' Then a flock of carrion crows flew down on to the wagon and began to eat the heart of the lion.[2]

The Ordinary Man said to me, 'Tell me what you think of this.'[3]

I said that I am an ignorant person with little understanding of such things. Nevertheless he insisted that I speak.

So I said, 'If the eagle was the king, then once he is dead the infidels and heretics will come and take from him the best of what he had.'

Without answering me so much as a word, he made the sign of the cross and said, 'My companion has gone because they have the nets on the sea, and I must go too.'

And then I awoke.

1. I. Lucrecia's dreams exist in a way that yours and mine never will. And Lucrecia exists now only because her dreams exist. Dukes, princes, bishops, ambassadors and generals have written their impressions of their times and much of our history has been founded on these accounts. Lucrecia is not the first 'ordinary' person to have spoken and been recorded but she is unique in having so much of the content of her mind preserved.

In September 1587, Lucrecia came to the attention of the unsurpassably well connected Don Alonso de Mendoza. Scion of the most powerful family in Spain outside the Habsburg monarchy, he was also brother to the great Bernadino de Mendoza, ambassador to England and then France. Don Alonso was a clever and determined man and was well set for a good career in the Church and an influential role in the life of his country. But something in his cast of mind disqualified him from high office (it was later testified that he had once walked in the streets dressed in secular clothes and white shoes, and had precipitated an unfortunate affair by shouting inside the Cathedral at Toledo; another witness said that Mendoza 'does not have all his senses'). He was overlooked, and this turned him against those with power in the Church and court and against their master the king. Despite his disaffection, Alonso de Mendoza remained powerful at one remove and utterly confident in his abilities. When it came to it, he would look the officials of the Inquisition in the face and, instead of repenting, tell them they were wrong.

Lucrecia's dreams were recorded because Mendoza transcribed them and then, when he returned to his duties in Toledo, persuaded Fray Lucas de Allende to continue this work. The eventual arrest of these three placed the transcripts in the possession of the Inquisition, which further extended Lucrecia's existence. She was rediscovered in passing in 1890 by Henry Lea and again in 1903 by Manuel Serrano y Sanz. In 1947 she surfaced again and this time Beltrán de Heredia told the world exactly where Lucrecia was buried – the all-important numbers of the *legajos* or bundles in which Lucrecia's dreams are held among the many thousands of such files within the Archivo Histórico Nacional, Sección de Inquisición in Madrid. The bundles containing transcripts of Lucrecia's dreams have been investigated by Spanish and American scholars in the last two decades. Should Lucrecia ever disappear again, our successors will know where to find her. She has now, by some momentum of interest, been changed from documented fact to a part of history.

2. *Then a flock of carrion crows flew down on to the wagon and began to eat the heart of the lion.* An indication that Lucrecia's dreams owe something to those who dreamed before her and evidence perhaps of her knowledge of classical, Spanish and biblical dreamers. Lucrecia was to plead her innocence as an ignorant illiterate, but she either dreamed as others because she knew of their dreams, or because dreaming in this way is a shared human experience. Birds are commonly used in classical and traditional dream stories to embody particular human

qualities. One of the great medieval Spanish romances retells the story of the French poetic ballad the *Chanson de Roland*, in which Roland ('Roldán' in Spanish) is killed in the Pyrenean pass of Roncevaux while returning from fighting the Moors of Spain. These legends were part of the oral culture of Europe, available to the illiterate and the scholar. The story of 'The Dream of Doña Alda' was widely known throughout Spain in Lucrecia's time.

> In Paris lives Doña Alda,
> the wife of Don Roldán,
> three hundred ladies with her to keep her company . . .
> At the sound of their soft music
> Doña Alda has drifted asleep;

Doña Alda wakes in terror and tells her dream to her attendants. In a bleak and deserted woodland she saw a hawk fly down from the mountains pursued by an eagle. The hawk sought refuge beneath Doña Alda's dress but the eagle drew the hawk out and tore it to pieces with its claws and beak. Doña Alda's lady-in-waiting told her that the dream was easy to explain:

> 'The hawk is your very husband,
> returning now from Spain:
> you then are the eagle
> who will wed him presently,
> and the woodland is the church
> where you'll don the wedding veil.'
> But the next day in the morning
> letters arrived from afar,
> darkly stained on the outside,
> within written in blood,
> that her Roldán had perished
> in the battle of Roncevaux.
> (quoted in Palley, 1983)

What can be understood can also be misunderstood. The interpretation given by Doña Alda's companion turns out to be wrong. What though did it matter? The dream was not intended as a warning on which Doña Alda could act – she could not possibly have had any influence over the battle at Roncevaux. What, then, is the dream for? We are often given to believe that, in these mythic responses to the world, dreams are merely convenient plot devices. Doña Alda's dream shows they are more subtle and complex. The dream and its false interpretation has the effect of doubling Doña Alda's grief, it disorients her by playing with her own trust in her feelings, it teases her and makes her grief and our pity for her more attenuated, more poignant, more poetic. Legends are normally regarded as being utterly predictable in outcome but here we see the presence of that essential element of the art of fiction – provoked and confounded expectation.

'Dreams,' as Penelope, wife of Odysseus and another woman who dreamed of birds, rightly says, 'are awkward and confusing things.'

But why should they be clear; and why should they be helpful? To be a dreamer is to place yourself in a game whose rules you do not control and may not understand.

3. *The Ordinary Man said to me, 'Tell me what you think of this.'* Having asked Lucrecia what she thought of the vision that he showed her, the Ordinary Man might have responded to her interpretation. She is clearly a little put out when he later turns away 'without . . . so much as a word'.

The Ordinary Man came and said, 'Arise for there is more to see this night.' Looking out of the window[1] I saw the sky coloured like blood. I asked him how this had happened and he said, 'In the year in which your king will die, the moon will be eclipsed on three successive nights[2] and within the fortnight following, there will be a comet of the colour of blood with a white tail. As this star fades your king will die.'

I asked him, 'How shall I know that I can truly believe that this will be so?'

He answered, 'Do you wish me to give you a sign such as the angel gave to the father of John the Baptist?[3] I will clarify the meaning of the star another night.'

Just then the buffalo wagon appeared again, and the Ordinary Man said, 'Now it is time for the battle to commence.'

I saw rising on the southerly wind a vast cloud of crows and rooks. With them there was a dark eagle which wrenched from the dead eagle the greater part of the world which it held in its talons. The crows and rooks plunged towards the dead eagle on the wagon and began tearing at its heart. Then from the west came great flights of doves, white and speckled, to defend the dead eagle. The Ordinary Man, raising his eyes to Heaven, said, 'Lord God, may it serve your will that these buffaloes depart with this wagon before the crows devour the eagle; for you spare us no corner of what you have promised us.'

The buffaloes started to draw the cart away, and the final battle between the crows and the doves began. During the battle the crows killed all of the doves while the dark eagle remained on a nearby roof. Then the crows, the rooks and the dark eagle flew away to the north leaving all the dead behind.

*I said to the Ordinary Man, 'Explain this to me, for this is
the third night.'*

*But he would not and said that the Old Fisherman must do
so.*

*The Old Man came but said, 'You are weary so I will not
explain the dream. But tomorrow night I shall, for believe, we
are men who will tell you the truth.'*

And I awoke.

1. *Looking out of the window.* Lucrecia often began her dreams by being taken
to the window of her room to look into the street below or across the
city. She lived in the heart of Madrid, within a short walk of the royal
palace. She had even worked in the royal household for a time.
Although nineteen years old when her dreams began to be transcribed,
Lucrecia de Léon was unmarried – in sixteenth-century Spain this was
unusual – and lived with her parents, three sisters and one brother in
a modest house rented from the estate of the Duchess of Feria. Her
father, Alonso Franco de Léon, was a solicitor working in and around
the royal court. His main client was the Genoese banking community
in Madrid, a group of men whose loans were vital to the prosecution
of King Philip's policies and who were not always well served in return.
Alonso Franco came from Valdepeñas in La Mancha, a town famous
for its wine.

Lucrecia's mother, Ana Ordoñez, was from northern Spain. The de
Léons were living in Madrid when Lucrecia was born in 1568. This
was only seven years after the establishment of the royal court at
Madrid, an event which turned the small town into the capital of an
empire and began a rapid expansion in its population – from 15,000
in the year 1500 to 80,000 in 1600. King Philip's choice of Madrid as
the site of his court was criticised by his father Charles: 'If you desire
to expand your kingdom, move the court to Lisbon; if you wish your
kingdom to remain as it is, stay at Valladolid. But if your desire is to
destroy it, take your court to Madrid.'

This was not simply a personal prejudice on the part of the old
emperor; the move to Madrid was, Hugh Thomas writes, 'a fateful

THE SKY OF BLOOD

choice, which has for ever after affected, and severely weakened, Spain, and perhaps, through example, the entire Spanish world.' The reason was simple enough:

> For Madrid, unlike other capitals of Renaissance Europe such as London and Paris, or Vienna and Amsterdam, had no navigable river. All goods, therefore, had to be carried to it by land, mostly by mule, at great expense . . . Heart of the country though it was geographically, heart too of an empire which stretched from Peru to the Philippines, Madrid bred a population ignorant of business . . . In the sixteenth century, the only people to know anything of commerce in Madrid were the Genoese banker friends of the soon-to-be-ruined royal favourite Antonio Pérez. (Thomas, 1988)

Philip may have chosen Madrid because the more significant towns of Castile had joined the *communeros* rebellion against his father. If so, this act of revenge may have cost his country dear. Nevertheless, Madrid flourished in its infancy and Lucrecia's family was there in its midst, living the story of its growing glory; her window looked on to the streets of the centre of the world's empire – the city of the court of the Spanish king.

Philip installed himself in an old Arab *alcazár* or fortress on a plateau above the small Manzanares River. The building was refurbished as a royal palace so that the old mud walls butted up to the stone and marble of the new court-cum-residence. A continual procession of visitors, supplicants, civil servants, soldiers and officials passed through the main gate from the city into a series of courtyards. Around the courtyards were the offices and meeting rooms of the various councils of government – the Council of Castile, the Council of the Indies, the Council of Finance and so on – while in the plazas great crowds milled about, arranging meetings, delivering messages, awaiting commissions, requesting favours, picking up gossip, pushing a cause, hoping for a word, or simply being seen. The centre of each rectangle buzzed with activity while in the cool side-rooms the policies of half the world were reckoned.

Above the council chambers were the royal apartments. Some rooms were public, at least to the members of the court and esteemed visitors, while others were the residences of the royal household. There was a multitude of rooms in the palace, as Marcelin Desfourneaux (1970) describes:

Some were huge and well lit, others small and dark; they were all connected by narrow corridors and staircases. The public salons were covered with magnificent Flemish tapestries and graced with admirable paintings.

The etiquette at court was extremely strict and inflexible – an inheritance of the Burgundian court of Philip's father – and the bureaucracy notoriously tortuous. It was said by more than one courtier that if he had to wait for news of his own death from the Alcazár he would live for ever.

Desfourneaux mentions the *mentidores* – literally 'lie parlours' – where people gathered to exchange news and gossip and intrigue. Some of these were inside the Alcazár itself and were known as the 'flagstones of the palace'. Here groups of courtiers tried to garner the innermost secrets of the councils, waylaying couriers and advisers and trading political tit-bits with anyone and everyone. The maze of rooms, corridors and courtyards, the rigid codes of behaviour, the slowly grinding officialdom, the hissing of gossip, evoke an atmosphere riddled with favours and frustration. It was the most powerful court in the world and the most difficult to know.

Outside the palace the courtiers and nobles built their grand houses. Philip had decided on Madrid in 1561, so Lucrecia must have seen many of the mansions of the royal quarter being put up. The Calle Major and the other main streets fanning out from the palace were lined with impressive houses. Further to the east wealthy families escaped the dirt of the city by building alongside the Prado, an area of open gardens and promenades.

Between these grand houses and the great churches and monasteries the narrow streets and small houses of the old city crowded in. This was not the most pleasant place to live. The lack of any sewerage system was aggravated by the absence of a great river to wash away the city's effluent. The stench in the streets was remarked on by visitors and would have been worse but for the unusually fresh air of this elevated plateau. A clean and abundant supply of water to the city, devised by the Arabs, helped to make life tolerable. Life was by no means unremittingly grim for the poorer citizens of Madrid but city life brought dangers of disease as well as work, excitement and the prospect of making money.

The street where the de Léon family lived was to the east of the Plaza Major, off the Calle de Atocha. The parish of San Sebastian was a hive of small streets built after the arrival of the court, its inhabitants generally middle class rather than poor. In the late sixteenth century both Cervantes and Lope de Vega lived in the neighbourhood.

The de Léons' dwelling was the ground floor of a house. It was a relatively spacious apartment with a large living room and several bedrooms. Most Castilian houses had no dining room; food was served on small tables in the main room. The Arab influence on Spanish life showed in the etiquette for mealtimes – the men sat on chairs to eat while the women squatted on cushions on the floor. Richard Kagan (1990) writes, 'Of the apartment's several bedrooms one was reserved for Lucrecia, at least when she was ill. The window in this bedroom afforded a glimpse of passersby in the street of San Salvador as well as those on the Calle de Atocha.'

The streets were the meeting place of the inhabitants of Madrid. Desfourneaux (1970) writes: 'The most celebrated of all these meeting places was, however, on the steps of the church of San Felipe el Real which was at the top of the Calle Mayor near the post office. The habitués gathered together at the end of the morning to hear the latest news from each other . . . Liñan y Verdugo remarks: "They are informed about the intentions of the Grand Turk, revolutions in the Netherlands, the state of things in Italy, and the latest discoveries made in the Indies."'

From a small city Madrid grew rapidly at the centre of a world-wide web. Having no other importance, the city was the court and the court the city. Lucrecia grew up in it and with it. Her mind reflected its gossip, its self-importance, its excitement and its international outlook.

2. *'In the year in which your king will die, the moon will be eclipsed on three successive nights . . .'* There were to be two eclipses of the moon in 1588. Notice of these appeared in almanacs published throughout Europe and it is likely that Lucrecia or her transcribers knew about them. If so, her dream was forecasting Philip's death within twelve months. Moreover the year 1588 was forecast to be an apocalyptic year in the Christian world.

3. *'Do you wish me to give you a sign such as the angel gave to the father of John the Baptist?'*

And Zacharias said unto the angel, Whereby shall I know this? for I am an old man and my wife well stricken in years. And the angel answering said unto him, I am Gabriel, that stand in the presence of God; and am sent to speak unto thee, and to show thee these glad tidings. And, behold, thou shalt be dumb, and not able to speak, until the day that these things shall be performed, because thou believest not my words, which shall be fulfilled in their season. And the people waited for Zacharias, and marvelled that he tarried so long in the temple. And when he came out, he could not speak unto them: and they perceived that he had seen a vision in the temple: for he beckoned unto them, and remained speechless. (Luke 1: 18–22)

This mention of the striking dumb of Zacharias is an intemperate threat to Lucrecia, who was, after all, only trying to understand. But here is the first mention of John the Baptist – the figure that the Ordinary Man was believed, by Lucrecia, Mendoza and others, to represent. By invoking John the Baptist Lucrecia is entering the entanglement of prophecies that binds the Judaeo-Christian world. If Lucrecia is a conduit for messages from God about the future, then her position is strengthened by association with such an important prophetic figure, in the same way that John was given credence and stature by his embodiment of previous prophecies.

In the Christian Scriptures, as John was sent to tell of the coming of the Christ, so he was foretold in his turn by the prophets Isaiah and Malachi. And now he is seen by Lucrecia in her visions of the future. The Old Testament prophets spoke of the coming of John the Baptist and the Christ but the world and the Christian religion do not come to an end with the departure of Christ from the earth. In order for the sense of prophecy and fulfilment to be continued the Scriptures need to say something about what will happen after the ascenscion of Christ into Heaven. Christ, being the Son of God, does not prophesy but informs. He comes to tell humanity that there will be a terrible Day of Judgment.

Every prophet, visionary and dreamer who comes after Christ can only speak, as Lucrecia does, of how Christ's vision will come to pass, and when; and who will be saved, and who condemned.

John the Baptist was, we are told, sent to bear witness of the true Light. And though he told of Christ, he was a 'preparer' more than a prophet. He was not allegorical or philosophical, but direct and robust. John the Baptist is introduced to us by passages of unparalleled power and grace:

There was a man sent from God, whose name was John. The same came for a witness, to bear witness of the Light, that all men through him might believe. (John 1: 6–7)

Yet he is not a graceful man. This man in his 'raiment of camel's hair and a leathern girdle about his loins', whose meat is locusts and wild honey, is angry and unforgiving. He is that voice crying in the wilderness, and the people come to hear what he has to say. He calls the Pharisees 'a generation of vipers', and sees through their requests for baptism. Though he cannot refuse them, he says that 'he that cometh after me' will baptise them with fire. And in case this is not clear, he tells them that the wheat will be gathered in and the chaff will be burned up with unquenchable fire. His anger at the hypocrisy of the world is evident. Then the people ask him 'What shall we do?' and we learn that John is radical as well as unforgiving. He answers, 'He that hath two coats, let him impart to him that hath none; and he that hath meat, let him do likewise.' John's vision of the Kingdom of Heaven may be the same as that of Jesus, but John is more explicit. He says those things which Jesus does not quite say, or at least says them differently.

Then Jesus is baptised by John and at this most exquisite moment of spiritual history the heavens open and Jesus sees the Spirit of God descending like a dove – a meek, harmless, pure and lowly creature, symbolic of the vast and sudden change which is taking place beside a watering place in the desert of Judaea (why, otherwise, was the Spirit of God not represented by a whirlwind or a flood or an avenging angel?). John continues to rant against the Pharisees and is thrown into prison by Herod. John, we are to understand, is the end of this line of prophets (a line that might have gone on indefinitely were it not for the need for the arrival of the Messiah). He is the last of the old, the final flash of anger of the God of the Hebrews, before the forgiving light of the Son arrives. John is constantly brought forth by Lucrecia because she is not in forgiving vein. She has seen the Pharisees and seeks, and therefore foretells, their eternal damnation.

John is the inheritor of the tablets of stone, and their 'Thou shalt not' commandments. But he is the precise point where the old proscriptions give way to a new succour and inspiration. John remains full of warnings and vengeance, Jesus of promise and forgiveness. Even to the last, it seems that the great prophets may not really have understood the nature of the Messiah that was to come. Perhaps it would be surprising if they had – such an alteration in the mind of humanity cannot surely be foreseen.

This change is confirmed in the events that immediately follow the baptism of Jesus. As John lies raging in the heat and dirt and squalor of a Judaean prison, Jesus flees northwards to Galilee, most remote of the four provinces controlled by Herod. After attracting multitudes by his preaching, he goes up into a mountain and teaches his disciples the new Word of God. This is the Sermon on the Mount in which the poor, the meek, the persecuted, the reviled, the salt of the earth are blessed. This astonishing exposition of moral grace unites at a stroke the inheritance of Socrates with the God of David. John remains in prison, unheard and apparently unlamented, calling down vengeance on those who have sinned; while his cousin Jesus spreads the Word – we are all sinners, and we may all be forgiven.

For Lucrecia, though her Christianity oscillates between the old and the new, this night there is no Light. It is the God of Isaiah and Job and Moses that she requires, and John is the man who will prepare the way. As for her prophecies, Lucrecia carries within her the universal desire to see her God on earth. But God will only come to earth in order to destroy and rebuild it.

The Ordinary Man took me by the hand and carried me on high towards the east, where he sat me upon a tower. 'You are upon the highest tower in all the world – now look for there is much that you should see.'

I looked and saw all the lands of the earth laid out below[1] with many rivers flowing in all directions. While I gazed out from the tower, the Ordinary Man descended and called out to me from far below on the ground saying, 'Now find the place where you are to climb down.'

I said, 'There is no way for me to come down; I will stay here and warm my face in the rising sun.'

But he said I must descend. So I lifted myself over the parapet and began to climb down the vertical walls, clinging with my hands to the slippery stones. But half-way down I could see that the walls sheared away inwards so that there was nothing but a vast emptiness below me.[2] I called out to the Ordinary Man that from here I would plummet straight to the ground.

But then a man in a mask and black clothes, with shackles on his feet and chains around him, appeared next to me on the wall of the tower. He reached over and took my hand and helped me down and placed me on the ground beside the Ordinary Man.

I said to the man in shackles and chains, 'Are you Piedrola?'[3]

He replied, 'Take care to whom you tell your dreams and visions, for look what has become of me.'

Then the Ordinary Man took me to the seashore and there I saw the two fishermen.[4]

I said to the Old Man, 'Tell me what the buffalo wagon is that I have seen these past nights.'

Grasping his beard in his hands he said, 'The buffaloes signify life and the wagon, death.[5] *The wheels of blood are the many just people of no fault who are nevertheless dead because of your king. Those who hold on to the cart, crying so loudly, are the king's evil counsellors. When he dies there will come a judge so just and severe that he will cause them to follow the king into death. The crows and rooks are the heretics and infidels who, when they see the king dead will take from him what little he may have.*

'I will not tell you who is the dark eagle who came with them so that it may not be said, "How is it that a man who is now worth so little is to become so powerful?" The lion and the castle which were borne upon the wagon are the arms of the king, which the dark eagle will scornfully take to give to his people.'

Having finished telling me this the Old Man spoke again: 'Would you like to go to England?'

I said I should be glad to but, 'Before I go, tell me who you are.'[6]

He said, 'Who are the fishermen brothers that Don Alonso told you about?'

I said these were St James and St John.

Then he asked, 'Are there any other brothers who are fishermen?' and I answered, 'St Andrew and St Peter.'[7]

The men laughed and repeated these names and the Old Man told the Ordinary Man to take me away to England.

When we came to England we went to a house and into a room where Sir Francis Drake,[8] *dressed in crimson damask lined with sable, was writing at a desk of silver. A gentleman entered, to whom Drake gave a chair, and said 'I am writing to the Great Turk.'*

Then this man read out the letter, in which he said that war in Poland was imminent, and that the king of Spain was sending help to his nephew Maximilian. Drake himself undertook to send aid to the Turk. As he sealed the envelope containing the letter Drake said to the gentleman, 'If the Turk gains Poland, we have Spain in our hands.'[9]

Then the Ordinary Man took me home, and I awoke with a great thirst.

1. *I saw all the lands of the earth laid out below.* 'Again, the devil taketh him up into an exceeding high mountain, and sheweth him all the kingdoms of the world, and the glory of them; and saith unto him, All these things will I give thee, if thou wilt fall down and worship me' (Matthew 4: 8–9).

2. *there was nothing but a vast emptiness below me.* Remember that this is the highest tower in the world. Lucrecia is suspended far above the ground, clinging to the slippery stones with no way of either ascending or descending safely. It is a terrifying situation. Some dreamers, finding themselves in such an extreme position, decide to escape from the dream world by letting go and allowing themselves to fall, in the knowledge that they will then wake up – a risk that can only be taken from inside the dream but which requires knowledge of a waking state beyond it. Lucrecia rarely steps outside her dreams in this way, and was, in this instance, condemned to live out the story which her mind has brought forth. In this dream Lucrecia begins to be an active part of the story rather than simply a passive observer.

   The mention of falling in dreams makes us think, inevitably, of Freud's work on dream interpretation. Recent works on dreams in Spanish literature have, in spite of their numerous virtues, found it impossible to escape Freud's influence. His requirement that every mental phenomenon should have an explanation led him into a 'this means this' formulation that modern psychologists have wisely circumnavigated. In the context of Lucrecia, there is an interesting suggestion that the weighing of debts between Spanish dreamers and Dr Freud should tip the other way. Julian Palley in his 1983 book *The Ambiguous Mirror: Dreams in Spanish Literature*, relates a connection between Freud and Spain investigated earlier by S. B. Vranich (1976):

Freud himself, in a curious manner, may have been influenced by the author of *Don Quijote* in the choice of his future vocation. Freud taught himself Spanish when he was in school and was fascinated by Cervantes' 'Colloquy of the Dogs', Cipión and Berganza; in correspondence with a school friend, he referred to himself as 'Don Cipión' and to his friend as 'Don Berganza'. In Cervantes' picaresque novel, Cipión plays the role of the listener and Berganza that of the narrator of his life history. It has been speculated, no doubt apocryphally, that Freud conceived of the doctor–patient relationship in psychoanalysis (the physician who asks probing questions, the patient who recounts, through free association, the details of his life) from Cervantes' tale, which, incidentally, takes the form of a dream.

3. '*Are you Piedrola?*' In 1587 a certain Dr Guillén, a representative in the Cortes (the secular parliament of Spain) wrote that 'One of the most important issues facing the kingdom is to determine whether Piedrola is a prophet.'

Miguel de Piedrola Beamonte is a decisive element in Lucrecia's story because, it seems, Lucrecia's role was initially that of a kind of substitute for the man known as the 'Soldier-Prophet'. In a stark demonstration of the different loci of power in Counter-Reformation Spain, at the exact time that the Cortes was debating Piedrola's status, he was arrested by the Inquisition and removed to their prison in Toledo. But how had this man become of such great concern to the Spanish political world?

Piedrola first came to Madrid in 1570 after soldiering for the king in Italy. Men calling themselves prophets shouted their assertions from every street corner of Catholic southern Europe. A few even went so far as to write memorials to King Philip, suggesting that he change his conduct and prevent the disasters that they unanimously foresaw. Piedrola did all this and more. Writing to the king on how to make a peaceful end to the war in the Netherlands, he suggested that the king's children would die if he did not follow this advice. Piedrola proclaimed in the streets the source of his prophetic information – it was God who spoke to him. He was Elijah, he was the connection between the Lord and His people. But lost in the babble of voices he was ignored – as a prophet and as a danger to the king.

By 1579 the tone of Piedrola's prophecies had become strong enough to attract attention and he was advised to leave Madrid. Five years later he was back. He was now notorious as the illiterate soldier-prophet who had memorised the Bible with divine assistance (how else could it have been done? but then how had an illiterate written to the king?) and as a true prophetic visionary. Piedrola was from the province and ancient kingdom of Navarre and advocated a new constitutional monarchy of the kind that some in Navarre had fought for. He predicted the destruction of Spain and urged his followers to emulate the legendary heroes of old Spain by hiding out in caves before emerging to re-conquer the kingdom.

By the summer of 1587 he had become famous enough for a strange possibility to be considered – that Spain should have an official national prophet and that Piedrola should be the first holder of this post. The idea reached, as we have seen, the floor of the Cortes. How did this degree of importance accrue to such a man?

Piedrola was a relentless and determined promoter of his own cause (unlike Lucrecia who was promoted by others). But the political situation in Madrid was probably more important to his advancement than his personal qualities. Piedrola advocated political reform which would limit the power of the king. His supporters and promoters shared this objective and found it convenient to disguise their criticisms of the regime (and their own ambitions) as support of a simple, yet holy, man. But general reform was itself perhaps a disguise. Piedrola's backers were influential and powerful people who were concerned, as such people are, that their influence and power was not what it had been and not what it might be. Their anxiety did however have a stronger basis than the constant paranoia of those who walk the shifting sands of political life. Their concerns were centred on one of the most fabulous and puzzling men in the history of Spanish politics; a man who practised the art of politics with a truly delicious diabolical aplomb, who rose to hold a degree of influence over the most powerful man in the world and who ended both as a traitor to his king and a loss to his country; a man who might, had he not fallen, have kept Spanish supremacy in the world for longer. His name was Antonio Pérez and in 1587 he was in prison on suspicion of involvement in murder – a case to which we shall return.

Piedrola became entwined with the Pérez affair because both were a manifestation of discontent with the king's policies. As long as this discontent was tolerated, Piedrola's cause flourished as an echo of Pérez. Once Piedrola was imprisoned, the discontented elements at court sought another figure to articulate their concerns. This was the role that Lucrecia de Léon was to fulfil. All of this meant that Lucrecia's fate became tied up with Piedrola's and that the dénouement of the Pérez affair was to prove fateful for Lucrecia and her supporters.

4. *Then the Ordinary Man took me to the seashore and there I saw the two fishermen.* The map of Lucrecia's mind has Madrid at its centre with Toledo, holy city of Spain, close by. The remainder of Spain is a featureless expanse stretching to its boundaries – the kingdom of Navarre in the north and the sea on all sides. The seashore is where Spain faces the world and to where any attacking force must come, unless it comes through Navarre, the land border with France. From the seashore which Lucrecia visits, the two companions can show her the rest of the world. From here Lucrecia can see above all the English, masters of the seas, tormentors of the Spanish fleet and enemies of the Spanish people.

5. *'The buffaloes signify life and the wagon, death.'* In this dream the Old Man at last tells Lucrecia the meanings of the symbols in her recent visions. The explanations are an anticlimax that deaden the vitality of the dreams but help us to see the reasons why Lucrecia is being shown visions rather than being given information.

6. *'Before I go, tell me who you are.'* Another attempt by Lucrecia to discover the real identity of her constant dream-companions – and another demonstration of their reluctance to be known. Here they delight in teasing both her and the earthly interpreter of her dreams, Alonso de Mendoza. We may wonder with Lucrecia who these men might be, and we may wonder that they need be anyone at all, other than who they seem to be.

7. *St James and St John . . . St Andrew and St Peter.*

> 'And Jesus, walking by the sea of Galilee, saw two brethren, Simon called Peter, and Andrew his brother, casting a net into the sea: for they were fishers. And he saith unto them, Follow me and I will make you fishers of men. And they straightway left their nets and followed him. And going on from thence, he saw other two brethren, James, the son of Zebedee, and John his brother, in a ship with Zebedee their father, mending their nets;

and he called them. And they immediately left the ship and their father and followed him' (Matthew 4 : 18–22).

'Why us?' they never asked. 'We are fishers.'

8. *Sir Francis Drake.* On 11 April 1587, eight months before Lucrecia de Léon dreamed this dream, Francis Drake left Plymouth intent on causing damage. Unfurling their sails behind his flagship *Elizabeth Bonaventure* were three more galleons of over 400 tons, three heavily armed tall ships from London merchants, seven men-of-war at 150 tons apiece and a dozen frigates. The heavy ships were packed with such brass cannon as Drake could muster, and as much iron as they could carry. That spring, there was more fighting tonnage in this one fleet than in the whole of the Spanish waters. And it was for Spain that Drake was bound.

Two months before Drake sailed, a half-botched decapitation had disturbed the delicate balance of power in Western Europe. The removal of cousin Mary Stuart's head in February 1587 had made Elizabeth's own more secure but demolished with two swipes the delicate structure of peace of which she was the chief architect. Elizabeth's fury at the execution of Mary Queen of Scots surprised her closest courtiers as much as it has stimulated historians. The sequence of Lucrecia's dreams obliges us to treat this subject later; it is enough to know that Elizabeth felt that open war with Spain was now likely, but might still be avoided. Drake and others had been harrying the Spanish Atlantic fleets for years, but Elizabeth was always careful to disown their activities in public. They were not official English warships, they were privateers. But now the shadow boxing was becoming irrelevant and the time had come for the puppet-masters to show their hand. It was no longer a matter of a few ships for bounty (though God knows it cost money to run a war). Now kingdoms were at stake. Let no one be deluded. For a generation the English had lived in peace and unheard-of prosperity but they knew of the butchery just across the Channel where the Spanish Catholics had massacred Protestant Dutch. Now there was just England and Spain. For the most part Elizabeth's Council urged action. The Dutch wanted more help. Her captains begged for permission to strike at the enemy. The men around her seemed tired of peace and relished the end of pretence.

Still Elizabeth weaved and watched. Queen Bee. She would not abandon peace so easily and, while most of her advisers said the opposite, she guessed that time might be on her side. Drake, pleading in Greenwich while his ships sat in Plymouth, thought the queen advised by traitors. Elizabeth has often been accused of prevarication in military matters but she was a good politician, not a bad general.

All the world knew that an Armada was being built and stocked in the shipyards of Spain and Portugal. Drake wanted to stop it before it started. Even without actual engagement he could sit off the Spanish coast and prevent the delivery of coastal supplies to the shipbuilders and chandlers of Lisbon and Cadiz. No Spanish galleasses would venture out of port without a prodigious escort if Drake was known to be lurking off-shore. Come March 1587 Elizabeth decided the time was right. She granted Drake six of her ships and her commission 'to impeach the purpose of the Spanish fleet and stop their meeting at Lisbon'. In order to execute this order Drake might go as far as 'distressing the ships within their havens'.

These are clever words. Elizabeth was not at war with Spain and still wanted not to be. The subtle language of Drake's commission may have had a particular purpose since, when it was too late to stop him, Elizabeth apparently changed her mind. An order signed by the Privy Council on 9 April was immediately sent by courier to Plymouth. Her Majesty instructed Drake to 'forbear to enter forcibly into any of the said King's ports or havens or to offer violence to any of his towns or shipping within harbouring, or to do any act of hostility upon the land'. The same was not to apply to the sea, where 'you should do your best endeavour to get into your possession such shipping of the said King or his subjects as you shall find'.

No subtle verbs here – violence and hostility were plainly forbidden. But the order missed Drake by such a distance (he was at sea by 2 April, nine days before the Privy Council met, and this was almost certainly known in Greenwich since it was known in Paris) that we must assume the queen's intention was that even a fast frigate would not catch Drake in time. Then why send the message?

The queen's secretary of state Francis Walsingham straight away wrote to Stafford, the queen's ambassador in France, that Drake was forbidden by the queen to go into any Spanish port or harbour. Stafford was known by Walsingham to have a strong vestigial loyalty to the Catholic faith and a tendency to keep the Spanish informed – he knew that the information would be passed to the Spanish ambassador in

Paris. This ambassador was none other than Bernadino de Mendoza, lately expelled from England on suspicion of plotting against the English queen, and brother to Alonso, mentor to Lucrecia de Léon. Don Bernadino was thus to learn that Drake was sailing to Spanish waters but that the queen was not at war with Spain. Drake meanwhile was free to go about his business.

The Spanish would not have been duped by this elaborate charade into thinking that Drake would not attack, but that was not the point. Elizabeth's manoeuvrings helped her to keep the situation outwardly calm and helped to delay the Armada by a further year. Elizabeth's overall objective, as Garrett Mattingly (1959) writes, 'was to make the best of two lines of contradictory policy, simultaneously pursued'.

Though Lucrecia and her fellow citizens feared Drake above all others, it was Elizabeth who presented the most danger.

9. *'If the Turk gains Poland, we have Spain in our hands.'* Here Lucrecia shows a broad and partial knowledge of the politics of Europe. The Habsburg Emperor Maximilian had long coveted the throne of Poland but had been defeated by Stephen Bathory, who was elected king by the Polish parliament in 1575. Twelve years later, at the time of this dream, another king had been elected in Poland and another Habsburg turned down by the parliament. This time Sigismund III, who was also king of Sweden, overcame the claims of the Archduke Maximilian, the late emperor's younger son and nephew of Philip of Spain. The Archduke Maximilian invaded from the south as Sigismund entered Poland from the north in October 1587. In December 1587 therefore Maximilian remained an active claimant to the Polish throne. Three months later the Habsburg army was defeated at the battle of Byczyna and Maximilian taken prisoner. He escaped two years later and continued to press his claim. Other members of the Habsburg family withdrew their backing for Maximilian after reaching agreement with Sigismund, and Maximilian was left with only one Habsburg supporter – Philip of Spain. Maximilian eventually renounced his claim to the Polish throne in 1598, the year Philip died.

By the late 1580s Turkish forces had spread as far north as modern-day Hungary and Moldavia, hovering near the southern borders of the Habsburg realms. Ottoman expansion had been extremely rapid in the early 1500s, though the late sixteenth century was to see its high-water mark. Lucrecia often dreams of the Great Turk and his plans to invade Spain. Turkish expansion in the Mediterranean coincided with the increase in Spanish ambitions and these two great powers fought for control of the western Mediterranean. The death of Suleiman in 1566 and the subsequent infighting halted Turkish expansion. A series of truces were signed with Spain which were still in force in Lucrecia's time.

The Ordinary Man came to me[1] and brought a red water vessel shaped like a Zamoran jar with two handles and a tall neck. He said, 'Notice that it has four holes in the neck and a mouth at the top which makes five.' And he told me to drink from the vessel, not from the mouth at the top, but from one of the holes at the side. When I finished drinking, the Ordinary Man took the jar and gave it to another man. He said that the water belonged to 'Our friend Aguiar.[2] He wishes you to know that it was drawn on St John's Day[3] before sunrise, and is from the river which runs over the land.'

Then the chained man who rescued me from the tower came to me. He made me lean out of the window of my house which looks to the south. As I looked there came down the street from the east twelve young women[4] wearing elaborate gowns and head-dresses in silks with much gold and many precious stones and pearls. In their style of dress they did not look like Spanish women for their breasts were bare as painters sometimes depict foreign women. They passed in front of the window where I stood and went on towards the west.

Following them came a very beautiful woman, so tall and full-figured that she seemed a giant, like those I have heard called Roman Matrons. This woman had a snake twined around her bare left breast. By way of a head-dress she had something like the twisted bulk of cloth that mountain women wear, but hers was formed out of serpents coiled and plaited together. Her sleeves were rolled to the elbow showing arms like those of a man, strong and hairy. In each hand she carried a copper cauldron full of water.[5]

As she reached the place level with where I stood, she stopped and gave a great cry, calling out: 'Although I am upon the earth, this voice will be heard in heaven.'

As this great voice resounded, all the men of all the nations of the world came from all directions to set themselves about her. And, having them there before her, she said to those of the Spanish nation, 'Drink, O you thirsty ones, since your shepherd has left you without water and you are dry.'

These people came to drink from the cauldrons until they were satisfied. Then the woman gave another cry, but did not speak. And all of the smallest birds of the world came round about her and she said to them, 'Drink, for you too have been deprived of your nests, which caused so little inconvenience in this world.' The little birds came down to drink and then perched on the woman's breast and head and from there flew off.

The giantess moved away down the street towards the west, making a noise with her cauldrons as she ran to catch up with the others.

Then a man approached from the east from where the giantess had come. He was dressed in black, and had the same size and features as the woman, though he was dark-faced. He stopped in the same place and gave a great cry, saying, 'With this voice I shall cause all of the earth's serpents and wild beasts to come to me.' I saw, approaching from every direction, lions, tigers and wolves, and serpents and lizards, toads and snakes and other venomous creatures.

As all these creatures surrounded him, I saw his entire body become a fountain with clear water springing from all of its parts. The wild beasts came to drink at the fountain, but when they left it the water was turned to blood. And when the snakes and venomous creatures came they tumbled into it and made it turbid and black like muddy water that has been stirred.

At that moment the two men who called themselves Elias[6] and Moses appeared on either side of this man-become-

fountain. I saw that Elias took up a lizard and Moses a toad. I saw that the man who called himself Moses was the Ordinary Man who often accompanies me. But when I said this, he hid his face.[7] *Then he turned to Elias and, turning the toad belly upwards and placing his hand on it, said, 'Do you remember how, the other night, I stood on a castle, the highest one in the world, and had a person there with me who was very fearful? But this is why I took her there, and made her lose her fear: I have to show her all of those kingdoms in all of their detail, like the belly of this toad.'*

Then the chained man took me away from my window and returned me to my bed. The Ordinary Man was at the side of my bed, and I said to him, 'Do you not look like a man who calls himself Moses?'[8]

He answered 'Leave me be, do not involve me in this.'

I saw that he had the gourd and esquero that he carried with him at other times. I asked him what the gourd was and he answered, 'Do you not remember when I gave you the flesh of this gourd to eat?' Then I asked, 'What is the leather bag you are carrying?' and he answered, 'This is to show that I am not a man of these times.' Then he disappeared.

Present during all of this was the chained man who then said to me, 'Look to the manner in which you tell these things; you know that Piedrola is in prison.'

And with that I awoke.

1. *me*. Each morning Lucrecia makes herself presentable for Fray Lucas de Allende or Don Alonso de Mendoza, holding the jumble of voices and faces in her mind that her mind has brought to life. Her sleeping brain has already worked these sounds and pictures into stories. So now her

waking mind looks at its own work in a kind of fear mixed with wonder. These visions are not something over which she seems to have any control. The events and images are not, on the whole, very pleasant and, though she says she relishes their arrival, they come to her unbidden.

The dreams always begin in Lucrecia's room giving her and us the nice illusion that these events could, indeed, be happening to her, the Lucrecia of the woken world. If she goes anywhere in her dreams, she is generally careful to say that she was taken there by someone, and that she was returned to her room before she awoke. This illusion of being just one step from reality is very strongly maintained by Lucrecia throughout her dreams.

If these events are just one step away, then where does that step lead? Lucrecia clearly does not believe that these events are simply taking place inside her head. But then where are they occurring? Where is the place that she is seeing each night? If she is taken into the street or to the seashore or to England then are these the places she says they are? Is she simply visiting them at a time when normal life is ended and dream-life can begin, like a group of players stealing into a theatre in the dead of night to perform a parody of the real drama of existence? If we cannot imagine her believing this, then is she entering a parallel world, recognisable yet profoundly different? Is this dream world, inhabited by humans and creatures of terrifying description and filled by events of shuddering unpleasantness, another of God's worlds? If it is the place where God chooses to show his visions to those chosen to see them, is it like a constructed stage set, imitating the world in order to mock its existence? Does it show Lucrecia an ugly parody which is in fact the 'true' world – the world stripped of its hypocritical illusions of piety, security, order, longevity; a world where the reality of human sin and its consequences are openly visible?

A place of this kind, though not quite as Lucrecia sees it, has been said by some theologians to exist. This place is lodged between the unformed, chaotic, perfect location of God, where time has no meaning and no dominion, and the prescribed, shackled, sinful, physical and ageing world of the earth. This in-between place has been called the *aevum*. Here things happen but time does not hold sway. It is here that the angels are – a nether, dreamlike world between the perfection that has no shape and the shape that is corrupt.

2. *'Our friend Aguiar'.* Was it wise, this telling of dreams? Was it holy? Was
their transcription a sacred act? More pressing, was it likely to mean
trouble for Lucrecia?

Lucrecia was to say later in her defence that she told the dreams
'in confession' and it is likely that Alonso de Mendoza told her as much.
But she herself was worried. She repeatedly asked Don Alonso and
Fray Lucas whether telling her dreams would lead her into trouble
with the Holy Order, the Spanish Inquisition. They were reassuring
but Lucrecia sought other advice.

She went to her former confessor, a local Dominican with a high
reputation as a preacher, named Fray Gerónimo de Aguiar. Domini-
cans were orthodox Catholics and strongly opposed to superstitious
aspects of religion – a quite different attitude to that of the Franciscan
order to which Fray Lucas de Allende belonged. It was Dominican
priests who founded and sustained the Holy Order.

Richard Kagan (1990) writes that Fray Aguiar, when asked for
advice, 'strongly urged Lucrecia to put an end to the copying, warning
that, "they would all be arrested by the Inquisition"'.

Juan Blázquez Miguel (1987) goes further and says that Aguiar
'threatened to denounce Lucrecia to the Inquisition if she were to
continue her accounts to Fray Lucas and Don Alonso de Mendoza'.

A worried Lucrecia sought more assurance from Fray Lucas de
Allende. He is quoted by Kagan as giving an enigmatic reply to
Lucrecia's concerns, which must have left her in a state of sublime
confusion: 'The Inquisition has no interest in these dreams unless you
believe in them.'

3. *St John's Day.* There was an old religious (and rowdy) custom of *Madrileñas*
bathing in the Manzanares River on St John's Day, which falls on
Midsummer's Eve, 24 June. The custom was banned in 1588 in the
newly puritanical atmosphere of the Catholic Church following the
Council of Trent.

4. *As I looked there came down the street from the east twelve young women
. . .* The symbolism of the twelve and one is obvious but explication
risks reducing the gorgeous richness of this vision. Though Lucrecia's
apocalypticism may sometimes feel overcooked, she more usually presents images of great clarity and original beauty. We can picture the
line of women winding slowly towards us from the distance, growing

in stature and focus, arriving not suddenly but graciously, using all the possible space of our vision to transform their presence from an objective distant reality into the full possessor of our senses. They pass beneath the window and then fade again into the distance with no backward look, only to be followed by the Medusa-like giantess with great cauldrons and voice enough to reach the heavens, all the birds of the world swooping about her. That we all should dream so well.

5. *In each hand she carried a copper cauldron full of water.* Water runs through this and other dreams. In the arid world of New Castile, as in the eastern Mediterranean in the time of Christ, water, by its transforming properties, became a representative of something else.

In the earliest Judaeo-Christian creation story (though not the first presented in the Bible) the earth began barren and lifeless,

> And every plant of the field before it was in the earth, and every herb of the field before it grew: for the Lord God had not caused it to rain upon the earth, and there was not a man to till the ground. But there went up a mist from the earth, and watered the whole face of the ground. And the Lord God formed man of the dust of the ground, and breathed into his nostrils the breath of life; and man became a living soul. (Genesis 2: 5–7)

Water then life. And for New Testament authors, something else beyond mere earthly life. An acknowledgement of the dual meaning of water is given in John's Gospel. Jesus meets a woman of Samaria at a well; they are alone and she is surprised that he speaks to her since 'Jews have no dealings with Samaritans.' The story continues,

> Jesus answered and said unto her, If thou knewest the gift of God, and who it is that saith to thee, Give me to drink, thou wouldest have asked of him, and he would have given thee living water.
>
> The woman saith unto him, Sir, thou hast nothing to draw with, and the well is deep: from whence then hast thou that living water? Art thou greater than our father Jacob, which gave us the well, and drank thereof himself, and his children, and his cattle?
>
> Jesus answered and said unto her, Whosoever drinketh of this water shall thirst again: But whosoever drinketh of the water that I shall give him shall never thirst; but the water that I shall give him shall be in him a well of water springing up into everlasting life.

32

The woman saith unto him, Sir, give me this water, that I thirst not, neither come hither to draw. (John 4: 10–15)

Lucrecia herself meets Christ at a well in her most affecting dream, with which this book ends.

6. *Elias.* Elias is the name used in the Gospels for the Old Testament prophet Elijah (it is the Greek version of a Hebrew name). The last words of the Old Testament are spoken by the Lord of Hosts: 'Behold, I will send you Elijah the prophet before the coming of the great and dreadful day of the Lord: And he shall turn the heart of the fathers to the children, and the heart of the children to their fathers, lest I come and smite the earth with a curse' (Malachi 4: 5–6).

The arrival of Elijah would therefore signal that the coming of the Lord was at hand. When John the Baptist declared, 'He that cometh after me is mightier than I,' he was asked if he was the prophet Elijah ('Art thou Elias?' John 1: 21). Lucrecia, having been told that the Ordinary Man might be John the Baptist, now sees the pre-incarnation of John in her dream.

7. *I saw that the man who called himself Moses was the Ordinary Man who often accompanies me. But when I said this, he hid his face.* A depiction of the blurring of identities which can make dreams so difficult for the conscious mind to untangle. How did Lucrecia identify this figure as both Moses and the Ordinary Man? We should bear in mind that Lucrecia did 'know' what Moses looked like in her waking life because he was depicted in paintings that bedecked the walls of the churches of Madrid. Did the dream figure look like the Ordinary Man in some sort of Moses disguise?

The extent of Lucrecia's participation in the visions changes radically from dream to dream and within different phases of the same dream. So on this night Lucrecia simply watches the parade of women and the giantess (or rather watches, if that is what a dreamer does, herself watching), while she later interrupts the vision of Moses and then becomes a subject of discussion. The point here is not so much the existence of a continuum of levels of intervention by the dreamer, but that there are some visions in which it would be inappropriate for Lucrecia to participate. The vision of the giantess calling out to all the heavens and all the corners of the earth positively precludes the intimacy of an individual intervention. It is on too grand a scale to allow Lucrecia herself to do anything more than observe it and wonder at it. But this quickly changes when the vision's panoramic feel becomes telescoped into the intimate scene between Elias and Moses. Now and only now can Lucrecia speak and be heard and become an active player.

8. *The Ordinary Man was at the side of my bed, and I said to him, 'Do you not look like a man who calls himself Moses?'* Lucrecia's question is sly and teasing and the Ordinary Man is irritated that this puts her at a distinct advantage. Up to now we have believed in the Ordinary Man's omnipotence within this world; he summons up visions, he takes Lucrecia where he thinks she ought to go, he gives and withholds explanations. But now he is caught out. If the Ordinary Man is not in control of these visions then who is?

*The Ordinary Man came to me and took me to the castle with
the high tower[1] where he had taken me on a previous night. The
tower had a steeple of slate like the one on the tower of Santa
Cruz. He took me to the top of the steeple which opened up like a
pomegranate and I sat inside. The Ordinary Man left me there,
and then the masked and chained man came. I asked him who he
was and he said, 'Do not seek to know more. He knows I am of
royal caste.'*

*I asked him what was inside the castle and he said 'I will
show you.' The floor beneath me opened and I fell into a
sumptuous chamber. Lying on the bed was a most beautiful
woman. The chained man said that she was the master of the
castle. Then the floor on which we stood opened up and we fell
into another room. There I saw a serving woman by the hearth
trying to blow life into a fire, but she was so small and her
blowing so weak that the fire would not burn. Then this floor too
opened and we found ourselves in a room where an old man sat
at a table filled with a great variety of food, but no bread. The
chained man said to this man, 'I wish to show this maiden all
that there is in the castle.'*

*Then he took me down to the cellar or crypt where I saw
many dead people lying. Each body had a nameplate above its
head but I could not read them and was told that they were in
Latin. One label was just a single M. When I had seen all this,
the chained man took me back to the top of the castle.*

*The steeple of the castle closed so that it was as before. As I
stood on the tower the Ordinary Man brought before me many
kingdoms,[2] much reduced in size, and it seemed as though they
approached of their own accord and settled in front of me.
Among them he showed me the kingdom of Navarre where I*

saw that many young men in Moorish costume[3] entered from the south and set fire to the city with tapers. But I saw no people in the city.

Then I saw Italy come before me in the same way. A man dressed in black wielded in his right hand an ancient lance, and said, 'The time will come when I shall act to my advantage against Spain.' I saw also the city of Venice which seemed very beautiful, all of her buildings were so clear that they might have been made of crystal. She represented great power and wealth, and I saw that the Great Turk sent her a message asking for help in a war he wished to undertake. Venice answered that indeed she would help and, as a token of friendship, sent an impressive gift by galley. The Ordinary Man said that this would be found to be true, that today on the 8th day of December of 1587, the Venetians were sending such a gift and that the Turk would receive it.

Then I saw the kingdom of Poland. I could see King Maximilian in his palace and I understood that half of his people viewed him with favour and that the other half were ill-disposed. These rebels were murmuring and plotting some treasonable act which was to take place when he went to hear Mass.

Then I said to the Ordinary Man, 'Spain is missing.' But then I saw that in Spain all the men were dressed in dark clothing and were lying on the stubble of the fields. And as I looked I saw that a ploughman came and tied his ox to a vine. Then, as he led it by the halter, the ox dragged the vine, uprooting it, and the root ran with blood. The man who dragged it said to the others, 'Did you see that it reached as far as England?'

And hearing this, I awoke.

1. *the castle with the high tower.* Lucrecia has, as she says, paid a previous visit and will return to this castle and its enormously high tower – the highest in the world. At each visit things change slightly so that their significance lies not only in themselves but in their alterations.

2. *the Ordinary Man brought before me many kingdoms.* Lucrecia's visions credit Spanish people with an outlook beyond the borders of their kingdom. Spain was a dominant force in Europe and the Spanish were much concerned with the politics and diplomacy of the continent. Lucrecia had her views on what each of the kingdoms was up to – not much good, usually – plotting and boasting of Spain's downfall, making meetings where Philip could not see them. But Lucrecia, from her high tower, could see it all.

   King Philip's inheritance and Spain's military power had given her control of large tracts of Europe, including the Netherlands, Burgundy, Franche-Comté, Naples and Savoy-Piedmont; her seafarers and conquistadores had taken the silver-rich Americas. She had lately got the better of the rebellious Dutch and had been extending treaties with the troublesome Turks. Portugal had been annexed. France remained a complicated mess but was at least no immediate threat. Only the English remained a serious problem.

   But the war in the Netherlands was ruinously expensive, absorbing most of the bullion from the Americas; the Dutch were pinned back but not defeated; the English were openly attacking Spanish shipping and ports in Europe and America and giving aid to the Dutch; the effect of the silver bonanza was to devastate manufacture and agriculture in Castile, to treble the price of goods and to drive the common people into poverty and emigration. Meanwhile it was no secret that Spanish troops were resented in Philip's Italian dominions; how long would it be before they rebelled as the Dutch had? And how long could the Grand Turk be trusted to keep his word; would he not be bound to combine with the enemies of Spain to his own advantage? How long would France remain Catholic?

   What was Spain – golden ruler of half the world, a fragile state surrounded and tormented by her enemies, or the bully who could not feed her own?

Navarre appears in Lucrecia's dreams as the part of Spain most vulnerable to attack since it comprised most of the country's land border.

The ancient kingdom of Navarre, which straddled the Pyrenees, was until the early sixteenth century a satellite state of France, having been separated from the other Spanish kingdoms since the twelfth century. Ferdinand and Isabella annexed Navarre in 1512 and it has since remained part of Spain. The part of France bordering Spain was the power base of Henry of Navarre, Protestant pretender to the French throne. France had traditionally been a great threat to Spain but by Lucrecia's time the internal difficulties of the French had made the country a potential pawn of outside powers. The 1580s was the period of the three Henrys in France. The king was Henry of Valois a ruler with apparently little support and a feeble character, though this was belied by his occasional political coups. Then there was Henry of Guise, leader of the ultra-orthodox Catholic League, and champion and vassal of the king of Spain. Guise controlled a third of France and came close to usurping the throne on several occasions. Henry of Valois was to invite this dangerous rival into his court and, on 23 December 1588, have him stabbed to death in the corridors of the Council of the Estates General. Henry of Valois was himself to be assassinated a year later and Henry of Navarre then spent four years fighting for the French throne. Ironically, given the fear he engendered in Catholic Spain, Henry IV would convert to Catholicism to gain the throne.

In Lucrecia's time Navarre was the dangerous route by which Spain might be invaded and this dream combines the two principal enemies of Spain – the heretics without and the suspect Moors within.

3. *I saw . . . many young men in Moorish costume.* Lucrecia's first mention of the Moors. This English word comes from the Spanish *moros* meaning dark-coloured. These were people of Arab and Berber descent, the remnants of the Arab rule of Spain which came to an end with the fall of Granada in 1492. In Lucrecia's visions the Moors are a threat to Spain – internal enemies aided by their friends the Ottoman Turks.

The vision of these nations, so strikingly seen from on high, is a pageant of paranoia about plots being made and deals being done in secret places. Spain is embattled, everyone is out to get her. Just as Lucrecia thinks she has seen all of Europe, the final two are shown: Spain and England – connected by a trail of blood.

Now the apocalypse is not shown as a symbol-laden wagon, nor a fountain turned to blood. Spain herself is shown to be vulnerable to her enemies. The visions are real, the world is a dangerous place.

The Ordinary Man came to me carrying the branch of a palm tree from which sprouted many dates. I asked him what palm this was and he answered, 'I shall tell you. Look at the dates that are on it. All of these dates that you see are born of this palm. Tell me, which of these dates is the best?'

I said, 'I do not know. They all seem good and of the same size.'

He said to me, 'Can you tell if any of these dates is rotten within?'

I answered, 'It is even less possible for me to tell that.'

Then he said, 'This palm is a king and from him have descended all the monarchs of Castile, and none of them has pleased God except the one signified by this smallest date.'

Looking at the dates I saw one that was smaller than all the others and said 'Tell me who he is.'

He said, 'I shall take you to where you may see that.'

Then the Ordinary Man took me from my house to the small courtyard of the palace.[1] There I saw King Philip seated with his back to the east on a chair drawn near to a column. There was another king in a similar chair at the right hand side with his back turned. Behind King Philip I saw two men writing letters.

The Ordinary Man said, 'Behold that there are traitors in Spain and know who they are.'

I observed them closely. One was the Marquis of Carpio, elder son of Don Diego de Córdoba,[2] and the other, a thin-faced man with red hair and blue eyes, bore on his breast the cross of the order of Culutrava. Him I recognised though I do not know his name.

Then the Ordinary Man said to me, 'Identify the king who is next to Philip.'

Looking, I saw that he had a palm with three dates in his hand, and I said, 'This king is Ferdinand the Catholic for I have seen him in other dreams with Queen Isabella his wife,[3] and I was told that it was he.'

The Ordinary Man took me away from the palace to the castle where I had been the night before. I saw again the beautiful woman still lying on the bed.[4] And I saw gathered before her many men of good fortune arguing one with another, for each wanted to lie with the lady. But I heard her say, 'None of you will lie with me unless he can put his head through the hole in this bread ring.' She showed it and I saw that the hole was so small it seemed impossible that anyone should succeed.

Then the Ordinary Man took me down to the room where, the night before, I had seen the woman blowing on the flame, which was now burning well. One of the men who had been arguing over who should lie with the lady (he seemed to be a foreign youth with a fair face) came to the chimney-breast and extinguished the fire, pouring on to it a jug of water that he carried. He said to the woman, 'Your lady is not to have the pleasure of this fire.'

I remembered that in other visions I have seen it had been explained to me that fire signifies life and extinguishing it, especially with water, means death.

From there the Ordinary Man took me down to the cellar where the dead bodies were. I saw that the nameplate of each began with the letter R. I managed to read one that was inscribed 'Rey don Pedro'. This body had many thorns at the feet and its shroud was of black Hondschoot[5] cloth with a red cross upon it. I wanted to read the rest of the nameplates but the Ordinary Man would not allow this, saying, 'It is necessary to go to the seashore where the Old Fisherman is.'

*   *   *

The Ordinary Man took me to the seashore, where I found the Old Fisherman alone. He said, 'Have you seen all that has happened?'

I said, 'Yes, explain it to me.'

He said, 'Those dates represent your kings who have descended one from another, as you have been told. The small date is Ferdinand the Catholic, whom you will not find among the other dead bodies.'

And then he said to me, 'Do you not know of the evil that has come to pass?'

'Tell me of it,' I said.

And he answered, 'Then the man who goes with you has not told you? He is to tell it, then I must explain it.'[6]

And with that I awoke.

1. *the small courtyard of the palace.* Lucrecia had an intimate knowledge of Madrid, its streets, its public buildings, its churches and even the royal palace. The Alcázar was less than a mile from Lucrecia's house and though access to the palace was not entirely open, neither was it cut off from the city. Madrid's importance came only from its status as the site of the court and the two grew up together. Lucrecia knew more than most ordinary *Madrileñas* about what went on in the court because she was, for a short time, employed in the royal household. Her position as an eighteen-year-old was as a maidservant to the governess of the infante, the king's son and future King Philip III. Lucrecia was, it seems, observant and had a good memory for what she saw. She had access to parts of the royal household that were closed to all but the most important members of the royal staff – and the royal household servants. Her dreams often contain details of the appearance and layout of the innermost reaches of the palace. The small courtyard (*placetilla*) was also known as the *plaza del rey*, the king's courtyard.

She was also familiar with many of the personalities of the court – important councillors, clerics, tutors as well as members of the royal family. Lucrecia probably came into contact with the Infanta

Isabella (a regular and sympathetic character in her dreams) and the Infante Philip. It is not known whether she ever spoke to the king himself. Lucrecia worked at the palace for periods in the years 1586 and 1587.

The proximity and interdependence of court and city infused Madrid with gossip and rumour about every aspect of political life. Lucrecia's father was not untypical in being, as a lawyer to the king's bankers, closely dependent on the doings of the court. The streets and houses of the parish of San Sebastián were packed with people eager to hear, discuss and embellish every tit-bit of information from the Alcázar.

Although she clearly spent a lot of time out and about in Madrid, Lucrecia did not have to go out of her front door to know what was going on in the world. The de Léon household itself was open to a constant stream of visitors bringing news, stories and arguments. We know, for instance, that an Arab woman lived as a lodger in the house for a few years and, as Richard Kagan writes, 'allegedly taught Lucrecia about the Moorish tradition of dreams and prophecy'. She came across a few men who styled themselves as prophets and healers, some of whom are known from the records of their arrests by the Inquisition. Lucrecia also met Miguel de Piedrola Beamonte before his arrest. More concrete news about the world came from friends and neighbours, and news about the New World from Lucrecia's mother's sister María who lived in Yucatán. People returning from the Americas would bring news to relatives back home in Spain. One regular visitor to the de Léons at this time was Don Guillén de Casaos, a former official in Yucatán who returned to Spain in 1585 and moved on the fringes of the court. He was a source of news and information and was interested in the prophetic nature of Lucrecia's dreams. Don Guillén was to feature in the plans to save Spain from destruction, both in Lucrecia's dreams and in real life.

By the simple fact of living in Madrid Lucrecia breathed the sweet and tainted air of political intrigue.

2. *the Marquis of Carpio, elder son of Don Diego de Córdoba.* One of the king's tasks was to keep a check on the ambitions and personal aggrandisement of his nobles. This grandee of the Spanish court had been arrested by Philip in 1587. Several of the highest aristocrats in the land had been severely punished and even executed for crimes against 'ordinary' people. Lucrecia's identification of Carpio as a malign presence was a

piece of retrospective wisdom. Córdoba features as an irresponsible father in later dreams.

3. *'This king is Ferdinand the Catholic for I have seen him in other dreams with Queen Isabella his wife . . .'* Lucrecia, like most Spaniards, considered the era of Ferdinand and Isabella, known as the 'Catholic Monarchs', to be the golden past. During their reign from 1479 to 1504 the reconquest of the peninsula from Arab rule was completed, all of Spain's Jews and Moors were forced either to convert to Christianity or to face expulsion, and the Holy Order of the Spanish Inquisition was founded under Fray Torquemada to promote and police the Catholic faith. By their marriage Isabella (the senior partner) and Ferdinand united the squabbling kingdoms of Castile and Aragón. They thereby created the unified Catholic Spain that endured for five centuries and created for the Spanish people a focus for nostalgic longing.

So much for the past. Lucrecia also believed in a golden future, and her visions are a curious mixture of the prophetic and apocalyptic – words whose meanings are not always clear. The literature of apocalypse is not quite what it seems and not quite what we normally take it to signify. An apocalypse is different from a prophecy. In the Bible prophecies were made in times of relative freedom and prosperity. They were proclamations and warnings to the rich and powerful about their flouting of religious observance and their ill-treatment of the poor. Prophets such as Amos, Hosea, Isaiah and Jeremiah did not, in their original sayings (later additions made their speeches more palatable) see or predict a golden future. Quite the reverse – they saw only doom and destruction ahead. In a sense, although the prophets spoke on God's behalf and often directly relayed His words, they had no need of direct communication with God to make their point. If you were a devout believer then you would agree that the Lord would be angry at the flouting of His laws, and you might be grateful to the prophets for reminding you of your duties. If you were a cynic or an unbeliever, then the claim of the prophets to be in direct connection with God would be irrelevant. This is not to deny the importance of faith, but to show that in this type of preaching the moral and charismatic force of the preacher is as important as his divine vision.

Apocalypticism is different altogether. In its original meaning, but contrary to the sense it has now attained, an apocalypse was an uncovering of God's plan for the world which always involved final salvation for the faithful. It is not a doom-laden prophecy. As Enslin (1971) says of apocalyptic writings:

> they were intended as sources of strength and confidence for contemporaries of the author who were in a period of crisis and needed encouragement to stand firm in the testing days immediately at hand . . . In a word, this type of writing may properly be styled a shot of adrenaline to nerve those who well might falter in despair just as the glorious day was about to dawn.

Apocalyptic writings were composed at times of crisis but were, confusingly for later readers, set in previous and similar times of national despair. Through this device the author could show a historical figure predicting that at some time in the future (i.e. at the time of actual writing) things would become very bad, but that this was simply a prelude to the opening of an era of splendour in which those who remained faithful to the Lord would find eternal reward. In other words, stick with God and He will see you right in the end – and you won't have to wait too long. Prophecies of doom were made in good times and revelations of a golden future came in times of crisis.

4. *I saw again the beautiful woman still lying on the bed.* The beautiful woman is likely to represent Spain surrounded by her enemies. She is the lady of the castle in which the kings of Spain are buried, so she may be seen as the living spirit inhabiting the body of her country. She is perhaps Lucrecia's evocation of her nation's soul.

5. *black Hondschoot cloth.* This is the cloth used for monks' habits and is presumably meant to signify King Pedro's holiness. Black habits were worn by members of the Dominican order. The town of Hondschoot (or Honschoote) housed the biggest cloth-making works in the Netherlands. The war between the Spanish and Dutch had a devastating effect on the country and its prime industry. In *The Dutch Revolt* (1985), Geoffrey Parker writes that Hondschoot's 'population fell from 18,000 in the 1560s to 385 in 1584. Cloth production fell from 90,000 pieces annually in the 1560s to 9,000 in 1587–8.' Textiles had been Europe's prime manufacture and the source of its growing, though fragile, wealth.

6. *'He is to tell it, then I must explain it.'* Within the dream world each figure has a role to play. The Ordinary Man must show Lucrecia places, events and people and is ever present. The Old Fisherman, or Old Man as he is more usually known, appears frequently and will explain some visions. He also instructs the Ordinary Man as to what he may or may not do or say. The Young Fisherman (also known as the Lion Man) who appears less frequently, at least in the early dreams, has a similar role and stature to the Old Man yet seems to have greater authority – he is certainly more assertive, though this sometimes leads to disputes between the 'two companions', as the fishermen are called by Lucrecia. It appears to the reader of her accounts that Lucrecia does not so much dream of these figures as enter an alternative world where they are waiting to receive her.

*The Ordinary Man took me to the seashore where I met the two
fishermen. The one with the lion[1] said to me, 'Has last night's
vision of the tree been explained to you?' I said that Don
Alonso had told me his understanding of it.[2] The Old
Fisherman said, 'I would say; the trunk of the tree is the king,
the branches his Armada and the leaves his troops. The crow,
bringing a leaf to Drake, is a sign that he is receiving news
from Spain.[3] The tearing off of branches means that the
Armada will be lost.[4] The splinters that flew from it, wounding
and killing the people that fired upon it, indicates that the
troops of the Armada will defend themselves and inflict
damage on their enemies.'*

*Then he told the Ordinary Man to take me to a certain place of
which he had already told him. He took me towards the south to
a very high and very dry island[5] where I saw neither men nor
trees nor anything green upon the ground. Neither was there
any water but only a soil like white sand or burnt earth.*

*Then came the two fishermen. And the one with the lion
said, 'Now look, for my companion has insisted that I show you
these visions. As you see there is no tree nor any green plant
upon this island.' Indicating with his hand a small patch of
earth, he went on, 'Take notice of what may arise from here. It
will seem, and indeed is, very little, but it is to mean much.'*

*Then I saw that from the soil there arose a tiny tree, slender
as one just planted and without a single leaf, so that it seemed
more like a dry stick than a plant. Then I saw that from the east,
to my left, there came a river running towards the little tree. It
was really a brook of very clear water. Then from the other three
directions, west, north and south, came others in the same way.*

And they all flowed towards the tree. I saw that, with all this watering, the tree was rising from the ground and growing strongly. It became a large and powerful tree of many branches which bore more fruit upon them than leaves.

Looking at the fruit I saw that they were muscatel pears, of the largest, most beautiful and aromatic kind. The aroma of the pears spread about the island as though it were happy to be there. Round about the trunk of the tree sprang up many more tiny trees, like children of the first. These too grew large very quickly. Some bore fruit, like the main tree – these ones were watered by the streams. Others, from which the waters seemed to shrink away, bore only leaf. The Lion Man said to me, 'You will tell the man who explained the other dream to you, that you have seen this tree.'

Now, looking round the island again, I saw that it was fresh and green and flowering like a garden, populated by trees that had all been born from that first one and that now occupied all the open spaces. Then my three companions disappeared and I awoke.

1. *The one with the lion.* The younger of the two companions has recently been accompanied by a lion. In later dreams Lucrecia calls him the Lion Man. In this dream she receives the explanation of an earlier vision. This is given, as ever, by the two companions and not the Ordinary Man.

2. *I said that Don Alonso had told me his understanding of it.* The reference to Don Alonso is instructive. We might have taken the three men to be omniscient but it appears that they rely on Lucrecia to inform them of events in her waking world. She might have allowed the Lion Man to know about Don Alonso's conversations with her without having to ask her. Lucrecia is, though, quite consistent in this. It is Lucrecia and Lucrecia alone who informs the waking world of events in her

dreamlands and she alone who can bring the real world to her dream companions.

3. *The crow, bringing a leaf to Drake, is a sign that he is receiving news from Spain.* Drake, again. Confirmation that in Spanish eyes the enemy they faced was, above all, Drake. He himself was aware of this and played up to it. He felt much the same way in reverse – the conflict between England and Spain was to Drake a personal fight between himself and Philip. Drake had regard for the men he faced in combat but he had a visceral hatred of Catholicism born out of his Puritan upbringing and his belief that it was the principal threat to his queen and his country.

Drake relished his growing fame and knew that it could be useful to him. If the Spanish feared him as some sort of demon then a little more demonic behaviour would both delay the fulfilment of their plans and give them further cause for concern. To find the foundations of Drake's reputation, we return to the events of April and May 1587 – seven months previous to this dream – with Drake tacking out of the western approaches setting course for the Spanish coast.

It was decided, either in Plymouth or off Portugal, that Cadiz should be the first target of the raiding fleet. Dutch traders had reported an unusual build-up of ships there, clearly intended for the Armada, whose preparations were an open secret. (There is a claim that the English had spies in Spain whose information about the Armada was crucial to its defeat, and that this is what this part of the dream signifies. But this may be too conspiratorial. The Armada was to be the largest fleet of ships ever seen. It was to be gathered, built and provisioned in harbours that remained open to trade with most parts of the world – the supply of wine from Jerez to England via Cadiz continued right through the conflict. Though the precise date of sailing was not known in advance it would have been impossible for the English not to have known of its imminence.)

Drake's small fleet came into sight off Cadiz harbour at around four o'clock in the afternoon of 29 April 1587. The only seaborne defence was a squadron of eight galleys commanded by Don Pedro de Acuña that happened to be standing in the harbour in the course of a patrol of the coast from Gibraltar to Cape St Vincent. They immediately put out and strung a line across the harbour entrance. At this point many of the citizens of Cadiz crowded to the waterfront to see what might happen next. The squadron of huge ships, forging in on a steady south-westerly, did not look or behave like Spanish vessels, but what were they? A galley was sent across the outer harbour to find out. Before it got within hailing distance the leading ships opened fire and, as Mattingly writes, 'If he followed his usual custom it was then that Drake broke out English banners and trumpets brayed from the quarter deck. In the town something like panic ensued.'

Naval warfare was about to enter a new era and the events in Cadiz harbour were very nearly the last of the old: the Spanish galleys, low in the water, powered by sail and oars, with their terrifying bronze ramming spikes and decks crammed with soldiers and small cannon, against the English galleons, massive ships with long-range guns, well-trained gunners and good experience of handling sail. In the Mediterranean it might have been interesting; on the Atlantic it was no contest. The English pounded away with their brass culverins and gave no possibility of close-quarter action. The galleys had to give way and run for shelter behind an offshore shoal – they knew better than to allow themselves to be reduced to matchwood or to end up surrendering half a dozen prize ships to the enemy. Apart from the galleys and a couple of cannon taking optimistic pot-shots from the shore, Drake sailed into Cadiz harbour unopposed.

The population and small local garrison retreated into the citadel and sent to Jerez for reinforcements. A Genoese galleon put up resistance and was sent to the bottom of the harbour for its pains (the English much regretted the loss of several prize brass cannon) and some brave soldiers and citizens made things as difficult as possible for the invader by hauling more cannon into place. But the armaments and the garrison and the fort had all been arranged to keep possible invaders at bay and Drake had no intention of invading. His weapon was surprise and he meant to be in and out before the Spanish came to. He anchored among the confusion of ships stranded in the harbour, many without sails on board. His crews set to work, methodically sorting out which cargoes and which vessels were worth taking and which were to be emptied and destroyed. Mattingly writes, 'As night fell the first hulks were towed free, fired and set adrift on the flood-tide. Soon the blazing ships lighted up the bay and cast a glow on the white walls of Cadiz.'

The following morning there was some skirmishing within and without the harbour until at about noon the wind cut to nothing and the English ships were still as statues. Now the Duke of Medina Sidonia (future commander of the Armada) arrived from Jerez with 6,000 infantry and cavalry. With the English ships becalmed, the townspeople scented revenge for their indignities. But Drake had anchored far enough out to deter any troop-carrying boats and the new cannon that were hauled into place on land were at hope-for-the-best range. Even without a wind the English could swing their ships with the skilful use of anchors and ropes to give a decent broadside to any adventurous galleys. The fireships that were inevitably launched as the second night fell were likewise gelded by lack of wind – the English boats had plenty of time to tow them out of harm's way.

A wind eventually started off the land around midnight of the second day and the English ships sailed out through the harbour channel. They were followed at a cautious distance by Acuña's galleys. Drake turned to offer combat but the Spanish commander once again showed commendable sense. 'Instead he sent the English admiral a complimentary message, along with a present of wine and sweetmeats, and after an exchange of courtesies worthy of two knights in a romance of chivalry the two commanders began to consider an exchange of prisoners.' (Mattingly, 1959)

The overwhelming of the Spanish galleys by English men-of-war was not just a matter of technology. The galleys had been ideal fighting ships in the Mediterranean since before the time of Xerxes. For 2,000 years they had been a key weapon in the building of empires, but now they were swept away by ships built for the Atlantic. The raid on Cadiz was not just a fleet of galleons swatting a squadron of galleys, it was an indicator of the burgeoning of the northern and western and the subsidence of the south and east, of the coming of the age of the Atlantic and the marginalisation of the Mediterranean nations. Spain, though, washed by both seas, was still in the game.

4. *The tearing off of branches means that the Armada will be lost.* Why did Elizabeth weep and rail over Mary's severed head? Because she knew that ships must now come from Spain against her throne. How was this chain of consequence foreseen?

As long as Mary Queen of Scots lives, everyone tells Elizabeth, her own life and throne are in danger. Mary is the only claimant to succeed Elizabeth, a fact that makes her a tempting target for a Catholic assassin William of Orange, Europe's other great Protestant leader, has been assassinated in his own house by a Catholic fanatic. Mary's accession would instigate a civil war – a religious bloodbath. Then why not be done with her? Well, why not? Elizabeth has lived with twenty years of 'why not' from her advisers.

When Elizabeth came to the throne England had been a country slipping into internal strife. There was no money, the national religion had changed three times in twenty years with bitter consequences, it had lost its last bridgehead in France, it hadn't a friend in Europe and the authority of its monarchs was in deep question. Elizabeth's claim to the throne was shaky, her authority restricted by a constitution made for feudal knights, her revenue pathetic, her armies dependent on the goodwill of her courtiers.

She has, in thirty years of governance, made England secure for her throne, stable, prosperous, strong. Juan da Silva, a Spanish courtier was to write in 1589: 'Only England preserves its spirit and increases its reputation . . . these last twenty-two years that the queen of England has spent in the service of the world, will be the most outstanding known of in history' (quoted in Kamen, 1997a).

Elizabeth of course knows that England has prospered through stability and she has made herself (and England) powerful by becoming indispensable to this. In her foreign policy she works for stability in Europe to feed her own nation's power and prosperity.

Wars are expensive and achieve little, but now Elizabeth feels that war is being forced upon her. The day before Mary's death at Fotheringay, envoys of the Dutch rebels ask for more money and support. The Netherlands has become a swamp into which she pours money and men, which the Dutch misuse, and where the Spanish advance goes on regardless. Her people need the open wool and cloth markets of the Netherlands and access from there to the fat towns of southern Germany and the Rhine. The Spanish are closing that route and English exports in 1587 will be drastically reduced. The economy of her kingdom is at risk and without money she cannot wage the war which she does not want, but which she must feel is inevitable.

But up until now it has been clear to Elizabeth that as long as Mary Queen of Scots is alive Spain will not attack England. Why should this be true? Mary Stuart is the daughter of a king of Scotland and a French noblewoman, Mary of Guise. For the past few years Philip of Spain has been busily pursuing his goal of placing Henry of Guise, Mary Stuart's cousin, on the throne of France. All well and good. He would be a good Catholic king and grateful to Philip for his help. He would not be a threat to Spain and would be an effective ally. But then, what if Elizabeth were to be assassinated or dethroned? Half-Guise Mary Stuart would become queen of England. The two strongest rivals to Spain, England and France, would be ruled by one family. This is not Philip's wish. Though he may desire each – Elizabeth gone and Guise on the throne of France – he does not want them both.

But now Mary Stuart is dead and Elizabeth looks through Philip's eyes at the English question: Scotland is potentially hostile to the English; France is neutered and neutral and will not interfere against Spain; the Netherlands is for the time pacified and full of crack Spanish troops within three hours' sailing of Margate; and England is both Protestant and a nuisance.

Philip can, Elizabeth knows, envision a world in which England is a Spanish ally-cum-client. Where his ships can sail the North Atlantic and the North Sea unharassed, where he can use English friends to help quash the rebellious Dutch, where the treasures of the Americas can pour unhindered into Spain and where Europe can be at peace. Elizabeth must know that this vision is so tantalising that Philip must attempt to grasp it.

History has often said that Philip was a prudent, over-cautious ruler who procrastinated over his papers, while Elizabeth was decisive and pro-active. But we can see it another way. Elizabeth wanted what she could get, Philip what he could not. Elizabeth had no grand vision: she wanted peace and prosperity – not simply out of altruism but because her wit and her life had shown her what their absence meant. Philip's vision was devout and, he thought, practical. He saw a peaceful, religiously harmonious world at the end of his struggles, and he was prepared to go to war to get it. But the creation of this world was always just beyond his grasp and that was the tragedy of his reign.

Had Spanish troops successfully landed in England in 1588 would Philip's vision have been brought into being? Colin Martin and Geoffrey Parker have pointed out how feeble the English land defences were. The experienced Spanish forces might easily have advanced to London and even taken the capital. But what then? Martin and Parker also argue that Philip had little sense of tactical or strategic compromise, no feel for the matching of military and political objectives, no flexibility, no alternative plan in the face of changing circumstance. His troops might have conquered England only to see Philip turn it into another Netherlands.

Philip was an apparently meticulous planner who, when difficulties were pointed out, retreated into the chant that the outcome would be decided by the will of God. Elizabeth, with her revolutionary pragmatism, is unlikely to have so exposed her fate. Philip's wars were ultimately unwinnable because the victory he desired was always unattainable.

5. *He took me towards the south to a very high and very dry island.* Dream visions from the centuries before Lucrecia were often set in idyllic gardens. This evoked both the scriptural paradise of the Garden of Eden and the pastoral ideal of classical authors such as Virgil. A. C. Spearing (1976) writes:

> It [the medieval vision] is typically set in bright southern sunlight (perhaps augmented or transformed into the jewelled brilliance of the Apocalypse), but it also provides shade against the sun, and is therefore furnished with a tree or trees, often fruit trees.

Lucrecia fashions this archetype for herself. The land is barren and is transformed. The meaning was undoubtedly clear to her and her transcribers – the tree is a sign of growth out of nothing; the manifestation of the barren become fertile.

The Ordinary Man came and took me to the seashore where we found the two fishermen. The Young Fisherman, who was now without the lion, was painting, in vivid colours, the tree which he had shown me the previous night on the island.[1] He said to me, 'Girl, why do you call me fisherman, for I have never fished?'[2]

I answered, 'I have seen you with your companion who carries the nets and I understood you both to be fishermen together.'

He said, 'No, once I used to fish, but not for fish.'[3]

Then I saw in the distance the many-towered city that I had seen in a previous dream, and now it was burning with a tremendous fire. It was not like the burning of some house but like the burning of brick ovens – all flames and smoke that was thick and black. This flame and smoke was advancing towards Spain.

I asked the Lion Man, 'Who is being burned there?' and he replied, 'It is not important to tell you now, another day you will know.'

The Lion Man took me to the island of the previous night, and when we were there he asked, 'Has Don Alonso explained to you the meaning of the tree you saw last night?'

I said yes and related what he had told me about it.

The Lion Man said, 'As to that I have no more to say. It is well.'

As I looked at the trees I saw that those around the main tree which bore only leaves were consumed by fire, although they were still upright. And then I saw that three trees equal in size which were watered by the brook that came from the east, stood in front of the principal tree as though looking at it.

I said, 'I can see how all these trees share the water of this king!' (I said this because Don Alonso, in his explanation, had said that the large handsome tree signified a good king whose virtues and exemplary works were shared by his children and subjects.)

As I said these words, I saw that the ground we stood on was white, as though dry, and sloped away from us. At the bottom of the slope we encountered King Philip. He was dressed in shepherd's clothes and had seven ewes.[4] *I saw that the king settled himself among some brambles and then lay on his left side and slept while holding his shepherd's crook in his right hand.*

While he slept, from the direction from which we had come, which is also the direction in which England lies, there came a foreign man (I knew him to be such, for I had seen others like him). He wore a low-crowned round hat, a long-skirted garment and tight red hose; his right sleeve was rolled up and in that hand he carried a knife.

Reaching the ewes, the foreigner took them each by their ears and cut their throats. Then, flaying them he cut away all the meat. He took this up to the top of the slope and cast it into the sea. Next he filled the pelts of the ewes with straw and set them upright on their legs as if they were still alive. This horrified me for it seemed to be a very new way of stealing. Having carried out this injury and theft he went away in the direction from which he had come.

The shepherd awoke. He touched one of the ewes which was near him with his crook so that it should go and graze with the others, for there was no grass where it stood. Being full of straw this sheep fell to the ground at the touch of the crook. The shepherd got up to look at his sheep, grasping them by their heads and finding them to be only pelts. At this he began to cry out with overmuch noise and feeling.

The Lion Man said to me, 'He would have done better not to have slept among the brambles.'

From the island the Lion Man took me to a room in the royal palace in Madrid where I saw a writing desk draped with a black cloth. Upon the desk was a royal crown covered with a transparent black cloth such as is placed over the cross which is venerated on a monument. By its side lay a royal sceptre also covered by the veil and, on the same desk but uncovered, a small bell such as may be seen on sheep. The end of the bell's tongue or clapper was tied and fastened around the outside to the handle at the top.

The Lion Man said to me, 'Ring that bell.'

I took hold of it but since its tongue was tied it made no sound whatsoever.

The Lion Man said, 'You may understand that when the king is dead the bells of El Escorial, which have never been pleasing to God for having been made at the expense of the poor, will be of no benefit to him.'[5]

Then he returned me to where the Ordinary Man and the Old Fisherman had waited. The Ordinary Man took me home and I awoke.

1. *The Young Fisherman, who was now without the lion, was painting, in vivid colours, the tree which he had shown me the previous night on the island.* The painting of Lucrecia's visions went on within her dreams and within the woken world. There is a record of Don Alonso de Mendoza having commissioned an artist to paint the visions that Lucrecia described. This visual record, which would perhaps have been shown to Lucrecia for her opinion on its versimilitude, has not survived.

   Is it possible though to catch the evanescent world of dreams in a static image? Those dream visions that have been painted have generally been manufactured to give an impression of what a dream seems like. Though a painting of the 'real' world has a similarly refracted relationship to its source, the idea of holding up a dreamscape and asking, 'Is this what you saw?' is a degree more absurd than attempting the same with a landscape. Dreams and works of art are both products of the imagination but one cannot easily be used to represent the other.

On occasion Lucrecia or her patrons thought the Lion Man to be St Luke. Generally believed to have been a physician (though even this is contentious), Luke was by legend an artist and is the patron saint of both doctors and artists. Belief in Luke's artistic vocation led to the story that he painted the picture of the Blessed Virgin Mary in the church of Santa Maria Maggiore in Rome.

2. *He said to me, 'Girl, why do you call me fisherman, for I have never fished?'* This man who inhabits the seashore and once took a lion about with him is a prickly character. He half resents having to deal with Lucrecia at all and persuades us to assume that he is somehow doing his duty. This reluctant voice gives us a stronger sense of the reality of Lucrecia's visions (in the sense that they existed for her) and of their divine authenticity. It induces the sense that God's choice of this unremarkable woman is not without its difficulties for those who serve Him. The Lion Man, as Lucrecia learns to call him, gives the impression that he would rather be dealing with someone else – perhaps a saintly nun or an intellectual prelate – rather than this 'girl'.

Lucrecia's concrete, consistent and believable depictions of the characters of the three companions has the effect of making the extraordinary situations in which she has her visions seem quite workaday. Yet as we begin to know more about these characters the dreams take on the atmosphere of a fairy tale. A young naive girl-woman is shown an unbelievable and incomprehensible world by three variously more knowledgeable men who alternately welcome her, resent her, explain to her, are exasperated by her, patronise her and tease her. We might be on the far side of Alice's looking-glass.

3. *He said, 'No, once I used to fish, but not for fish.'* 'And Jesus, walking by the sea of Galilee, saw two brethren, Simon called Peter, and Andrew his brother, casting a net into the sea: for they were fishers. And he saith unto them, Follow me, and I will make you fishers of men' (Matthew 4: 18–19).

4. *King Philip . . . was dressed in shepherd's clothes and had seven ewes.* This strange and beautiful fable echoes the deep symbolism (rather than the manufactured symbols of tradition) of rural societies. If the shepherd sleeps, all is lost. The image of the sheep stuffed with straw is close to being comical, giving the story a disturbing tone. The shepherd is robbed *and* ridiculed. But the most potent image in the tale is a throwaway line that is incidental to the story. After killing and flaying the sheep the stranger takes the meat to the top of a cliff and casts it into the sea. The conjunction of cut flesh and ocean is visually and profoundly startling.

5. *'You may understand that when the king is dead, the bells of El Escorial, which have never been pleasing to God for having been made at the expense of the poor, will be of no benefit to him.'* Spanish armies defeated the French at the battle of Saint Quentin on 10 August 1557. King Philip of Spain decided to build a monastery dedicated to the saint on whose feast day the battle was fought – San Lorenzo. El Escorial, situated 30 miles north-west of Madrid, was begun in 1563 and finished in 1584, just three years before Lucrecia dreamed this dream. It was and is a vast complex of buildings – a monastery, royal palace, church, library, mausoleum and museum – resembling a fortress rather than a place of spiritual contemplation. Now one of the most visited sites in Spain, the complex, a modern guidebook tells us, 'has 16 courtyards, 2673 windows, 1250 doors, 86 staircases and 88 fountains, and the corridors have a total length of 16 km'.

By the time of Lucrecia's dream, when the citizens and churches of Castile were being squeezed for more taxes, the king's extravagant monument did not go well with the people.

A less controversial consequence of the battle of Saint Quentin was peace between Spain and France, or more properly between the Habsburgs and the Valois, rulers of France. A treaty was signed on 3 April 1559 in Câteau Cambrésis in France and it was this treaty that was the springboard for Spain's emergence as a world power. Unencumbered by its nearest powerful neighbour, and for the time being on neutral terms with England, in control of most of Italy and the Low Countries and master of the New World, Spain had only to deal with the last throes of Turkish power in the western Mediterranean to find itself in an extraordinarily advantageous strategic and economic position.

There was, though, a bizarre outcome to this peace which gives us a sense of the personal connectedness of European power politics in this era when monarchs, rather than emperors or popes or dukes, were becoming the key figures in the emerging nation-states. Philip of Spain, the world's most eligible widower, having lately lost his English Queen Mary (his second wife), has allowed her sister and successor Elizabeth to consider him a suitor (her Protestantism is not an obstacle to him). She has thought on it then thought a little more. But now she has heard he is casting his line in other directions and tells his ambassador that his king 'could not have been much in love with her, since he did not have the patience to wait four months'. In the wake of the new treaty, Philip now favours Isabel de Valois, daughter of Henry II, king of France. The marriage is agreed, and the peace of Europe is sealed.

Notre Dame Cathedral, Paris, 22 June 1559. A midsummer wedding. All Catholic and Habsburg Europe is there except, curiously, the bride-groom. Philip is still in Ghent and cannot come to Paris. The Duke of Alba therefore takes his place at what is termed a proxy wedding. This strange affair emphasises the symbolic nature of these matches, but Philip did, it seems, come to love Isabel.

There is a strange aftermath to the wedding. A young Scottish nobleman, the Count of Montgomery, is in Paris for the celebrations as one of the Scots Guards. His still half-Catholic country's ties with France are close and suddenly more important with the recent acces-sion of Elizabeth to the English throne. He is given the honour of jousting against the French king at the traditional tournament which follows the wedding. Henry II is a forty-year-old veteran of many battles who relishes the opportunity to show off in front of his court. Mont-gomery must offer spirited competition for the spectacle to be exciting – any obvious pandering to the king will lower him in the eyes of onlookers. Unfortunately the young Scot is a little too keen. His lance pierces the king's helmet and right eye and wounds him fatally. Within ten days Henry II, king of France is dead. His son François, aged just fifteen, is declared king alongside his teenage bride – Mary Stuart, Queen of Scots.

Move on eighteen years . . . Mary has survived her French king and two more husbands before dying in an English castle. Philip has built his monument to the battle which brought him peace and a new bride. He now sits in his vast Escorial and fusses his way through the papers that overwhelm him. He has more rooms in which to worry.

The Ordinary Man came to me and took me to the seashore where I found the two companions as usual. The Lion Man said to me, 'I had no wish to explain anything to you but I must.'

He took me by the hand and led me to the same island as on other nights. We looked at the trees and he said to me, 'This one (indicating the large tree) is the king that is to come. The burnt trees round about it are the rich men who will try to get close to him, as they now are to your king.[1] But he will not permit it, rather he will destroy them and exalt the poor, who are represented by the small trees which bear fruit. And you see, of course, those three trees in front of the big one; you will say to Don Alonso that these three emerge from a single trunk and that all are one. This is something whose meaning you will come to understand well.'

The Lion Man then took me back to where we had left the Old Man and the Ordinary Man (which is towards England). As we went I said to him, 'Don Alonso asked me to tell you that although he will do what you command, explaining these visions in so far as he understands them, he still wishes you to clarify them. Tell me now, what was being burned in the fire in that English city?'

He replied, 'You saw how that fire, together with the smoke that arose from it, advanced towards Spain. That signifies the great evil that is to come from that city.[2] Many people will be lost in that evil.'

Then, arriving before the Old Man and the Ordinary Man, he said to them, 'Take your woman away for I have nothing further to do with her, and give me paints and paper.' They did so and he began very ably to paint the dreams of the previous nights in vivid colours.

The Old Man told the Ordinary Man to take me to England. We flew across the seas[3] and came to a seaport, where there were many ships, medium-sized and large, being made ready. Entering into the city we saw many newly-arrived foreigners who were to be paid by Drake. In order to pay them Drake went to his house, and we saw how he took out from a safe place a hoard of treasure that he had hidden – this was something I had seen in another dream.

From there we came into another room, where I saw a woman who looked a little more than fifty years old. The Ordinary Man said to me, 'Look, there is Elizabeth, queen of England.'

The queen was sitting on a low stool and holding on her lap a dead lamb, cut open at the belly. The queen was putting her hands into the place where the belly of the lamb was cut and was pulling out its guts and entrails. She was taking up with both hands the blood that was held inside the lamb and was drinking it with great relish. At the queen's side was a very beautiful woman, though very pale and dressed in the black of a widow. The queen spoke to this woman, telling her to drink some of the blood of the lamb but the woman in black said that she would not do this. The queen became very angry at this and stood up and, taking a sword from her side, she struck suddenly at the woman, cutting off her head.[4]

The queen washed the blood of the lamb[5] from her hands, and the body was taken to Drake. He ordered that the remaining meat and skin should be shared out among his soldiers. He told them that they should hang the flesh of the lamb[6] from their banners to give insult to our king and that soon they would be giving the old and wrinkled king of Spain a slap on the face.

Then the Ordinary Man took me back across the sea to the Old Man. As he did so I heard the sound of war drums.

When we arrived I asked the Old Man, 'Who was the
beautiful woman in mourning?'
   He said that he would answer me another night.
   The Ordinary Man took me to my house and I awoke.

1. *'the rich men who will try to get close to him, as they now are to your king'.*
All visionaries have imparted a religious message and in some cases
this has become political as well, but few have been so openly political as Lucrecia. Before and after Lucrecia there was a strong tradition
of dissent within religious life. Prophets and preachers, taking their
cue from the likes of Jeremiah and Isaiah, predicted disaster unless the
Church and their rulers mended their ways. The inspiring example of
St Francis, seen by some as a second Christ, laid bare the unnecessary
grandeur of the lives of the clerics as early as the thirteenth century.
The corruption and greed of the Church was thereafter contrasted
with the humility of the common people. Kings and emperors are often
included in this criticism of the powerful, though generally as a by-
product. While the clergy should not live in grandeur the monarchy
certainly could and did, but this should not be at the expense of the
poor.

Although Lucrecia does occasionally criticise some church officials,
Philip is the main focus of her anger. He is to blame for the ills of Spain
which will only be righted when he is gone – to be replaced by a new
king (maybe Piedrola) who will reign in a golden time. We may find
this paradoxical since Lucrecia was living at a time history has called
El Siglo de Oro, the Golden Age of Spain, but for the ordinary citizens
of Castile life was hard and getting ever harder.

Lucrecia is almost always unfair to Philip but why should she be
otherwise? She is wrong about his lack of personal devoutness (he was
a pious man; had he been less so it might have been better for his
country), but this error was born out of her own belief in God's dispen-
sation. If the Spanish people were suffering, as Lucrecia and her
associates believed, then it must be because God was punishing them.
This in turn must be because they were offending Him. As the common
people were devout and ascetic (though probably not through choice)

their rulers must be to blame. Philip must therefore have offended God by impious behaviour.

Lucrecia was more accurate in her other criticisms. Raising money from the populace and from the Church for the fighting of wars was painful and highly unpopular – though Lucrecia also wants Spain to be protected from her enemies. The problem was that Philip was both a Spanish king and a Habsburg emperor. Though the Habsburg lands had been divided into separate realms, Philip's share was large and, inevitably, troublesome. He felt a great responsibility for his dominions – not only for defending them from without but for policing them within.

Castilians might have hoped that Philip, being one of them, would have treated them better than his father had, and perhaps learned something more about money from his early experiences. Philip's father Charles V, Holy Roman Emperor, had left Philip to look after Spain when only seventeen years old while he went off to fight the French and some unruly Germans in other parts of his vast realm. Philip quickly learned the difficulties and expense of fighting wars. With dreadful regularity messages would arrive from his father requesting immediate funds from Castile. The Cortes would meet and point out that they simply had no money to give – and anyway why didn't the German lands pay for their own wars? Philip, then a kind of Prince Regent, was in total agreement. He wrote to his father in March 1545, when he was eighteen years of age:

> With what they owe for other things, the common people who have to pay the taxes are reduced to such extremes of misfortune and poverty that many of them go naked without clothing. And the misery is so universal that it afflicts not only Your Majesty's subjects but even more those of the nobility, for they cannot pay their taxes nor have the means to do so. The prisons are full, and all are heading for ruin. Believe me, Your Majesty, if this were not true I would not dare write it to you. (quoted in Kamen, 1997a)

Given this youthful awareness, what did Philip do when he was king and in command of military and financial policy? He too turned to his subjects for money to prosecute ruinously expensive wars. But despite this heavy taxation, several times in his reign the king had to declare the national treasury bankrupt and unilaterally reschedule his debt repayments with his German and Genoese creditors. He also forced the Church to hand over part of its wealth – a particularly sore point with the Spanish clergy including Don Alonso de Mendoza and Fray Lucas de Allende.

Fourteen months after this dream, in the wake of the Armada defeat, Philip introduced the notorious *millones* tax, levied on the purchase of everyday essential items – the first time such a levy had been made. Naturally enough, this only added to most Spaniards' disillusionment with their king. Posters displayed on public buildings in Avila read, 'Spain, Spain, look to yourself and defend your liberty; and you, Philip, be satisfied with what is your own and do not claim what is another's.'

All of this was happening at a time when gold and silver were pouring in from the Americas. This should have made Spain a rich country but the Spanish people failed to benefit from their apparent good fortune. They saw only the inflationary effects of the American bullion and the neglect and subsequent collapse of their agriculture and textile industries. The gold and silver from the New World brought a boom to the Atlantic seaboard and it enabled Philip to go on fighting wars, some of which he might have done better to have been unable to afford.

All this would have been more bearable had Philip been easier to love. The interpretation of Lucrecia's dream given by the Lion Man here is politically adroit. Subjects and citizens are always wary of the people that surround their leaders. We do not like to feel those we have placed in power disappearing beyond our reach into the midst of a self-interested clique. In democratic times those with nous understand this concern and make regular direct contact with the populace. But even for monarchs the respect of the people needed to be nurtured. Philip's reign coincided with Spain's apogee but his people shared only the illusion of glory. He never reached out to them except with a collecting plate.

In the late 1580s as events went against him, the king had no reservoir of affection to call on. Lucrecia's scorn and mockery could not be pushed away. They struck a chord and thereby became dangerous.

2. *'That signifies the great evil that is to come from that [English] city.'* On first reading, Lucrecia's dreams of the end of the world and of the destruction of Spain appear interchangeable; a kaleidoscope of images of

portent and destruction, each as lurid, grim and doom-laden as its predecessor and successor. But steady immersion in the dreams reveals that there is, at least for the period covered by the dreams in this book, a strongly progressive pattern.

Lucrecia dreams first of symbols of destruction and vengeance, of strange events and strange people whose import is clear but whose meaning is deliberately displaced. Then, as the nights pass, she begins to see men and women of the world she inhabits. These are the real people who will destroy Spain and bring her world to an end, or they are those who will be victims of the destruction. The portents hardly need interpretation: something terrible is going to happen.

Later Lucrecia will see exactly what it is that is going to happen and what her own involvement will be. This will draw her on towards the only ending that she can foresee – the end of the world. While we naturally try to empathise with Lucrecia, our anticipation is entirely different from hers. She knows that the end of the world will come soon; we know that it did not. We therefore wonder how the ending that Lucrecia expects will be confounded.

3. *We flew across the seas.* Artemidorus' *The Interpretation of Dreams*, the principal dream-guide for Europeans for nearly 2,000 years, is, for all its oddities, a very commensensical book. This may account for its lasting appeal – from the second century when it was written until well into the nineteenth. Its explanations doubtless gained authority from their parallels with everyday life. The experience of flying, Artemidorus says, means different things, according to altitude:

> To dream to fly a little height from the earth, being upright, is good; for as much as one is lifted higher than those about him, so much the greater and more happy shall he be. It were better for him not to be in his own country, for it signifieth wandring, or not resting, or returning to his Country. To fly with wings is good generally for all, for servants it is liberty, to the poor riches; to the rich office and dignity. To fly very high from the Earth and without wings is fear and danger; as also to fly over the houses and through the streets and forlorn ways, it is trouble and sedition. It is always good, after having flown on high, to descend low, and after that to awake, but it is best of all to fly when one will, and come down when one will, for it is a sign of facility and good disposition in affairs.

4. *The queen became very angry at this and stood up and, taking a sword from her side, she struck suddenly at the woman, cutting off her head.* Queen Elizabeth went to great lengths to assure the Catholic rulers of France, Scotland and in particular Spain that she regretted the death of her troublesome cousin, Mary Stuart. She even imprisoned William Davison, the secretary who had allowed the signed execution warrant out of his hands (though he was quietly released once the fuss had died down). Some historians have decided that Davison behaved nobly and his queen badly over the affair, but this may be unjust. On the bare facts Davison honestly dispatched the death warrant that Elizabeth had signed under pressure from her Council and, it might be said, the populace. But Elizabeth was not the sort of queen whose orders were simply to be carried out. She demanded to be understood, above all by her secretaries.

First there is the question of death. Elizabeth quietly suggested that Mary might meet hers unexpectedly. Davison and Sir Amyas Paulet, Mary's official custodian, sternly refused to act without legal authority. (Mattingly writes that 'Davison would not understand her, and when he did would not pretend not to be shocked.') Her later reaction showed her frustration at having to deal with men whom she regarded as hidebound Puritans. They did not seem to understand that it would not be moral cowardice to end Mary's life behind closed doors, but political astuteness. Every monarch appreciated the need occasionally to murder one's close relatives; but this should be done with discretion. For Protestant Elizabeth to make a public event – it was not quite that but too near for her liking – of the killing of Mary would be close to a declaration of religious war against Catholic Europe. If her Council and her people wanted to be rid of the woman then so be it – there were, surely to God, ways and means to have it done! But Davison could see none of this, just his legalistic duty. (Walsingham, her chief interpreter, lay ill in bed at this crucial time – though some say this was a convenient sickness.) So the proper channels were followed and Elizabeth, though not surprised, was nevertheless infuriated by the outcome – the execution of an ex-queen of France, mother to the Scottish king and bulwark against Spanish ambitions in England, in front of a solemnly gathered group of Elizabeth's own advisers. The outcome, which will be disastrous for Spain, will not do much for England either.

Lucrecia's vision is closer to what Elizabeth would want (not herself as executioner but the privacy of it) than what she got. It also shows how little the English queen's disowning of the deed persuaded the Spanish people. The widow in the dream is, of course, Mary Queen of Scots. Her first husband, Francis II of France, crowned in 1559 on the tragic death of his father Henry II, died seventeen months later. Mary was then seventeen. On her return to Scotland she married Henry Stuart, Lord Darnley in 1565. During this brief marriage Mary fell for her Italian secretary David Rizzio, who was dragged from the royal supper table and murdered in front of her. Darnley was then also murdered, in 1567, probably by the Earl of Bothwell who then married Mary himself. This all became too much for the increasingly Calvinist Scots, who forced her abdication and imprisoned her in Lochleven Castle. She escaped in 1568 and raised an army, but was defeated at Langside and was forced to cross the border and seek sanctuary with Elizabeth. She remained under house arrest in England for twenty years. Her story has enlivened the dull afternoon of many a British school-child.

5. *the blood of the lamb*. If the Greeks sought perfection and the Romans power, what did these Western Europeans, with their piety and their visions of blood, yearn for? Perhaps their ultimate goal was purity. Anything could be forgiven of him who was pure, while impurity, even though hidden, would in the end be revealed. And as one's own soul must be constantly purified, so all the world must be made pure in the same way. If blood must be shed, including one's own, then so be it. If every heretic, infidel and unrepentant sinner must be bled, then that would be done. And at the Day of Judgment the blood of the Lamb would wash all things clean.

Sancho Panza says, 'I am an Old Christian' and we laugh at the absurdity of such a man claiming superiority through the purity of his ancestors. But we should not laugh too much. Sancho Panza speaks for all bigotry born out of self-pity and is a satirical creation (Cervantes was a contemporary of Lucrecia de Léon). But his narrow-mindedness was formalised and used as an instrument against his fellow citizens.

The story of the Spanish Inquisition, its origins, its impact on the people of Spain, whether Christians, Jews, *conversos* (Jews who had converted to Christianity) or *moriscos* (Muslims who had similarly converted), and the Spanish people's view of it is far more subtle and complex than some caricatures of its work have allowed. Though associated in northern minds with the Counter-Reformation, the Inquisition began its work in Spain in 1480, three years before Martin Luther was born (and one hundred years before Lucrecia dreamed her dreams).

At that time Spain was a country of three faiths – Christian, Muslim and Jewish. The accession of Ferdinand and Isabella in 1474 united the realms of Castile (of which Isabella was queen) and Aragón (ruled by Ferdinand from 1479). This brought an end to inter-provincial hostilities in the north and east of the Iberian peninsula and enabled them to turn towards the conquest of al-Andalus, the Arabic south, of which only the province of Granada remained. Though the Reconquest of the south of Spain was a bloody, intolerant business (the entire population of Málaga was enslaved after its capture in 1487) it was seen thereafter as an heroic and chivalrous defeat of infidel forces.

In setting up the Spanish Inquisition and reconquering the south (the two were crucially linked), Ferdinand and Isabella acted for political rather than religious reasons. They were, like many of their subjects, reasonably tolerant of other religions and content to live alongside Moors and Jews. But, as Kamen (1997b) writes:

> All this was changed by the successful Reconquest . . . It appears that the rulers, seeking to stabilize their power in both Castile and Aragon, where civil wars had created disorder in the 1470s, accepted an alliance with [regressive] social forces that prepared the way for the elimination of a plural, open society. The crown accepted this policy because it seemed to ensure stability, but the new developments failed to bring about social unity, and the machinery of the Inquisition served only to intensify and deepen the shadow of conflict over Spain.

Once all of Spain's Jews and Moors were forced to convert to Christianity they fell within the remit of the Inquisition, a body which had no command over people of other faiths. These communities retained much of their separateness (and continued practising their faith without much attempt at secrecy) and were policed only sporadically, but occasionally with great intensity, by the Inquisition.

Sancho Panza's remark gains its potency from a singular social phenomenon. Converted Moors and, in particular, Jews had, over the generations, married into many of the noble families of Spain. This was a reflection of the generally liberal and tolerant attitude of the educated and aristocratic class. (On a practical level the landowners also liked and admired their hard-working and peaceful *morisco* work-force and tenants.)

Sancho Panza, being of humble stock, has no such 'impurity' in his blood and can therefore call himself an Old Christian. It is the perverse pride of the unworldly and uncurious. By Philip II's time toler-ance of *conversos* and *moriscos* was a complex and fragile business, but it seems that the king, though occasionally liberal, fell, as in so many other things, on the intolerant side of pragmatism. Henry Kamen (1997b) writes:

> The king became a more convinced supporter of blood purity. In 1554 he approved purity statutes in the four cathedrals of the realm of Granada. In 1566 he introduced a purity statute into the city council of Toledo against the bitter opposition of most of its members . . . In reality his prejudice . . . was out of step with the thinking of many educated Spaniards of the day.

Let us be clear about what this meant. No cleric could be appointed to a position in these cathedrals if any of his ancestors, going back through any number of generations, was Jewish or Arab, even if that ancestor had, in good faith, converted to, or lived all through life as, a devout Christian. Soon it was not good enough to declare your blood purity, you had to prove it. People set up as genealogists publishing the infamous 'green books' which showed all the great families of Spain, and many others, to have Muslim or Jewish roots. The best known of these, the *Tizón de España*, was a great popular success, reprinting many times. Aspiring officials had to hire alternative inves-tigators to draw up their 'true' family trees, showing them to be of the purest blood.

This obsession with lineage, given implicit royal sanction, threat-ened to get out of hand. Artisans in occupations associated with Arabs came under suspicion of impurity and were looked down on by unskilled peasants whose rural isolation had kept them unsullied. We are back to Sancho Panza.

All of this is distasteful to us but did it, in the swing of Spanish history, mean much? There was a long tradition, now discarded, of writing about the history of Spain as an extension of what the his-torian perceives to be the Spanish character. For these writers, the importance of purity and of a certain type of honour led Spanish society to fossilise. From this perpective Cervantes satirised an aspect of the human condition that his fellow countrymen determined to live out.

6. *the lamb.* We may take it that the lamb in this vision stands for the Catholics in England. Elizabeth is seen as taunting the Spanish king by her persecution of the followers of the true faith. Recent work on Philip's reign has countered the long-held assumption that he was engaged in a life-long war against Protestantism. Instead his conflicts can be interpreted as heavy-handed responses to insurrections (as in the Netherlands) or strategic campaigns to protect his kingdom (as in the later war against the English). We might add that in both cases the enemy happened to be Protestant but even this is not true. In the suppression of the original Netherlands revolt, which was against the imposition of religious restrictions known as *placards* and the subsequent barring of certain Dutch nobles from the ruling Council of Estates, dissident Catholic nobles were arrested and even executed along with Calvinists.

But even if Philip was not engaged in a religious struggle his subjects may have believed *they* were. There is no question that Lucrecia sees the enemies of Spain as the enemies of the faith – both within and without the country. And even if the king was more concerned with rebellion (while acutely aware of the disastrous effects of religious dissidence in France) it was his own religious laws imposed on the autonomous Netherlands following decisions made in Spain that began the conflict. Moreover the sending of the Duke of Alba to the Netherlands in 1567 (a decision which Geoffrey Parker, 1985, tells us is still incomprehensible to historians) at the head of an army of 10,000 Spaniards bent on punishment of all heretics was, though a short-term success, a disastrous failure of diplomacy and politics. It was to cost Spain everything it had gained.

*The Ordinary Man came to my house and took me away to the
seashore.*[1] *I saw that the Lion Man was painting and I heard
him ask the Ordinary Man what we had seen in England. When
he had related this, the Lion Man showed me in his paintings all
of the dreams that he had revealed to me these past nights. It
was done with such perfection that all seemed as alive as when I
had seen it.*

*The Ordinary Man said, 'We went to England and saw Drake
and his preparations for war.'*

*The Lion Man replied, 'Truly that was well done. They know
what they are doing. They are indeed enemies although I have
always had some regard for them.'*

*As we spoke we saw that Drake's fleet approached, and the
soldiers had parts of the lamb's flesh and skin displayed on their
banners. This fleet made directly for that of the Marquis of
Santa Cruz.*[2] *They battled and the victory went to the
Marquis's fleet, although little damage was inflicted on Drake's
ships. He retreated to England, the Marquis pursuing him as far
as the port.*

*Then the Old Man told the Ordinary Man to take me to
Turkey, and set me in the hall of the Great Turk. There I saw
that the Great Turk was saddened at Drake's loss, which he had
learned about from letters from Spain. But then letters arrived
informing him that he had gained the kingdom of Poland and
that Maximilian had retreated. He derived much satisfaction
from that. I saw him write a letter to Drake saying that Poland
was taken and that, if he was under pressure in the port to
which he had retreated, he should come to Turkey so that
together they might advance on Navarre.*

At this point I saw enter the hall a very beautiful Turkish

woman.[3] *In her right hand this woman carried the world. On it
many men were painted, among them some men I recognised
from the streets of Madrid, including Don Diego de Córdoba
who appeared very troubled. In her left hand the woman
carried the head of a man, which she grasped by the hair and
which was running with blood. In front of the Great Turk, she
indicated with the head that she carried the world. Of all the
men painted on the world she dripped blood only on Don Diego
de Córdoba.*

*I remembered him from a previous dream, so I said to him, 'If
the sons that you engendered were not such as they are, you
would not find yourself so afflicted.'*

*Then the Ordinary Man took me out of there and back to the
seashore where he recounted everything I had seen to the Old
Man and the Lion Man. The two of them spoke together with
some appearance of discord, for one said it meant one thing and
the other another.*

*So, speaking to them both, I said, 'Look, until you can be of
one mind on this do not come again to take me out of my
house.'[4]*

*The man who walks with me said, 'They are as much one as
is this foot of mine. Do not be frightened that there is discord for
it also exists among the doctors of your church.[5] It is a minor
matter that it should occur between these two for they have so
much more knowledge.'*

And with that I awoke.

1. *The Ordinary Man came to my house and took me away to the seashore.* The
   formal way in which each dream transcript begins and ends shows
   that this is not a 'free' account. It is a set of variations within a form.
   The form was developed out of Lucrecia's visions and Alonso de
   Mendoza's wishes. In the beginning the dreams were transcribed in

the third person – 'The Ordinary Man came to *her* . . .' This allowed the still-uncertain priests (Don Alonso de Mendoza and Fray Lucas de Allende) to keep a distance from Lucrecia by appearing to be merely interested scribes. Once they felt more confident of the importance of her visions Mendoza decided that the first-person voice would give authenticity and immediacy, allowing readers to sense that they were hearing directly from Lucrecia. It also implicitly involved the priests as her co-authors. Mendoza edited the transcripts that were sent to him and wrote up a fair copy himself. In this sense they were not exactly as Lucrecia related them but this is only one of the intriguing aspects of the voice of the dreamer.

Once she is awake Lucrecia's dreams must begin to fade in her memory. The act of remembering them is not simply the preservation of some recording in her mind, it is itself an act of creation. The dreams have been formed through her attempts to bring meaning and narrative to bear on fragments of sensation. Now that she is awake the process is gone through again and her dreams once more take form through the act of remembrance. This is something with which most of us are familiar – the gathering of a dream into woken memory. And then Lucrecia has a third task of reconstruction – the relating of her dreamed and remembered experiences to another person.

At each stage she must give a little more form to the object which she is creating. The dream itself can remain a barely connected string of images, events, sounds, sensations; the woken remembrance of it will bring more coherence as memory requires a sense of context; and then the telling of the dreams must involve yet more ordering as the act of communication depends on a shared set of conventions about form, meaning, progression, beginnings and endings. Through this process Lucrecia becomes the author of her dreams.

Although her patrons, her contemporaries, and perhaps even Lucrecia herself, viewed her as merely an inert medium for the transmission of the content of her dreams, we can see her in a different light. In essence Lucrecia used her imagination to create the narratives of her dreams. By this we do not mean that Lucrecia was making things up; rather that the imagination, as Frank Kermode has argued, far from being some ethereal luxury which invents the unreal, is the part of our minds which gives form. Lucrecia is not simply the messenger of her dreams, she is the imaginative force engaged in their creation.

2. *the Marquis of Santa Cruz.* Many histories of the Armada have blamed its defeat on Santa Cruz's absence and the inexperience of his replacement, the Duke of Medina Sidonia, but recent detailed accounts tend to support the view that Medina Sidonia played a bad hand well. He behaved with great courage and his exquisite sense of honour deliberately invited the blame and shame of the defeat to fall on his shoulders rather than where it truly belonged.

3. *I saw enter the hall a very beautiful Turkish woman.* The vision of the Turkish woman shows Lucrecia at her most captivating and disturbing. The balance between the world and a man's head, one held in each hand, is an instinctive and meaningful relation. We do not know the identity of the man who has presumably recently been executed and his anonymity is discomforting since he potentially stands for every possible victim of such violence.

   The faces painted on the world – which we take to be a globe – are a strange enough image. Then we see – and we really do see this action in our mind's eye – the woman wave the severed head across her body, so that the blood drips on to the surface of the world. It is a conjunction of a familiar everyday human gesture – look at what I hold in my hand – with a vision of epic sweep.

   The woman stands before the Grand Turk in a scene it is impossible not to envisage. And then Lucrecia, having drawn us into this compelling and repellent scene, reminds us both that this is *just* a dream, but that this *is* a dream. She discards her role as observer and speaks directly to Diego de Córdoba, or at least to his image. This breaks the spell and Lucrecia then leaves the scene.

4. *So, speaking to them both, I said, 'Look, until you can be of one mind on this do not come again to take me out of my house.'* The change in Lucrecia's tone is worth noting. She feels confident enough of her own status to be able to scold the two companions.

5. *'Do not be frightened that there is discord for it also exists among the doctors of your church.'* The Ordinary Man is right but discord over the minutiae of the dreams' interpretation will not be Lucrecia's main problem. In the sixteenth century belief in dreams was a complex and subtle business. Mostly they were thought to hint at future events in a minor way and not taken too seriously, rather like the astrology columns of

newspapers today. But sometimes they were believed to hold a profound meaning and in certain rare cases were thought to contain messages with divine authority. Lucrecia's visions of the king, the destruction of Spain, the courts of Europe, angels and apocalypses clearly contain something more mysterious and meaningful than guidance about her daily concerns. Those who read and interpreted them knew that they might be dealing with the voice of God or the voice of the Devil – but how to tell which?

In this context it was important for Lucrecia to be presented as innocent and unworldly, since a woman claiming to be a visionary who was thought to be clever would be suspected of invention or, worse, of being in league with the Devil. Visions were one of the few ways in which women of Lucrecia's time could express their views of the world. The price for this was that, to be taken seriously as a visionary, a woman must erase her own person.

The Ordinary Man came and took me to the seashore where I saw the Old Man.

He said to me, 'The Armada of the Marquis of Santa Cruz approaches England with much power.'

I said to the man who went with me, 'What are all of these wars about?'

He said, 'You do not understand it; talk about it to the people who explain your dreams, they will understand.'

Then I found myself in Turkey and saw that the fleet of the Great Turk was leaving for Poland, and behind all the ships and galleys was one which carried the Great Turk and Drake.[1] (In another dream I had seen the Turkish woman advise him to do this.)

From there I was taken to Poland. There I saw that Maximilian, the son of the Empress, was very anxious for he had but few troops and half the kingdom against him. I watched as he sent to ask a favour of his uncle, King Philip.

The man who goes with me said, 'Here you see Spain lost, because her enemies will fall upon her if Philip sends help to his nephew.'

From there he took me back to Spain, where I saw King Philip in a room cleaning swords from his armoury. My companion told me that we were in Toledo and said to the king, 'That sword that you are cleaning will do you little good for within sixty-four days you are to die in the same month as your wife Doña Isabel.'[2]

Then I saw that Toledo was besieged by Moors, Turkish, French, English and Polish soldiers.[3] The assault from the landward side[4] was so heavy and pressed forward so much that nobody came out to defend the city. Inside the city I heard a crier dressed in black anounce that the king would grant much favour to anyone who would go to its defence.

A man of moderate social standing came forward. He was dark-faced, well-built with strong limbs.[5] He assembled two hundred men who armed themselves. Upon their arms they wore white crosses that reached across their chests. I saw these men go out of one of the gates of the city which faces towards Madrid (in front of this there is much flat land) and they killed so many of the enemy that those who were left alive fled from that gate. It was then towards evening and when this man sought to gather his people together he saw that one hundred of them had been killed. They entered the city and there heard a great noise among the people saying that King Philip was dead. The man ordered that the news should not be broadcast throughout the city for fear that the enemy should take courage and return to the attack. Rather he wished them to inter the body quietly.

I saw the funeral of the king, the body borne shoulder high by a black-robed Cardinal Quiroga[6] and other clergymen whom I do not know. The archbishop wore something in the nature of a white linen bandage tied around his forehead and falling across his eyes.

I asked the Ordinary Man, 'Is that man ill, who wears a cloth in that way?'

He answered, 'That is the Marquis of Auñón. Either one or the other of them will die within a short time.'

I saw that they bore the king from the Alcázar fortress to the Great Church[7] and laid him in the chapel below the high altar. All of this was done with no bell-ringing. After that I saw the man who had gone out to defend the city. He had added another two hundred men to the hundred who had remained alive and with these three hundred he went out of the city by another gate which also faces in the direction of Madrid. Here the land slopes downwards, ahead and on both sides. There *they fought with the enemy and killed and captured many of them.*

From there and without seeing the end of the battle, the Ordinary Man took me to the seashore where I told the Old Fisherman all that I had seen. He said it was better to tell it at once so as not to forget anything.

Then the Lion Man called me and said, 'Do you wish me to show you a vision, for Don Alonso will receive kindly the news that you do.'

I said 'Yes' and he took me up above the seashore. We looked down on to the sea, and he showed me a thorn bush floating on the waters,[8] close to the shore. The bush was burning with a very vivid fire, the flames clear and without smoke. In the middle of this fire I saw a most beautiful angel (in form and dress like those depicted in images of the Annunciation to Our Lady) who, from the waist upwards, was clear of the flames and was beating his wings very fast over the fire. I could not tell whether this was done to extinguish the fire or to blow more life into it so that the thorn bush should be more quickly consumed. But then I saw that the fire died out, leaving no trace of the thorn bush. The angel disappeared as well and I saw that in the place where all this had been there was a dead body.

The body was wrapped in a white shroud which had been scorched by the fire above it. The sea, rough to the east, rose in great waves which swept towards the body and bore it away to the west.

The Lion Man who had shown me this vision said, 'Come now, go with God and tell what you have seen.'

And with that I awoke.

1. *the Great Turk and Drake.* By the time of Lucrecia's dreams Spain had renewed concerns about its neighbours. Lucrecia sees an unlikely alliance combining to attack Toledo, spiritual centre of Castile. But even if this was unlikely, there is some evidence that Philip shared Lucrecia's paranoia.

In 1580 Spain had quiet control of an empire ten times the size of Rome's – a triumph of military, political, administrative and diplomatic skill and adventurousness. Spanish atrocities in America and in the Netherlands and the publicity they attracted have overshadowed the country's achievements – not just as an empire-builder but as a major force in the development of modern Europe. Spain is seen, at its apogee, as an encumbrance to human progress rather than leading the world into a new age. There may be a particular reason why this view persists.

By the sixteenth century the centre of gravity of European power had shifted westwards from the Mediterranean to Spain and her Atlantic seaboard. This process continued in a further shift northwards to the English Channel, culminating in the rise of Britain to the world's greatest power. It has been argued that the seemingly inexorable increase in the power of Britain from Elizabethan England to the Victorian empire has diminished our appreciation of the achievements of Spain, and that the boldness and sense of making the world anew that excited the English Elizabethans into adventure had already been flowing through Spain for two generations. England followed where Spain led.

That Spain's supremacy in the world could be reduced so quickly tells us something about the fragility of power. History has tended to point the finger at Philip himself, but if he is to take the blame for Spain's misfortunes then perhaps he should be credited with her achievements. The conflict which did most to destroy Spain's power is hardly mentioned by Lucrecia – probably because it never threatened the territory of Spain itself.

The Netherlands was a semi-autonomous territory within the part of the Habsburg empire inherited by Philip from his father Charles V. The origins and progress of the Dutch rebellion are a complex intertwining of religious and political dissent but their root cause was a rising sense of resentment at Spanish interference in every area of Dutch life.

Philip was born and brought up in Spain. He acted as a *de facto* regent in the country while his father, Charles V, looked after the remainder of his empire. In 1548 Charles decided that his heir should visit the rest of the realms so that he could be formally acknowledged as heir to his father's kingdoms. Philip was away for two and a half years, travelling through Italy, Germany and the Netherlands. He left Spain again in July 1554 in order to marry Mary Tudor, queen of England. He left Spain as a prince but returned as king, as, in October 1555 Charles V gathered his court together in Brussels to announce his abdication. Philip was detained in the Netherlands by a military campaign by the Dutch against France and eventually returned to Spain from the Netherlands in 1559. He never left the peninsula again.

Philip's first action as king that angered his Dutch subjects was to leave 3,000 Spanish troops behind in 1559. These were ostensibly to guard the southern frontiers of the Netherlands – a federation of separate states roughly comprising the present-day Netherlands and Belgium. The Spanish troops were highly unwelcome and were later ignominiously withdrawn after intense lobbying by the Dutch.

Then came a reorganisation of the Catholic Church in the Netherlands which resulted in Philip's chief minister in the Netherlands, Antoine Perrenot, gaining a senior position in the Council of the state of Brabant (the most powerful in the Netherlands) and being made Cardinal Granvelle. The king's man suddenly had political and religious control of the supposedly autonomous country. Once again the Dutch protested and once again they succeeded – in 1564 Cardinal Granvelle was withdrawn from the Netherlands.

By now, though, dislike and disregard of Spanish interference had grown. The new religion of Calvinism was being practised in many Dutch towns and local rules often allowed Calvinist services in private or outside the city walls. This type of local autonomy was unacceptable to the king and his subsequent mishandling of religious dissidence led to political grievance and a rebellion that lasted for eighty years and did much to reduce Spanish power in the world.

In 1566 Philip made the decision to send the Duke of Alba to the Netherlands with 10,000 Spanish troops. There was no mistaking Philip's intentions – Alba's uncompromising views on religious dissidence and his intended methods were clearly known. The rebellions against religious laws and diktats were put down with fierce brutality. The Dutch nobles (many of whom had fought alongside the Spanish against the French) repeatedly asked Philip to come to the Netherlands and sort out the troubles in person. His continued absence while his troops slaughtered Dutch troops and civilians was diplomatically catastrophic. Henry Kamen (1997a) points out that Philip's policy was influenced by the recent success of his forces in putting down a rebellion in Mexico, but while this explains his actions they were nevertheless ill-judged.

Philip's father Charles V had been regarded by the Dutch as their emperor and they pleaded with Philip to play the same role. Their shock at the brutality of Alba's methods (over 1,000 people were executed within months of his arrival) was compounded by Philip's apparent deafness to their requests that he come to their country. The brutality had the predictable effect of bringing temporary and superficial order while sowing the seeds of deep resentment. Nor is this the product of hindsight. Philip was strongly advised by several members of his Council and by trusted ambassadors that sending Alba with repressive orders was the wrong strategy. The resentment of the Dutch found a physical outlet in the incursions of rebel armies led by William of Orange beginning in 1568. Once again Alba struck back. In October and November of 1572 the Duke recaptured the towns of Mechelen, Zutphen and Naarden and gave his troops free rein to massacre the inhabitants.

The outcry against Alba's methods was immense. Many in the Spanish court were appalled and, more importantly, Philip realised that his policy was failing. Although the king remained on Alba's side, he could not afford the drawn-out war that Alba's policies were producing. A shortage of money to pay the Spanish troops led to mutiny and the abandonment of the siege of Alkmaar (where Alba had decreed that 'not a living soul should be left'). After further military and naval reverses it became clear that success by force of arms alone would take many years.

In 1573 Philip ordered the Duke of Alba back to Spain and sent the governor of Milan, Luis de Requesens, to replace him. Philip's letter of appointment to Requesens is revealing:

Some say that the cause of the rebellions is religion, and that there is no solution other than punishment and rigour . . . Others say the contrary . . . and that the solution is moderation and a general pardon. [This was the view of] all those from the states and even some from Spain . . . With such difference of opinions I have found myself very confused. And since I don't know the truth of what is going on there, I neither know the solution that is necessary nor what to think. It seems to me that the most reliable is to believe neither one side nor the other, since I think that both go to extremes. I think that the best view to take, though with great discretion, is in the middle. (quoted in Kamen, 1997a)

Here, in a nutshell, is both Philip's mitigation of history's judgement and evidence for his condemnation. His nickname was Philip the Prudent: he studiously examined all evidence and consulted all opinion before acting. But how did such an impressively prudent process lead, finally, to such unimpressive results – a long and ultimately unsuccessful conflict that drained his country's wealth and put it into bankruptcy. It may be that Philip's position as ruler of the Spanish empire made him essentially conservative. If things stayed as they were his empire would remain intact, its people prosperous and devout, its borders secure. In every conflict he would wish to return to the status quo ante. Even his plan to invade England, while seemingly adventurous, was an attempt to return northern Europe to its recent Catholic past. This tendency may also have led Philip to believe that he could act in his own time. We have already seen evidence of the grinding slowness of the Madrid bureaucracy and Philip, while sometimes impatient, seemed to believe that deliberation was more important than speed of action. This tendency was in contrast to his principal rival.

Elizabeth of England also sought to keep the world in balance but hers was a more dynamic approach. She understood that, in the new world which was emerging at such extraordinary speed, time had become the essential ingredient of all human affairs. She saw that good statecraft was not simply a matter of doing the right thing, or even of acting 'in time', but that the achievement of stability is less to do with the placing of weights about a fulcrum and more akin to steering a boat along a restless and endless stream.

2. *'you are to die in the same month as your wife Doña Isabel.'* Enough of Philip's wives and children died prematurely and in his lifetime to give, even in an age of sudden mortality, breath to rumour. Betrothed at the age of fifteen to María, princess of Portugal, he was married at sixteen and a widower by eighteen. María died shortly after giving birth to Carlos – a son who was to cause Philip many difficulties before dying in his

father's prison. Philip next married Mary Tudor, Queen of England, on his father's instruction.

Philip arrived in Southampton on 20 July 1554 and proceeded to Winchester to meet his bride. (Philip was welcomed to England by Lord Howard of Effingham, future commander of the English fleet against the Armada.) Mary was eleven years older than the twenty-six-year-old prince. Both had seen portraits of each other before they met. They did not speak the same language but nevertheless managed to communicate. Philip spoke in Spanish, which Mary understood but could not speak well herself – she had not spoken the language since her mother Catherine of Aragón's death in 1536. Mary instead spoke in French in which she was near-fluent, and which Philip understood but could not speak.

In this fashion the two got on well enough. They were married in Winchester Cathedral on St James's Day, 25 July. Although Mary had apparently told the Spanish ambassador Simon Renard that 'If Philip were disposed to be amorous, such was not her desire, for she . . . had never harboured thoughts of love', the couple spent their wedding night, and subsequent nights, alone together.

Philip remained in England until September of the following year. Mary believed at one time that she had become pregnant but this proved unfounded. She died three years after Philip's departure.

Within two years of Mary's death Philip married Isabel de Valois, the daughter of the French king. Juan Blázquez Miguel (1987) writes: 'Historical tradition sees Isabel de Valois as Philip II's most loving wife. She is presented in [Lucrecia's] dreams as the king's mediator and protector. We see her on repeated occasions beseeching pardon for him.' It was certainly the first marriage he had made as a mature man in full assent. Isabel gave Philip two daughters, who both lived to maturity; then she died in October 1568 while giving birth to a stillborn daughter. Presumably Lucrecia's dream predicts that Philip will also die in October, but in fact he was to die in September 1598. Philip was devastated at Isabel's death and considered remaining a widower – he was then forty-one. But two years later he married his niece, Anna of Austria – a Habsburg family marriage. Anna was twenty and Philip was besotted with her. She gave birth to five children, four of whom died in infancy. The surviving son became his father's heir and later Philip III. Anna died in 1580. Philip was then a four-times widower at the age of fifty-three.

The king could not have been blamed for the death of any of his wives and was certainly grief-stricken at the loss of both Isabel and Anna. But dark deeds done out of sight were always possible for such a powerful man. Europe buzzed with unfounded rumours that he had a hand in the deaths of his wives and children.

3. *Then I saw that Toledo was besieged by Moors, Turkish, French, English and Polish soldiers.* Now Lucrecia's gloomy vision begins to clot. The symbolism of her earlier dreams has hardened into a comprehensible reality. These are now real people acting in real places. First she has been shown towers, wagons, eagles and giants, then told of how these portend the dark days to come. Now she is being shown how these days will be. The siege of Toledo, holy city of Castile, last remaining stronghold of the Spanish people, will become the focus of all her fears and hopes. Here the world might end in the final destruction of Spain and its people but here too might be the birth of a new nation under a new king. Every night as she drifts off to sleep Lucrecia knows that she will find out a little more of when and how her world is going to end.

4. *the landward side.* Toledo lies in a loop of the River Tagus (*Rio Tajo*); the landward side is to the north, facing in the direction of Madrid, 40 miles away.

5. *A man of moderate social standing came forward. He was dark-faced, well-built with strong limbs.* This new leader, emerging from the people, occupies the role that Piedrola envisioned for himself. Lucrecia sees more of him in her dreams and she too blurs his identity with Piedrola's. Though Lucrecia's supporters had no notion of placing this troublesome and well-known prophet on the throne, he was a convenient tool in their criticisms of the king and his advisers.

6. *Cardinal Quiroga.* Quiroga is the head of the Spanish Inquisition, the Inquisitor-General and Archbishop of Toledo. Though potentially a fearsome figure, Quiroga was actually more tolerant of unorthodox religious practices than many of his colleagues. Juan Blázquez Miguel (1987) writes that 'Cardinal Quiroga is not very well presented in the dreams which one may suspect had something to do with the personal hatred Don Alonso Mendoza had towards him. He is shown as inept

84

and ignorant and only interested in the inherent affairs of his office. It is also necessary to point out the friendship which linked him to the secretary Antonio Pérez but that is to enter upon complicated and unsteady territory.'

We will deal with Antonio Pérez a little later. Quiroga may have been hated by Alonso de Mendoza, Lucrecia's principal patron, but he was actually a valuable ally to her cause, believing her to be innocent of charges of sacrilege. This was to prove crucial when, within two months of this dream, she was arrested without Quiroga's consent. It was only when the king himself became involved that Quiroga withdrew from Lucrecia's and Alonso de Mendoza's cause.

7. *they bore the king from the Alcázar fortress to the Great Church.* The Alcázar is the Arab fortress used as a royal palace in both Toledo and Madrid. The one in Toledo still stands. From there it is a short step to the Great Church or Cathedral of Toledo which is now much as it was in Lucrecia's day.

8. *he showed me a thorn bush floating on the waters.* The contents of this vision are drawn from the Bible and show the ability of dreams to bring distant elements into the same time and place. This eclecticism can be liberating, allowing narratives to be constructed in strange and wonderful ways. But the cavalier plundering of our memory can give disturbing results.

In the story of Moses and the burning bush the angel is 'in a flame of fire', not above it. The Annunciation to Mary is more direct – the angel Gabriel appears to her as a messenger from God saying, 'Hail, thou that art highly favoured, the Lord is with thee: blessed art thou among women' (Luke 1: 28).

In her vision Lucrecia combines these scenes. The meaning of the body in the shroud, washed away by the rising sea, is connected to the earlier mention of the death of Philip.

The Ordinary Man came and took me to the same seashore where I saw the Old Fisherman who, on other occasions, is usually fishing. He was standing inside a large earthenware jar which must have been an oil jar,[1] for as he entered I saw that oil poured from the lip. He had a chalice and host in his hands and I saw many angels collecting up the oil as it poured. The Old Fisherman called to one of them and said, 'I wish you all to take this host to the place where it should be.'

I asked, 'Is that host consecrated?' and the Ordinary Man replied, 'It is as much so as the host which Fray Lucas consecrates in your Mass.'

I saw that two angels, dressed as acolytes but with wings, took the Old Man out of the jar and placed upon him the cape and mitre of the High Pontiff. Seating him upon a chair, they placed a book in his hands.

Seeing him thus I asked, 'How is it that you do not speak to me? Is it because you now hold papal office?'

He answered me, 'It is not for that reason but because I am celebrating the feast of the Lord and this is the eve of it.'

Then the Lion Man called to me, 'Come, I shall explain to you the vision of the angel while the Old Man completes his offices. The thorn bush on the sea and the angel above it, extinguishing it, is a sign that the life of your king is coming to an end by moments. You had only to see the thorn bush on the sea to realise that it meant Philip, but so that you should comprehend it better, you were shown a dead body.'

As he finished saying this the Old Man completed his offices and the angels removed his mitre and cape and went away, taking with them the jar of oil.

The Old Man said to me, 'To whom must you tell this vision in which you have seen me?'

I answered, 'To the same person as usual.'

He said to me, 'See that you do not tell it to Don Alonso but to Fray Lucas.'[2]

I said, 'I cannot tell it to Don Alonso for he is in Toledo.'

Then I saw the Armada of the Marquis of Santa Cruz pass on its way to England. I saw that in front of it, travelling upon the sea, were four women. These were the four Spanish queens that I had seen in the same garments in another dream.

I saw the English Queen Mary who appeared with a rope in her hands and about her throat. The Old Fisherman asked her, 'Why do you appear like that?'

She answered, 'Does it not seem to you that I deserve it since all of the sins committed by my sister fall upon me? There was a time when I could have remedied the situation and I did not. But the fault lies only partly with me for when I wished to do so my father hindered me.'[3]

The Lion Man said, 'What good has he done in all his life?' and then all of them disappeared.

Then three men came over the sea from the east, the one in the middle chained[4] and led by the others, all of them dressed in black. Having placed the chained man before the Old Man the two who had brought him disappeared. The Old Man spoke in Latin with the chained man and I did not understand what he said. At that moment I saw coming over the water two bloodthirsty lions which tore the chained man apart in front of the Old Man. The vision then disappeared.

Then the Old Man told the Ordinary Man to take me to Spain, which he did. In Madrid I saw countless Moors sacking the houses.[5] In the Plaza Cebada they were martyring many Christians, the majority of whom were women. The maidens

*were put to death in a different manner from the rest, being
flogged and burnt at the stake or subjected to other torments
while the other women merely had their throats cut.*

*As I watched, the Ordinary Man tugged at my arm and said,
'This is the time I told you about when there are to be many
Leocadias'[6] and I saw that the blood of these martyrs had
become a stream which was flowing into the church of San
Andrés. The Moors went to sack the church and found that there
was a priest standing inside the door.*

*The priest said to the Moors, 'Take all that there is in the
church but do not touch the body of San Isidro.'*

*They replied, 'The first thing we will do is to make a mess of
him.'[7]*

*Then I saw that as they tried to open the chest that holds his
body such a glowing light emerged that they were unable to
touch it. They fell back in dismay and the priest shut the doors of
the church.*

*From there I was taken to Toledo, where I heard so many
voices of men and women that they seemed to drown out the
world. I went into the Alcazár fortress where Fray Lucas
worked at a writing desk. I said to him, 'Fray Lucas, have you
not seen what has happened in Madrid? You must be sleeping.[8]
Many martyrs have been put to death and the blood that ran
made a great stream . . .' and I told him all the rest that had
happened.*

And with that I awoke.

---

1. *He was standing inside a large earthenware jar which must have been an oil jar.*
    'And they cast out many devils, and anointed with oil many that were
    sick, and healed them' (Mark 6: 13).
    'Is any sick among you? let him call for the elders of the church; and

let them pray over him, anointing him with oil in the name of the Lord' (Epistle of James 5: 14).

The pleasantly strange scene on the beach is a prelude to the horrors to come.

2. *He said to me, 'See that you do not tell it to Don Alonso but to Fray Lucas.'*
Having come upon Lucrecia de Léon and her dreams, Don Alonso de Mendoza has begun to write them down. He wants as many of them recorded as he can. He is interested and excited by them. Alonso is no fool, though he does not always behave wisely. There are things in these dreams which could only be said in dreams.

Do the dreams come from God? Mendoza could believe in a divine source while at the same time influencing the content of the dreams, or their transcriptions. It was Mendoza who circulated the dream transcripts to the right people. He sensed that the dreams were saying, or could be made to say, the right things – that the king was pursuing the wrong policies, that his advisers were corrupt, that his policies might bring disaster to Spain. But did he understand how dangerous these sentiments were?

He would first have circulated the dream transcripts to those who were likely to be sympathetic. But though these included influential courtiers, they were by definition on the fringes of the court; those with real power were not interested in making change. So the web must be widened to those with a little more influence and the dreams must come to the attention of some people who would regard them as dangerous and seditious. Mendoza was perhaps deceived as to his own power and influence. He may have thought himself untouchable and the longer things went on without official reproach, the stronger he may have felt.

Quite quickly Alonso de Mendoza saw that the task of transcription would be too much for him alone. Apart from the time needed to take down the details of the dreams, Mendoza had an official position as a magistral canon in the Cathedral of Toledo – he could not spend all his time in Madrid. But the transcribing of the dreams was a delicate task requiring skill, sensitivity, dedication and trust as well as an inordinate amount of time (sometimes the interviews with Lucrecia took several hours per day).

Mendoza introduced Lucrecia to Fray Lucas de Allende, prior of the largest Franciscan religious house in Madrid, friend and/or confessor of a swathe of Spanish nobility and a man known to be discontented with the policies of the crown. Allende had sat on councils dealing with royal taxes on the clergy and, as representative of the Franciscan order, had bitterly opposed them.

The Franciscans were open to, and interested in, unorthodox religious events and practices. Allende was an avid collector of reports of seemingly supernatural events and was keenly interested in anyone who showed prophetic gifts. Lucrecia must have been very appealing to this man.

So Fray Lucas de Allende became Lucrecia's confessor and then her scribe. But the arrangement did not go altogether smoothly. Having joined Mendoza in assuring Lucrecia that her dreams would not get her into trouble, Allende had a crisis of conscience in early November 1587. According to Richard Kagan (1990): 'After listening to Lucrecia relate a dream in which she described the interior of his cell – supposedly, a room she had not yet seen – Allende destroyed all the dream texts in his possession, asserting that the dreams were only a girl's foolish fancies.'

Mendoza hurried back from Toledo and somehow convinced his friend that he should resume his work. The dreams which have been preserved therefore date from 1 December 1587 and continue up to 18 April 1590. In effect Mendoza handed over the job of copying to Allende, who was absent only when indisposed. Mendoza remained in control of the enterprise, though. He gave Allende and the other occasional copyists instructions concerning the form of the transcriptions and on the details of the dreams which he wanted preserved. This may have been for his own interest, though it is likely that Mendoza knew that the church authorities would ask about certain specifics in deciding whether the dreams were genuine.

Lucrecia first related her dreams to Allende, who then asked her to clarify particular details and perhaps to try to remember or enlarge on particular episodes. Only then would he begin to write down an account of the dream, asking Lucrecia to tell or remind him of certain details as he wrote. As soon as he finished, the document would be handed to a courier and taken to Mendoza in Toledo. Mendoza used these transcripts as working copies on which he scribbled his own thoughts and ideas and interpretations, sometimes visiting Lucrecia to go over particular passages. Only then did Mendoza make a fair

copy which he wrote into one of a series of registers. It is these registers containing 415 dreams which have been preserved.

3. *'all of the sins committed by my sister fall upon me? . . . my father hindered
me.'* The content of Mary Tudor's speech from beyond the grave shows
a sophisticated knowledge of English politics on Lucrecia's part. The
clear inference is that Mary could, while queen, have somehow
prevented her younger half-sister Elizabeth from succeeding her –
presumably by having her executed – and thereby have saved the
Spanish the trouble they were now having.

    While Mary was queen and her half-sister under house arrest, any
messenger seen breaking the horizon was feared by the young Elizabeth to bear either tidings of the imminence of her own death or news
of her sister's; a message that she was to be taken to her execution or
her coronation. Lucrecia seems to believe that Mary was reluctant to
kill Elizabeth because of the influence of their dead father. This may
mean simply that Mary would not, in Lucrecia's view, have killed a
woman with whom she shared a father.

    It is not surprising that the Lion Man should be disparaging of Henry
in the last line of this section of the dream. Henry was well known to
the Spanish through his marriage to Catherine, Princess of Aragón.
His split from the Catholic Church, apparently for reasons of conven-
ience rather than conscience, must have seemed doubly heretical to
the Spanish people.

4. *Then three men came over the sea from the east, the one in the middle chained.*
The chained man is always Piedrola in Lucrecia's dreams. His grue-
some death here does not prevent him from appearing again later.

5. *In Madrid I saw countless Moors sacking the houses.* Arab or Moorish rule
over any part of the peninsula had ended in 1492 with the 'Reconquest' of Granada by Ferdinand and Isabella. All citizens were forced
to convert to the Christian faith or leave the country. Most Moors stayed
and became Christian in name only, continuing Islamic religious practices with little pretence and with little harassment. Every once in a
while the Inquisition would get excited about religious non-observance
and there would be some arrests, but for the greater part there was a
culture of live and let live. The governors, landowners and merchants
of the southern provinces were content to have it that way. The 300,000

moriscos were good workers and taxpayers and did no harm to them.

But the politics of the Church was fluid, and those who advocated less tolerance of Moorish culture gradually gained the upper hand. In 1565 a council of the Church, meeting in Granada, requested that the king should take steps to enforce the existing laws forbidding the use of Moorish language, customs or dress. The captain-general of Andalucía, Count Mondéjar, advised strongly against this policy and predicted a rebellion. The restrictions began to be enforced in 1567; the rebellion took hold in December 1568.

We are left to wonder again whether the dual channels of power – church and state – served Spain ill at times like this. Philip undoubtedly found it convenient to have the Church insist on actions which would achieve what he wanted without becoming overtly involved himself. On occasion the Church and its Holy Order could do things in secret which Philip, for all his power, could only do in public. But the *morisco* rebellion is a difficult case. Up until 1565 it seems that Philip was himself content to let things rub along. Why then did he allow the Church to interfere? The consequences, as we have seen, are not only obvious with hindsight, but were predicted by those with most knowledge at the time. It could be that Philip was once again seduced by the end, without considering the undesirable effects that the means would bring. Many believe it was the growing power of the Turks in the western Mediterranean that enforced the suppression of their fellow Muslims and there is some evidence of collusion between elements of the *morisco* population and Turkish forces. A purely integrated Christian Spain would help to lift any threat of invasion by Turkish armies. Philip may have seen religious suppression as a route to ridding the *moriscos* of solidarity with the Turks but did he foresee the bloodshed that would be provoked?

The *morisco* rebellion began in the countryside. The difficult terrain of the Alpujarra range was the initial stronghold of the small rebel army which grew rapidly through 1569. By early 1570 the whole of the province of Granada was involved in the war. Don Juan of Austria, the king's half-brother, was put in charge of suppressing the rebels. The repression was fierce and bloody, as the rebellion had been. This was a messy war with no front lines, a war of patrols and ambushes, with no havens for prisoners to be brought to. The occasional town that was isolated and surrounded suffered a terrible fate: Serón taken by the *moriscos*, 150 men killed and 80 women taken into slavery; Inox a promontory taken by the Christians, 400 men killed, 50 taken for galley slaves and 2,700 women and children taken for slaves. When Don Juan arrived he brought regular troops and made a sweep of the territory, changing the nature of the war. When Galera fell in February 1570 all 2,500 inhabitants were murdered, including women and children: 'the town was razed and salt poured over it' (Kamen, 1997a). The rebellion petered out from May to November 1570.

After all this Philip felt he could not allow this potentially insurgent population to remain in Andalucía. Around 80,000 *moriscos* were forcibly transported to other parts of Spain – a policy that was criticised by some of the next generation of Spaniards for placing a threat in every corner of the kingdom. Atrocities occurred on both sides but it was not altogether surprising that Lucrecia, a devout Christian, should dream of Moorish brutality, even though by 1588 the Spanish Moors were no longer any threat and the Turks had been at peace with Spain for some years.

6. *'This is the time I told you about when there are to be many Leocadias'.* The relics of Santa Leocadia had been returned to the city of Toledo in April 1587 in a celebration which drew massive crowds from all over Castile, including Madrid. Lucrecia may have been among the onlookers.

7. *'make a mess of him'.* The original Spanish is *hacerle una ensalada. Ensalada* essentially means a mixture, so this phrase could mean 'make him a salad' – a salad being a dish of mixed greens, or even 'sing him a little song' – *ensalada* also being a type of song with mixed metres. Both would be deeply ironic replies intended to ridicule the priest. We have here taken *ensalada* to mean 'a mess'.

San Isidro is the patron saint of the city of Madrid.

8. *'Fray Lucas, have you not seen what has happened in Madrid? You must be sleeping.'* Lucrecia seems to be telling Fray Lucas that he is not taking the content of her dreams seriously enough. It is unclear what more Lucrecia wished him to do but he may have expressed some reservations about the dreams' importance during their morning conversations.

The Ordinary Man came and took me to the seashore and said, 'I wish you to see how well my companions serve the Lord today as they celebrate His feast day.'[1] As he said this we arrived at the place. They were seated at a white-draped table upon which was a great bowl which ran with very clear water. I saw the Old Man wash his hands in the water first, and then the Lion Man and then the Ordinary Man. The Old Man sat down at the head of the table with the Lion Man at his side and the Ordinary Man at the foot.

Then the bowl was taken off the table without my being able to see by whom, more tablecloths were spread and I heard a voice saying, 'See how clear this water is after these men have washed their hands in it. All those who are to sit at this table are to wash in this fountain and he who muddies the waters shall not sit down.'

Then I saw that by the Old Man's side there was a crozier and a rock, and that the Lion Man set by his side the lion that he used to take about with him. The Ordinary Man was given a gourd and a leather bag. A voice said to me, 'What do you think of the signs and symbols of these men?'

I answered, 'I do not have sufficient knowledge to understand.'

And I heard the voice say, 'Placing the rock by the Old Man indicates that he is the rock of the Church and the crozier that he is given is the staff of a prelate. Setting the lion by the Lion Man does not mean that he will accomplish all, but rather that you should understand that, just as a lion when he has a person at his mercy will finish him, so this man will complete each task that he undertakes. And the leather bag and gourd symbolise the poverty that has been endured by the man who goes with

*you.' When this had been said the Old Man gave his benediction
and broke the bread.*

*At that moment a basket of muscatel pears was placed on the
table before the Old Man and he said, 'O Lord God, since the
good things that are made in the world do not last, these pears
belong to the king who is to come, whose works will be as
acceptable to God as the sins of the present king are
abominable.'*[2]

*Then many poor people arrived and were given bread from
the table. And the table was raised high, again without me
seeing it done.*

*The Ordinary Man said to me, 'Tell Fray Lucas to have white
cloths spread for that is the symbol of this feast day.'*

And they all disappeared and I awoke.

1. *His feast day.* The overwhelming impression on the feast day of Christ is
   of purity. The water in the fountain in the centre of the table must
   flow clear, the cloths must be white, everyone who comes must be
   clean. The three men who inhabit Lucrecia's dreamworld are at the
   table and forming the image which she sees – but the symbols must
   be explained. So, unusually for Lucrecia, the device of a disembodied
   voice is used. Following his previous appearance in papal dress, the
   Old Man is again seen as a church leader, while the Lion Man remains
   enigmatic.

2. *'the sins of the present king are abominable.'* The story that follows is of an
   affair which placed Philip's reputation in doubt among his own
   courtiers and subjects. History has not been able to agree on the extent
   of his guilt but there was enough circumstantial evidence for the court
   and people to suspect their monarch of being implicated in murder.

   On the evening during which he was to be assassinated, Juan de
   Escobedo, a prominent courtier in the palace of Philip II, made his
   way through the streets of Madrid. It was Easter Monday, 31 March

95

1578 and the streets were busy with the last night of the festival. Escobedo's passage was preceded by men carrying torches, his horse surrounded by a small group of other riders – for support, company and, possibly, protection. But this impressive entourage was a comforting illusion. Juan de Escobedo's life in Madrid was wrapped in the trappings of power while containing none of its substance. He had been an influential figure in the maintenance of Philip's global empire and had now returned to its centre. But here, instead of reward, responsibility and influence, he was granted a sedentary life and an occasional audience with the king or, increasingly, with someone 'close to the throne'. He was in danger of becoming one of a host of eager though resigned petitioners, clever in the ways of the court, cut off from any power base in the world beyond. Scheming, wasting.

If that was all that Escobedo threatened then he might have survived a little longer. But his previous positions had given him knowledge of certain questionable dealings that concerned the most powerful men in the Spanish empire. They had also given him a liking for independent action and ambition for greater things. This combination gave him a potentially strong position within the manoeuvrings of the court. It also put him in mortal danger. Though his life went on as before, it had by now been decided that Escobedo had become too much of a nuisance and must be eliminated. This had all been agreed some months before, but it was not until Easter Monday that the plans for his assassination could be realised.

Escobedo had spent the last afternoon of his life at the house of the princess of Eboli, the powerful head of the Mendoza family. We do not know precisely what he was doing at the house of the widow of Ruy Gómez – one of many things concerning the murder which we do not know – but we do know that the princess would eventually be arrested on suspicion of being involved in the assassination. Escobedo left the Eboli house at dusk to visit his mistress Doña Brianda de Guzmán. He stayed with her for a short period, leaving for the last part of his journey at around nine o'clock.

The district of Madrid through which Juan de Escobedo passed that evening was close to the royal palace and the location of many great houses as well as fine churches and other religious buildings. We have no knowledge of Escobedo's state of mind but it seems certain that he had no notion of the fate that was about to befall him. He may have had some general idea that his life was not without risk, but the worst he could contemplate would be a sudden demotion – and he had insurance against that possibility. Even if he was aware of the physical danger to his life (made real the previous day in a clearing outside the city where the murder weapon had been chosen – sword in preference to a crossbow) he must have felt safe in the royal quarter of the city. Indeed it was to be an uncomfortable surprise for the court of Madrid, and apparently for the king, that a well-known gentleman could be murdered so close to the walls of the palace. When he heard the news the following day, Philip was to write, 'It is all very strange, it was very bold of someone to kill so important a person under my very eyes.' But we will see whether the king's reactions are to be understood exactly as they were written. Before we arrive at Escobedo's murder, we need to retrace the path that led him to this end and discover the connection between his murder and the fate of Lucrecia de Léon.

The greatest military victory of the early part of Philip's reign was the defeat in 1571 of the Turkish fleet at Lepanto in the Gulf of Corinth. The Spanish forces were commanded by the king's half-brother Don Juan of Austria (an illegitimate son of Philip's father, Charles V). The victory brought great joy to Philip; it also brought him an unwanted difficulty. Don Juan was a hero to the people of Spain, to its armies and, increasingly, to himself. Despite his title 'of Austria', he had no territory to rule but was entirely dependent on Philip. He became impatient for greater glories and greater powers. Philip's half-brother was never felt to be a threat to the crown itself, but he showed worrying signs of wanting a territory of his own to rule. This might seem harmless enough and a convenient way to dispose of Juan's ambitions – to be prince of Naples or Flanders would be prestigious without being a threat to the centre. But Philip was concerned above all else with the integrity of his empire. If a prince of the royal blood was 'given' a territory would his heirs not then have a claim to it, in preference to Philip's own heirs? Quite apart from the protection of his dynasty, Philip perhaps realised that many of Europe's wars had been brought about by intra-family squabbling arising from such disposals. In any case he feared the consequences of Don Juan's ambitions and sought to curb and monitor his activities.

Philip turned to Antonio Pérez, secretary of state for southern Europe and one of his most trusted advisers. It is Antonio Pérez who binds this story and twines it with that of Lucrecia, and whose subsequent disgrace divided the court and came close to dividing the kingdom. In his official capacity Pérez had many dealings with Don Juan and in these dealings he showed the delicate touch which Philip prized so highly. Pérez obtained just enough for Don Juan from the king to earn the prince's gratitude, while at the same time demonstrating to Philip that he had the prince under control. Don Juan was at this time viceroy of southern Italy – a part of Philip's empire particularly vulnerable to Turkish attacks. Pérez used his own agents in Italy to report on Don Juan's activities. In his visits to Castile, Don Juan stayed at Pérez's country house and confided in this man who seemed to be the best promoter of his cause in the king's counsels. Pérez had secured more funds for the Mediterranean fleet which Don Juan commanded and had gained him the position of viceroy.

Despite Pérez's good work, Philip remained discontented with his half-brother's situation and feared that he might use the military resources at his disposal to conquer a territory in North Africa and then claim it for himself. In 1574, three years after the victory at Lepanto, Pérez decided, with the king's authority, to remove Don Juan's personal secretary and replace him with an old friend, Juan de Escobedo. The situation should now have been secure. Pérez would keep a steady eye on the behaviour of Don Juan, he would advise Philip as to the best course of action – giving a little here, holding back there – and would in turn instruct Escobedo on how to advise the wayward prince, while also presenting himself to Don Juan as his friend at court. Pérez was extremely adept at such play-making because he understood where real power lay. He kept close to the king – so near that when occasionally Pérez seemed to subvert the king's wishes, this turned out to be a deliberate illusion designed to fool others.

As an example of the schemes that Philip and Pérez devised, Geoffrey Parker (1995) cites a letter from King Philip to Don Juan on the subject of the prince being made a cardinal. This was itself a scheme to disinherit any possible heirs of Don Juan's by ensuring they were illegitimate. The letter has a covering note from Pérez to Escobedo, secretary to secretary. In this note Pérez writes that Don Juan should take no notice of the king's suggestion, and should 'disregard the harsh words in the accompanying letter, which were all added by the king; what mattered, said the secretary, were the parts written by Pérez himself. If Don Juan were to do as he said, Pérez continued, "we shall save our cause and make sure of Our Man [i.e. the king]." '

This seemed to be dangerous double-dealing by Pérez, but it turns out that he and Philip concocted the covering letter between them (there are extant drafts corrected by the king). By this and other double-dealing they hoped to flush out any disaffection felt by Don Juan for the throne.

Within a couple of years of Escobedo's appointment as secretary to Don Juan, two circumstances arose which upset the harmony so delicately achieved by Pérez. In October 1576 Spain's military situation in the Netherlands worsened. Philip sent Don Juan to take full control of the rebellious provinces and to restore the authority of the empire. His prestige as a warrior and brother of the king made him ideal for the task. The other change was that Escobedo, far from acting as the king's and Pérez's agent, began to relish the importance of his role as Don Juan's right-hand man. He could see great possibilities for this warrior prince, and consequently for himself. The man sent to keep Don Juan quiet began to encourage his ambition. To cap it all, Don Juan was swiftly successful in the Netherlands, and by May 1577 he 'was accepted as governor general by all the provinces of the Netherlands and made a triumphal entry into Brussels' (Parker, 1995).

This achievement should not be underestimated. To Philip the Low Countries were a constant problem from which Don Juan gained him a welcome few months' respite. But now Don Juan was once more the victorious hero and once more he became restless. Once he had pacified the Netherlands Don Juan wanted above all else to invade England. He believed its defences were insecure and its Catholic people ready to rise against Queen Elizabeth. He even fancied the idea of marrying Mary Queen of Scots and ruling England in her name. In July 1577 Don Juan sent Juan de Escobedo to Madrid to press Philip to send to the Netherlands a force large enough to invade England.

Philip never had any intention of allowing Don Juan to lead an army against the English, and he regarded the persistent Escobedo as a nuisance. As 1577 wore on, the Dutch rebels regained the initiative and Don Juan was fully occupied in defending his own army. Any thought of England rapidly dissipated. Escobedo's mission became futile but instead of returning to the Netherlands he remained in Madrid; he may have believed he would be of more use to Don Juan at court than by his side. But why, if he was such a nuisance, did Pérez and the king not send him away? Why was his presence tolerated for so long? In the answers to these questions lie the motives behind his murder. There were and are persistent rumours that Escobedo possessed certain information which others might not want revealed. Escobedo could not be dismissed because he was, in effect, blackmailing those who had power over him. What were the secrets that Escobedo possessed and who stood to suffer by their revelation?

During his time as Philip's secretary, Antonio Pérez played a delicate hand. On the face of it he belonged to that faction of the court known as the 'peace party', of whom the Mendozas were the central force. His efforts were therefore directed towards quiet resolution of the conflicts in the empire rather than towards military solutions. This faction believed that the rebellions in the Netherlands should be ended by negotiation, with the local leaders being given the degree of political and religious autonomy they sought: Philip never followed this route, to his own and his country's cost. During his term of office Pérez passed on pieces of confidential information. He told Don Juan and Escobedo about some of the king's thoughts, as we have seen. He also told Don Juan and others about decisions of the Council of State which he served. This much is clear, but what is not clear is whether this was done with the king's knowledge and connivance.

More seriously it is alleged that Pérez had secret dealings with the rebels in Flanders. The Spanish historian Gregorio Marañón (1954) gives a flavour of the intrigues of the court in his colourful, rambling account of the affair. He writes that contact between Spanish officials and the rebels was not as uncommon as might be thought. 'Flemish chiefs kept up a very large spy organisation at the Spanish court. Others before Pérez had been caught up in these nets of subornation and treason.' And moreover 'Everyone was mistrusted and rightly so.' We should bear in mind that these 'rebels' were often old friends-in-arms of Spanish courtiers, fellow members of the élite Order of the Golden Fleece, frequent visitors to Madrid and to the other Habsburg courts.

Marañón suggests that Pérez did more than consort with the rebels for political reasons and asserts that the king's secretary was using his position and his influence with the Dutch to make personal financial gain. Marañón writes that this is well known but provides no evidence to support the assertion. Leaving that aside, Pérez's game in the Netherlands and elsewhere was to try to prevent Philip from continually going to war. To do this it was necessary to control, among others, Don Juan.

Pérez probably did, therefore, have secret dealings with the rebels. He also made Don Juan and Escobedo believe they were receiving secret information and at the same time he was working to damage Don Juan's reputation in the eyes of the king. If all this came off he would bring peace to the Netherlands and persuade the king to have no more truck with this troublesome half-brother. In some parts of this strategy he was definitely abetted by his sovereign, and in others he may have been.

So Escobedo knew that, at the very least, Pérez had been leaking information to him and Don Juan. He may further have known that Pérez had been engaged in political and possibly financial intrigue in the Netherlands. He may even have known that the king was somehow involved in Pérez's schemes and he may have been trying to use all of this knowledge to further his own and Don Juan's interests at court.

A less likely source of Escobedo's leverage is sexual. As Geoffrey Parker (1995) writes, 'According to some versions, Escobedo found Pérez in bed with the princess of Eboli, widow of his former patron, Ruy Gómez, and threatened to tell the king; other versions of the story claim that Escobedo discovered that Pérez and the princess were selling state secrets to the enemies of Spain.'

These stories are improbable (it is close to inconceivable that, if Pérez and the princess were having sexual relations, Escobedo was the only one to know) but the latter assertion gains some currency from the subsequent arrest of Pérez *and* the princess of Eboli. (There is a truly ingenious suggestion that Pérez himself promoted the idea of a sexual blackmail in order to dissuade Don Juan from believing that the murder was political.)

As things stand, all of the theories of what Escobedo did or did not know and what, if any, of what he said he knew was true, are based on conjecture and deduction. All we can safely say is that by late 1577 certain people at court, including Antonio Pérez, decided that they wished Juan de Escobedo dead. Pérez's involvement in the murder is beyond doubt. Marañón tells us that Pérez poisoned Escobedo twice during February 1578, once at a dinner at his country house and once in Madrid, both times unsuccessfully. Pérez's chief-of-staff Diego Martínez then put Juan Rubio, a servant, to work on Escobedo's own cook. Several thimblesful of poisonous powders were added to a stew and Escobedo became very ill. Foul play was suspected and a Moorish slave girl was hanged for the crime (the rebellion in Andalucía was about to break out and she was a convenient victim). Pérez visited the sick man at his house, presumably hoping to see him on his deathbed. He made a full recovery.

Next a man called Antonio Enríquez (from Pérez's home state of Aragón like all of his most trusted servants) was sent to Barcelona with a bag of gold to find a small crossbow ('of the sort they use in Catalonia to kill men') and someone capable of using it. Enríquez returned with his brother-in-law Miguel Bosque, 'a man of the same crooked stamp as himself'.

The two were joined by Diego Martínez and Juan Rubio together with Pérez's previous secretary Juan de Mesa, summoned from retirement in Aragón for the purpose, and a man he brought with him called Insausti whom Marañón calls, chillingly, a 'specialist'. These six met to discuss and decide the place and method of assassination. The Catalan crossbow was considered and rejected. Instead they together decided that Insausti should use his sword to kill Escobedo, the others assisting as necessary. The plan was agreed at a meeting on the outskirts of Madrid from where they all returned to their lodgings. The deed was to be committed in Madrid the following day. Antonio Pérez meanwhile constructed an alibi. He departed for Alcalá de Henares, taking with him a certain Gaspar de Robles, recently arrived from Flanders and a close friend of Don Juan. It was essential that the deed be done before the end of the Easter festival when Pérez would have to return to Madrid.

On the evening of Easter Monday the three assassins – Rubio, Bosque and Insausti – tracked Escobedo's movements while the other three stood further off, ready to help if required. The main streets were still crowded when Escobedo's party left the house of Doña Brianda. The assassins dared not strike where they might be easily detained, but then Escobedo turned his horse into the narrow Calle de Almudena, leading alongside the church of Santa María to the main thoroughfare of the Calle Mayor. It was now or never for Insausti. The three men launched themselves at the Escobedo party and in the deliberate confusion Insausti expertly pushed the tip and blade of his sword into Escobedo's body and threw him off his horse. Rubio got clean away and out of Madrid that night while the other two lost their cloaks in the fighting and managed only with difficulty to extricate themselves. They melted away into the web of streets and crept quietly back to their lodgings.

The news spread loudly through the immediate neighbourhood with people running to and from the scene. The three other accomplices hastily returned to their houses. Escobedo's men searched for the assassins in the inns and streets but without success.

Rubio made it to Alcalá early next morning to tell Pérez that the deed was done and none of them arrested. He then returned to Madrid, met Bosque and headed for the relative safety of Aragón (a mule was provided by Pérez for their journey). Insausti, the principal assassin, was the last to leave. After spending a few days outside Madrid he was smuggled into Aragón by Juan de Mesa, disguised as a worker on the estate of Princess Eboli. All involved were rewarded for their efforts and all apparently disappeared into respectable livings. That should have been the end of the affair.

The central point at issue in what became 'the Pérez affair' is whether Pérez, in conspiring to murder Escobedo, acted with the knowledge or connivance of his king. Escobedo was a royal secretary. The investigation of his murder was therefore a matter for the king's magistrates. And yet they did nothing. The court and city seethed with rumour and accusation, all pointing to the guilt of the king's secretary Antonio Pérez. And yet the king did nothing. The Escobedo family and their allies were furious and vengeful. Philip managed to keep them at bay but it began to be clear that his own inaction was serving only to implicate him in the murder. He offered Pérez posts abroad, including as ambassador to Venice, but Pérez refused – he perhaps saw that acceptance of a foreign posting would be both an admission of guilt and a dangerous invitation to a hired assassin. Eventually the king succumbed and, in July 1579, fourteen months after the crime, allowed Pérez and Princess Eboli to be placed under house arrest (the princess was to die in 1592, still confined to a suite of rooms in the family castle at Pastrana). The charges though concerned bribes and were unconnected to Escobedo's murder and Pérez was able to keep on working much as before. The murder remained beyond investigation. All of this was to change in 1584.

After the murder Pérez had rewarded the assassins with gold escudos, obtained for them the rank of ensign in His Majesty's army and packed them off to Italy. It seems that agents of the Escobedo family (or even possibly of the king) followed them there. They probably boasted of their exploits to their fellow soldiers and told everyone that their gold came straight from the king. Insausti was dead soon after arrival in Italy. Miguel Bosque apparently drowned himself, though his family said he was poisoned. Rubio got nervous and returned to Aragón where he was protected by Juan de Mesa. That left Antonio Enríquez, who returned to Spain in 1584, sold out to the Escobedo family, confessed his guilt and implicated Antonio Pérez. The royal secretary was formally arrested and charged with murder in January 1585. By the time of Lucrecia's dream in December 1587 he had been in prison in Madrid for two years while his case was being investigated.

The arrest of Antonio Pérez did not stop the rumours of Philip's involvement in Escobedo's murder. Many at court were convinced both that Pérez had been acting on Philip's orders and that he should be released and returned to his previous position. Pérez became a focus for general discontentment with the king. This was partly because he had many friends at court, partly because many had agreed with the policies he advocated and partly because, since his arrest, Spanish fortunes had suffered a series of setbacks. Pérez might not have prevented these but his absence did not appear to help the king's policy-making.

The Pérez affair came to a head in late 1590, at a time of great disillusionment in Spain and in the Spanish court. Philip's advisers began to see enemies everywhere and took steps to eliminate them. Pérez was put to torture in February 1590, confessed his part in the murder and said he acted on the king's orders. He could not prove this defence since all of his papers had been seized. Before he could be sentenced, on the night of 19 April 1590, Pérez escaped from prison and fled to his homeland of Aragón where he was welcomed as a hero. Aragón was still an autonomous part of Spain with its own laws and it was not clear what powers, if any, Philip possessed to re-arrest Pérez. Over the next few weeks the escaped convict published documents showing Philip's involvement in the murder of Escobedo. This was a serious problem for Philip and a potential crisis for the integrity of Spain. One part of the country was defying the king, while in Castile, and even in the court itself, many supported the Pérez cause.

When Philip ordered his forces to the borders of Aragón and insisted on Pérez's return there were riots in Zaragoza in his support. Pérez decided that it was time to flee the country. He managed to escape to Paris and then to England, where he published a constant stream of evidence intended to prove the king's involvement in his crimes. He became friends with the Earl of Essex and is thought by some to have been the model for Don Adriano de Armado (listed as 'a fantastical Spaniard') in *Love's Labour's Lost*. He died in 1611 in a Paris monastery.

Did Philip sanction the murder of one of his courtiers, protect the man who carried out his orders and then allow him to be tried for murder? Or did Pérez act with his own motives, and invent the king's involvement to protect himself? Or did Pérez dishonestly persuade Philip that Don Juan and his secretary were untrustworthy so that the murder, committed for Pérez's own motives, would not trouble the king too much?

The two principal protagonists in the affair had their say without providing conclusive evidence. According to Pérez, Philip took him into a small room in the Escorial in late 1577 and said, 'Antonio Pérez, many a time, watching and waking, I have considered my brother's affairs, or rather those of Escobedo and his predecessor, Juan de Soto, and what a pass he is come to with his schemings. I find it very needful to make a decision quickly or we shall be too late. I find no fitter remedy for everybody than to be rid of Juan de Escobedo. And thus I am determined upon it and I will entrust this deed to no-one other than you, since I have good proofs of your fidelity and your diligence, which is as patient as your fidelity.' In a submission to the investigation of the murder, Philip wrote, 'All the things that he [Pérez] says, depend on what he said to me. They are most alien to the truth, though he made me believe them by deciphering letters so falsely that I sometimes answered in accord with what he wrote to me' (quoted in Marañón, 1954).

Pérez was tried not only for the murder but for the crimes which Escobedo may have threatened to expose. In 1584 the trial investigator wrote, 'Though he ought to have kept things touching his office secret, as he had promised and sworn, he did not do so. Rather did he reveal and uncover the said secrets by diverse channels, to certain persons, informing them and writing to them letters and recounting things and details in them he ought not, to His Majesty's disservice.' And it was later charged that, in addition, 'He deciphered falsely to make that glorious prince [Don Juan] seem a traitor' (Marañón, 1954).

What is the verdict of history? First Gregorio Marañón, writing in 1954: 'The planning of the execution was one of Antonio Pérez's masterpieces . . . But the king was also involved . . . We must insist on this last point, as the current of opinion has tended of recent years to hint and even affirm that the Prudent King was not responsible at all for the execution.'

Then Geoffrey Parker in 1995:

'I tremble with fear to see that there are people in the world who would strike down secretaries of the king,' wrote one minister, adding: 'I am astonished to see that it was possible for such a thing to have happened in the court of the king of Spain.' He, like many others, wondered why the crime went unpunished. The answer was simple: Escobedo had been murdered at the king's command, and the deed had been arranged by Antonio Pérez. Although whole books have been written denying Philip's complicity in the murder, there seems to be little doubt about the matter.

Then Henry Kamen in 1997:

No proof exists for the subsequent charges by Pérez that he acted at the king's instigation. There is no evidence that the king was implicated, or that he encouraged his secretary . . . Philip's innocence in the affair cannot be proved. But the most convincing argument against his implication in Escobedo's murder is that it was not his style and he stood to gain nothing by it.

Parker also quotes Ferdinand Braudel: 'In this mysterious matter no-one will ever have the last word.' Yet Parker himself gave as elegant a summary of the Pérez affair as one could wish for: 'Without either of them lying completely, the Monarch could say that the death was performed without his orders, and Pérez that the king had ordered it.'

The Pérez affair split the court and the country and when, in 1590, Pérez escaped, the king's authority over his own country was placed in serious question. Political dissent was suddenly dangerous. Among those placed in danger in this new atmosphere would be Lucrecia de Léon.

The Oxen and the Looking Glass | Chapter 15
29 December 1587

I dreamed that I was in the palace in Madrid. I was sitting writing an account of the visions[1] when a lady of the palace entered. She was distressed by a dream that she had had and asked me to explain it to her. This lady had a long and well-proportioned face, green eyes and fair hair, which altogether gave her a good appearance.

She said to me, 'In my dream I saw my father and his estate between the horns of a white ox.'

I told her that I had heard it said that white oxen represented the Moors and I said, 'If that is so then Spain is to be lost, as I have said before, and your father will be taken captive.'

At this point the king entered, very anguished. He commanded the lady to leave and said to me, 'I have dreamed that Madrid was surrounded by white oxen and that they were all attacking the palace.'

I said to the king, 'Prepare yourself, Your Majesty for this is a sign that Madrid is to be taken by the Moors.' The king walked through into another room in deep thought and looked out with me through a window above the main entrance to the palace. From there we saw three eagles coming from the south carrying a crown in their beaks. With great reverence they placed this crown upon the tower, on the side that faces towards the forests. The king asked me to explain this[2] and I said, 'The eagles have brought the crown for the king who is to come. You have little time left, for a year and a half have now passed. Your Majesty should look to what is needful and prepare a last testament.'

The king replied, 'If I had not been warned and were then lost, the fault would have been yours[3] and that of Fray Lucas since you would have known of it and kept silent. However, souls are so dear to God that He did not wish to lose mine altogether and He has informed you in order to warn me.'

This said, the king left me and Fray Lucas entered to study, as he does three times a day, at which time I woke up.

Then I slept again, and the Ordinary Man came to me and took me to the seashore where I saw the two companions. But on seeing me the Lion Man began to run away.[4]

I said, 'Do not go for I bring you a message from Fray Lucas.'

He answered, 'If I have listened to you from time to time it is because you are a messenger.'

I told him, 'Fray Lucas says that if the dreams are God's business, he will make up his mind to tell the king of it and further, that he is not a fearful man nor does he seek to gain anything from the king.'

The Lion Man said to me, 'Tell Fray Lucas to look at my words and see whether I have ever told him to act outside his priestly state or whether I have urged you to do any bad thing or to act against the will of God. That will remove any doubts he has.'[5]

Then, raising his hands to Heaven, he said, 'Blessed be Thou O Lord, a time has come when your word is doubted and I ask that you allow us to give further proof of who we are.'

And then to me, he said, 'Does Fray Lucas require that we give him a sign such as will leave him blind?'

I said to him, 'You have told us who you are and so has the Old Fisherman. Since these things have been disclosed to a woman, do not be surprised that they may well think them to be illusion or fraud.'[6]

Then the Lion Man seized me by the hand and took me to the top of a hill. There he showed me a closed book which he opened saying, 'Tell Fray Lucas de Allende to open a book of his that is closed, at all the pages whose numbers end in seven and there he will find a chapter where many things concerning prophetic visions are discussed.'

Then he opened a mirror case and showed the mirror to me.

In it I could see the infanta, Princess Isabella, looking very sad and at her feet three dead men running with blood.[7] And the blood was so black that it darkened all her skirts. Then he closed the mirror and showed me all of the world in a broken glass and said, 'I shall not see this world healed until another king comes.'

He turned to me and asked, 'Who has Fray Lucas told you that I am?'

I answered, 'Yesterday he told me you were St Luke.'

He said, 'For the kindness he has done me in saying that I am so great a saint, I shall, from today, take great care in all that concerns him.'

We were still standing on the hill and he said, 'I shall inform Fray Lucas when it is time to warn the king and when you enter to speak to him let it not be with sad faces so that he shall not think you hypocrites.'

I said, 'I shall not bear a sad face in to him for I do not wish to appear a hypocrite, and before then I wish to be married.'[8]

He said to me, 'Yes, in earlier times prophets were married and so continued their line.'

Then he took me down the hill to the Old Man who said to me, 'You will give this good news to Fray Lucas and tell him that we are all at his service.'

And with that I awoke.

1. *I was sitting writing an account of the visions.* At her trial Lucrecia was to maintain in her defence that she could not read or write. This was difficult for the authorities to disprove until a search of her prison cell revealed notes written on scraps of paper. It is not known when she first learned to read and write.

2. *The king asked me to explain this.* Within her dreams all three of Lucrecia's regular acquaintances have interpreted her visions for her. This ability

to explain things which she cannot understand reinforces the power they have over her. Now the king speaks directly to Lucrecia and asks her to interpret his own dream. The Bible is full of such requests, including the most well known of all, the one resulting from Pharaoh's dream of seven fat and seven thin cattle, and of seven good and seven blasted ears of corn. When Joseph interprets this dream for Pharaoh he is well rewarded:

> And Pharaoh said unto Joseph, Forasmuch as God hath shewed thee all this, there is none so discreet and wise as thou art. Thou shalt be over my house, and according unto thy word shall all my people be ruled; only in the throne will I be greater than thou. (Genesis 41: 39–40)

Pharaoh knows that the dream is a double cipher and of the two minds through which it must pass, the interpreter is greater than the dreamer. Joseph's demonstration of wisdom is a demonstration of power. Pharaoh knows this and ackowledges it. Lucrecia knows this too. The three men in her dreams have power over her and so, to a degree, does Alonso Mendoza. By asking her to explain his own dream the king now places her in power over him.

3. '*If I had not been warned and were then lost, the fault would have been yours*'. On Lucrecia's first arrest she will be criticised by the prosecutors precisely for *not* passing on her warnings to the king: '"This evil dreamer does not want these things to be told to the king, our lord, to whom it would matter if these things were from God. Rather she tells them to the common people in order to stir them up"' (quoted in Kagan, 1990).

This may seem an unfair accusation – what likelihood was there that the king would take any notice of the dreams of a common woman? – but there are two good reasons for the charge. First Lucrecia says that the dreams which seem to criticise Philip (and there are many which do so harshly) are really meant to warn him, but if this were the case how was he to be warned, if not by Lucrecia? Secondly it was quite common for visionaries, prophets, supplicants and anyone with a suggestion or grievance to write to the king – Piedrola did and Lucrecia could have. She might answer these charges by pointing out that it was Alonso de Mendoza who circulated the transcripts of her dreams and that she had little influence over the choice of recipients.

The eventual trial of Lucrecia and her patrons was characterised by such shedding of responsibility.

4. *on seeing me the Lion Man began to run away.* Lucrecia's relationship with this enigmatic figure continues to be uneasy. He is still disdainful, wishing to hear only her messages, not her thoughts.

5. *'That will remove any doubts he has.'* Fray Lucas de Allende was always less certain about the divine nature of Lucrecia's dreams than Don Alonso de Mendoza and consequently less enthusiastic about their dissemination. He seems to have voiced some doubts, which Lucrecia has got to know about and transmitted to her dream companions. (The conversations are so authentic that we momentarily forget that these are dreams and see instead Lucrecia living in two worlds and acting as a messenger between them.) The Lion Man has a better relationship with Fray Lucas than with Lucrecia and is keen to convince him that these are 'true' messages from God.

6. *'do not be surprised that they may well think them to be illusion or fraud.'* Richard Kagan points out that Lucrecia was at a disadvantage in her wish to be taken seriously as a visionary or prophet. She did not belong to a religious order, and her allegedly divine messages came not in waking visions but in dreams – traditionally a more suspect source. But above all it was the political and seditious content of the dreams that put Lucrecia beyond the pale. Warnings of catastrophes, denouncing of general corruption, even some criticism of princes might be tolerated, but outright denigration of the king was dangerous and it disqualified Lucrecia from official consideration as a divine messenger. But it was the political content that made Mendoza and others wish to believe that the dreams were truly prophetic.

7. *I could see the infanta, Princess Isabella, looking very sad and at her feet three dead men running with blood.* Lucrecia, who had worked in the household of the Infante Philip (the future Philip III) in the royal palace, seemed to identify with the Infanta Isabella, daughter of Philip II and Isabel de Valois. Lucrecia resented her own father's inability to find her a suitable husband – a parallel to Isabella who eventually married the year after Philip II died, when she was thirty-three years old (in contrast her sister Catalina, one year younger, married at the age of

eighteen). Isabella was just a few years older than Lucrecia; both were old to be still unmarried in Spain.

8. *'before then I wish to be married.'* It was not until October or November 1589, two years after this dream, that Lucrecia was to meet and fall in love with a man who came close to being her husband. Richard Kagan's assiduous researches have revealed that within Lucrecia's story there is a sorry tale of love and loss.

Diego de Vitores was a twenty-eight-year-old secretary 'of considerable learning' when he met Lucrecia. The circumstances of their meeting are not known but it is likely that Vitores had heard about Lucrecia's reputation as a dreamer. By February of 1590 they would become lovers and, it later emerged, make secret wedding vows known only to each other. Such marriages were illegal and in this case the couple may have wanted to preserve Lucrecia's image of a chaste woman – married women could not be innocent messengers of God.

In early March 1590 Fray Lucas Allende recruited Vitores to help with the transcription of the dreams. He had by this time used a number of different helpers but Vitores was the best placed of all of them and became the most frequent transcriber for the next few months. The arrangement was short-lived, because in May 1590 Vitores was arrested along with Lucrecia, Mendoza and Allende.

At Lucrecia's first appearance before the Inquisition tribunal in early June 1590 it was noted that she looked six or seven months pregnant. Lucrecia and Vitores were in the same Inquisition prison in Seville and, to start with at least, managed to communicate by sending messages written on scraps of cloth. In one of these Vitores addresses Lucrecia as 'My wife'. That summer Lucrecia gave birth to a girl who lived with her in the prison during the long-drawn-out trial procedure. As far as we know, Vitores had no chance to see them. When the sentences were finally passed the couple were sent to separate places, Vitores returning to his home town of Zamora. According to his own account, given in a letter to the court, Lucrecia did not attempt to join him there and the two never had the chance to formalise their wedding vows.

The Ordinary Man came and took me to the usual seashore. As we went along I saw three men's heads. I recognised them to be the two traitors[1] that I had seen in other dreams. The Ordinary Man told me to look well at the third head so that I should know the body. I saw that he was black-bearded with large eyes and a rather high nose.

'Look,' he said, 'this man is a close associate of the king and it is well that you should know him.' And since I told him that I did not, he took me before the two companions.

The Old Man said to me, 'Did you recognise the third head?'

I said no and he questioned me again, 'Those three heads, where did it seem to you that they were?'

I answered, 'Madrid.'

'The place is none other than Toledo,' he said, 'at the hawthorn gate, and these three will be prisoners when Madrid is restored.'

The Lion Man then asked the Old Man, 'Is this to come about when Philip is dead?'[2]

He answered 'Yes', whereupon an argument arose.

Just then I saw a great flock of crows approaching from England. The Old Man asked the Lion Man, 'Where are they going?' He answered, 'They are going to Spain, and so that you may believe it, come, all of you, with me.'

We went with him and saw that round about the palace there was much land that had been sown with seed. The crows came and settled on it and ate up all the seed. When they took flight again many mallows and weeds sprang up.

The Lion Man said, 'You see how the king will believe that his lands are all sown with good seed but he will find them full of weeds.'

Having said that, he sent the Old Man and the Ordinary Man away and took me inside the palace. There we saw the king lying in bed. Attached to the bed was a padlock and attached to the king's ear was a ring with an eyelet. A man came and took the padlock and passed it through the eyelet and locked it with a key which he placed in the breast of his garment. He then went quietly away.

I asked the Lion Man what this meant and he said, 'If Don Alonso does not understand it I shall tell it.'

He returned me to the seashore where we found the Old Man who said to me, 'Look again over England and France.' We saw a tree with many leaves. There came a wind, which the men who were with me called the Ice Wind, and they said, 'Wretched the land to which God sends you.' And this wind burned all the leaves from that tree and it did not have fruit.

At that moment I saw a dog with a black head and a white breast. It barked slowly and there came forth from its breath so much heat that a part of the tree became green again.

Now the Old Man told the Ordinary Man to take me to the castle where I had previously seen the bodies of the dead kings. I did not enter from above as I had done before, but by the door. Once inside the vault I saw that all of the dead kings had had their entrails removed. And in the empty space the first had gold, another silver, another incense, another myrrh and another balsam and precious liquors. When I came to King Pedro I could not see what he had in his belly for the foul stench that came forth from him. The king at his side had a tree in his belly which seemed to be an almond tree and the one beyond, a palm. Then I heard a voice which said, 'These are our vessels and in this way each one shows what is held within.'

Beyond the king with the palm I came to that man I had seen chained in other visions. He was wearing damask clothing. The voice said, 'This is Piedrola who is a descendant of the kings in

*this vault*³ *and very close to that king whose stomach gives forth*
a palm. Just then I saw that the chained man held forth his hand
*which bore an emerald ring,*⁴ *and said, 'You see here the hand of*
Piedrola. Know me by this and see how wretched I am.'
    And with that I awoke.

1. *the two traitors.* The business of traitors within the court is a difficult and
dangerous one. In Philip's court there were many men who had served
in the Netherlands and many others who knew it well. The Netherlands was the jewel in Philip's empire – a sophisticated, cosmopolitan,
autonomous territory, the centre of Europe's trade in textiles and other
manufactured goods. Straddling the Rhine delta, it controlled the flow
of water-borne traffic between the geographical centre of Europe and
its booming northern and western seaboards. A place of great thinkers,
architects, artists. A thriving teeming weaving spinning dyeing clock-
making lens-grinding shop-talking buying selling mecca for half of
Europe. The most grievous charge that history makes against Philip is
that he knowingly squashed this liberal humanist bazaar with the flat
sword of narrow dogmatic imperialist religiosity.

    A good number of Spanish courtiers were dismayed then horrified
by Spanish actions in the Netherlands. Some were good friends of the
Dutch dukes and had fought alongside them for Philip and his father
against the French. They even sympathised with their rebellion and
urged the king to negotiate a settlement. The main spokesman of this
'peace' faction was Ruy Gómez de Silva, Prince of Eboli, Portuguese
friend since childhood of the king, companion and adviser on Philip's
extensive early travels to Italy, Germany, England and the Netherlands. This group, formed around the king during his journey through
his empire, encompassed Spaniards, Germans, Burgundians, Dutch
and Italians based in Castile and elsewhere. This was, in short, the
Eboli party. As well as its cosmopolitan and outward outlook the Eboli
faction was tethered, through the marriage of the prince to Aña de
Mendoza (who then became princess of Eboli and was later embroiled
in the Pérez affair), to the great Mendoza family, grandest grandees
of Spain.

The other faction was headed by Fernando Alvarez de Toledo, the Duke of Alba, Spain's greatest soldier. When Philip assumed the throne Alba was already a powerful man in the kingdom and high steward of the royal household, a post which gave him the rule of the roost in the king's palace. Charles V warned his son Philip about Alba: 'You are younger than he: take care that he does not dominate you.' But the duke was a dominant figure in Spain for almost the whole of Philip's reign.

When the Dutch rebelled in 1567 Philip did not go to the Netherlands himself and did not send the prince of Eboli. Instead he sent Alba with an army and instructions not to compromise or negotiate. Now what should the Eboli faction do? As Marañón has said of the Pérez affair, the Dutch had networks of spies everywhere in the Spanish court: no one could be trusted. But these 'spies' were mostly Spanish courtiers who wanted desperately to end the conflict. They lobbied their king, and doubtless advised the Dutch on how best to do the same.

Is such behaviour, against the policies of the crown, traitorous? In some ways yes and some no. No historian has vindicated Spain's policies in the Netherlands, while all have been drawn to the conclusion that a negotiated settlement would immeasurably have benefited Spain, the Dutch, and probably the whole of Europe. The biggest beneficiaries of Spain's disastrous involvement in the Netherlands were, ironically, Philip's two greatest bugbears, France and England.

By the time of Lucrecia's dreaming career, Alba had been recalled, Ruy Gómez had died and the division of the court had been to some degree resolved. There was a peace faction that still pressed the Dutch cause, but if it was thought traitorous then Lucrecia and Alonso de Mendoza are unlikely to have held that view. Along with many others Mendoza favoured less expenditure on foreign wars (and less taxes), while also being intolerant of heresy and fearful of invasion. It is the prerogative of the citizen to hold to principles that, in practice, lead to opposing effects.

2. *'Is this to come about when Philip is dead?'* This section of the dream contains different visual allegories of Philip's predicament. First a flock of crows – enemies arriving from England – eat the good seed of his land, which then brings forth weeds. This is plain enough but is followed by a simple and imaginative vision. The eyelet, or ear-ring, and the padlock are

not explained, nor do they need to be. The story gives a disturbing sense of the vulnerability of the king (and by extension his realm) and of his semi-captive state.

3. *'This is Piedrola who is a descendant of the kings in this vault'*. The clearest indication yet that Lucrecia considered Piedrola the rightful successor to Philip as king of Spain.

4. *Just then I saw that the chained man held forth his hand which bore an emerald ring.* 'When the Incas of Peru were conquered by the Spaniards, vast quantities of emeralds, the most frequent stones adorning their temples, were looted and brought to Europe. The same thing happened when the native culture of Mexico fell . . . Emeralds were alleged to change colour or turn pale in the presence of deception and treachery' (W.B. Crow, 1968).

On the 31st of December I dreamed that, on the way from
Toledo to Madrid to warn certain people, I was captured.[1] I said
to myself, 'Knowing for such a long time that Spain has been
lost, how is it that I have been unable to take better care of
myself?'

The man who took me captive (who was a Moor) asked me,
'Where were you born?'

I answered, 'In Turkey.'

He asked me for some news of Turkey and I was able to give
him some because of the times I had been taken there. Then he
took me before the Great Turk who was lodged in the king's
palace in Madrid. It was already night when I arrived there and
I was taken to a room to sleep. While I was asleep the Ordinary
Man came to me and said, 'This is God's punishment because
although you have it in your power to warn the king you do not
do so.[2] Therefore God wishes you to be held captive. But come
with me, for I come to free you.'

The Ordinary Man took me to Toledo where I saw Fray Lucas
in the Great Church. I said to him, 'Fray Lucas, look how God
threatens us; we are responsible for this loss. If we warn the
king, so much evil will not have to come about.'

'Let us go and warn him,' said Fray Lucas, but I said, 'He is
already dying.'

He asked me who had told me so, and I said that it was the
Ordinary Man.

We made our way to the Alcázar which we found draped in
mourning and lit with many large wax candles. Robed in purple
and carrying a cross covered in green taffeta, Cardinal Quiroga
entered to help the king make a good death. We entered the room
where Philip was and found that he was propped up and was no

longer capable of speech.[3] *When the cardinal saw Fray Lucas he made way for him to approach the bed.*

The Ordinary Man said to me, 'Leave it to Fray Lucas to speak to the king, we are going to the seashore.'

When we arrived where the two companions were, the Lion Man said, 'I wish to show you a vision.' He showed me a very elegant lady, dressed in our fashion, and around her four men who, from their manner and good dress, seemed to be of the royal household. They were plucking out the woman's hair and she was standing very stiffly without any movement. They removed all of her hair and when they had reduced her to baldness they laid hands on her clothing and left her naked. After this they wished to dishonour her but she defended herself, though the four men inflicted many wounds upon her with their unsheathed swords.

When this had passed I saw the same woman to the south of where I stood. I saw that she was pregnant, for her belly was large, and she gave birth to a boy child and his name was that of one of the twelve peers of France, namely Urgel of the great strength.[4]

The Lion Man said to me, 'This child is made in sin and is to reign in Castile.'

I asked him who the woman was and he answered, 'I do not wish to say.' So I said, 'Then tell me what is the meaning of the tree that froze?'

He said, 'I do not wish to say until Don Alonso comes. Great is the favour I do Fray Lucas in showing, with my own hands, these visions and in pleading with God to grant peace with your Pope.'[5]

And with that I awoke.

1. *on the way from Toledo to Madrid to warn certain people, I was captured.* Now Lucrecia is the central actor in her dreamworld. She has not been taken by the Ordinary Man or ordered by the Lion Man or advised by the Old Man; she is not witnessing an event, she is not seeking an interpretation. Instead she is on a mission and suddenly in danger. Her incompetence at being captured is compensated by her deftness in using the knowledge of Turkey gained from her dream-visits. She was later to show this skill under questioning in her dealings with the Inquisition.

   As well as Lucrecia becoming more personally involved, the dreams are steadily becoming more real and more consistent. Madrid has now fallen, the Grand Turk uses the royal palace as his residence and King Philip is dying in Toledo, the last bastion of Spanish hopes. Lucrecia is increasingly torn (as were most devout believers) between fear of the terrible events to come and desire for destruction and renewal. Where will it all end and when will it begin again?

2. *'although you have it in your power to warn the king you do not do so.'* The re-emphasis of this warning that the king should be told of Lucrecia's visions is very striking. It is as though Lucrecia were now telling Mendoza (and she may have been warned by others to do this) that he should send copies of her dreams to the king in order to head off any future accusations of sedition. Lucrecia may have said this to Mendoza in person but the most powerful way of convincing him would be through the dreams themselves. This should have counted in Lucrecia's favour when she was arrested and accused, but in pointing to such things she ran the risk of appearing to be clever and manipulative, not ignorant and naive.

3. *We entered the room where Philip was and found that he was propped up and was no longer capable of speech.* Philip's death was not to come for another eleven years but when it did it was somewhat more unpleasant than Lucrecia's deathbed description. Geoffrey Parker (1995) writes: 'Dropsy set in; fever and arthritis combined to sap his vitality; a blood infection caused his skin to erupt in boils and sores.'

   Philip's valet later wrote a memoir in which he declared: 'He was forced to be incontinent which, without any doubt, was for him one of the worst torments imaginable, seeing that he himself was one of the cleanest, neatest and most fastidious men the world has ever seen' (quoted in Parker, 1995).

In the end Philip lay for fifty-three days in pain and filth, consoled only by his faith. He prayed for death, which finally was granted on 13 September 1598.

4. *his name was that of one of the twelve peers of France, namely Urgel of the great strength.* The twelve peers of France perished in the battle of Roncevaux as told in the twelfth-century French verse romance *Le Chanson de Roland*. The French warriors were folk heroes to the Spanish Christians because they fought against the Arabs.

5. *'pleading with God to grant peace with your Pope.'* The relation between Spain, Europe's most powerful Catholic nation, and the Papacy was fractious. Any accord on religious matters was clouded by the politics of the secular world. A messy war between France and the Holy Roman Empire had engulfed much of Europe early in the sixteenth century, dragging the Papacy in on the side of the French. Imperial troops of the army of Charles V, Philip II's father, entered Rome in 1527, sacked the city and took Pope Clement VII captive. The Papacy was forced to cede territory to the Empire. When Charles V died Philip inherited not only the Netherlands, Spain and the Americas, but Sicily, Sardinia, the Duchy of Milan and the territory of Naples. Since Spain also controlled the western Mediterranean, the Papal States were hemmed in to the east by the Ottoman empire and to the west, south and north (leaving aside the city states of Florence and Venice) by the Spanish.

Nor did Philip cede control of the Church within his realms. Though much has been made in England of Henry VIII's self-appointment as head of the Church of England, Philip was *de facto* and *de jure* head of the Catholic Church in Spain and its dominions. He appointed bishops and gave or withheld his approval of church statutes and he was the controller of the Inquisition.

Any pope (Philip saw nine of them come and go during his reign) must have wanted to regain the pre-eminence that his predecessor had held before the Reformation – once again to be the religious leader of the entire Christian world. Instead, given the size of Spain's empire and its expansion into the Americas and the East Indies (the Philippines), it became the dream of some at his court that Philip should become the ruler of the entire world – a world under one ruler and one faith.

The companions in Lucrecia's dream did not see it this way. They wanted Philip out of the way and replaced by a monarch who would reconcile Spain with Rome – perhaps even a Roman ruler. They wanted a holy man on the throne of Spain. The apocalyptic moment is one where faith and life are joined, where the ruler of Heaven becomes ruler of the earth.

On the 5th day of January of the said year[1] the Ordinary Man came and took me to Constantinople. There I saw many weapons being prepared. The Great Turk commanded that all those who received his salary should arm themselves so that he might review them. So they came two by two, armed, before his palace.

From there the Ordinary Man took me over the sea, passing above the waters, to England. I saw along the way how the sea formed a sort of arc encircling many lands. We saw Juan Andrea Doria's galleys,[2] in a poor state for having passed through a storm and bearing few arms.

Arriving in England I saw the port near to the city gate, and many people guarding that gate while others worked to strengthen it. We entered the city and I saw more people than on previous occasions. In all of the cities of England arms were being prepared and pikes and much gunpowder and shot were being loaded. I saw Drake emerge in dark robes lined with ermine to review his people.

Then we left England and went to the seashore to meet the two companions.

Once there the Lion Man asked me, 'Have you told Fray Lucas what you dreamed last night?' I replied that I had, and he then asked me if I had seen Drake and I replied, 'Yes, although I had heard that he was already at sea, I saw him there in his homeland.'

He replied, 'It is fifteen days since he went back among his people to recover.'

As he was saying this I saw that there came by sea a coffin bearing three tall crosses. Upon the first was the prince Don Carlos[3] and on the second, which was in the form of an X, was

King Philip. Upon the third was Queen Isabella his wife, but the cross seemed to be falling away from her shoulders.

The Old Man asked me, 'Do you know these people?'

I answered, 'Yes. Tell me why they are like this.'

And the Old Man said, 'It is not well that things are explained too much.'

At this time the coffin cover was raised and I saw in it the Marquis of Auñón. In the folds of his tunic he had a great quantity of playing cards and in another fold many papers with writing.

I asked who he was and they answered, 'The Marquis of Auñón and since he has falsified so many papers, God permits that he be seen with them.'

Then I saw at his side a gentleman lying face down. With him he had a fleece and with one of the points of the fleece he had written: he of Alba. Reading this I said, 'The Duke of Alba is the man who lies here.'

The Old Man said, 'It is not good that the great ones who, in their time, have ruled republics should be exposed.'

The Lion Man said, 'It is well done and if he had not done so much evil in Flanders and France, Spain would be at peace.[4] If he had done justice as was meet there would not now be so many Lutherans.'

And at this time the coffin disappeared and I saw that there came by sea a basket of chickens. I asked the Old Man what it meant and he said, 'Since the Lion Man has brought these visions there must be something to see.' The basket stopped before us and I saw that four of those chickens had women's faces, two of which I recognised and I think that if I were to see some portraits of ladies I would know the others. The rest had faces of men, two of which I also knew.

And with that I awoke.

1. *the said year.* The first week of 1588 – the millennial year. Regiomantus, a German seer had written a hundred years previously:

> A thousand years after the virgin birth
> and after five hundred more allowed the globe,
> the wonderful eighty-eighth year begins and
> brings with it woe enough. If, this year,
> total catastrophe does not befall, if land
> and sea do not collapse in total ruin, yet
> will the whole world suffer upheavals, empires
> will dwindle and from everywhere will
> be great lamentation.

Nicolaus Winckler wrote a book called *Considerations on Future Changes in Worldly Rule and the End of the World,* published in 1582 in Augsburg. Each year throughout the 1570s and 1580s he published predictions for the coming year (*Practica auff das Jar . . .*). These were avidly and widely read. Robin Barnes (1988) writes:

He [Winckler] showed that between 328 – an ostensibly significant year in the time of Constantine and Pope Sylvester – and 1588, there lay exactly 1260 years. That number appeared in Revelation 12:6 as the number of days (interpreted as years) that the woman clothed with the sun (the church) was protected from the dragon (Satan). In the second part of his work, Winckler examined the complementary evidence in nature. The signs for 1588 promised unimagined horrors, including worldwide religious upheaval and a bloodbath inflicted on Christendom . . . The terrible last days of the world were at hand.

For Catholic seers like Winckler the year 328 had been the start of the golden era which would come to an end in 1588. The first General Council of the Church had been called by the Emperor Constantine in 325 at Nicaea in Asia Minor. As a result the Church was united under one orthodoxy codified in the Nicene Creed.

Some Protestant prophets saw the Council of Nicaea as the beginning of a dark time for Christianity, a period when all dissent from the established doctrine was forbidden and called heretical. For them the Popes had been the incarnation of the Antichrist. The year 1588 was to mark the end of their torment and the beginning of a golden time.

The source for all of these calculations was the same: the last book of the Bible, 'The Revelation of St John the Divine', more usually known as 'The Book of Revelations'. Prophets who came after Christ not only made their calculations of the world's end on the basis of the Book of Revelations, they also borrowed its tone. Vengeance, prophecy, redemption and punishment are combined in a gaudy mixture which Lucrecia, among others, recreated in her own visions. The book's inherent strangeness has seduced both believers and non-believers into according it a profound mystery, but the early Christian leaders may have had a more practical purpose in including it within the approved Scriptures.

The God of the Old Testament was transformed through His son from a jealous, cantankerous, capricious and vengeful deity into a loving, forgiving father. But if all sin was to be forgiven how should sin be discouraged? The coming of the Messiah had been prophesied in the Scriptures; indeed the books of the Jewish Torah were rearranged by the early Christians to give the effect of building towards the coming of Christ. But what should happen after God's son left the earth? Should there be no more prophecies? Both of these points – the need for discouragement of sin, and of a final message from God about the future – were answered by the Book of Revelations. On a more practical level the early Christian leaders may have thought that their followers needed assurance that not only would they be saved, but that their persecutors would be damned – the 'beast' is widely thought to represent 'the Empire', meaning the contemporary Roman empire but also the past Babylonian and Assyrian empires. The desire for a strongly moral message of self-denial and humility needed to be combined with a promise that, in the end, not only would the good be rewarded, but the evil would be struck down. This combination was undoubtedly responsible for the success and endurance of the Christian religion.

The Bible is the entire history of the world but some of it had to be written while the world still existed. So the final book is a statement of what will happen at the world's end. It closes the circle and provides resolution. In this, the Bible provides a model for all the books that followed.

Lucrecia's task was to reimagine the end of the world (in her very first transcribed dream people 'cry out the end of the world') in a way that fitted with the Scriptures and with the world around her. The

Book of Revelations leads directly to the small house on the Calle de San Salvador.

Lucrecia shows all the certainty and confusion of the message of the Christian Church. She wants her loving Christ and she wants the enemies of God to be punished. She knows that the end of the world is coming, that the wrongdoers will soon be punished and the chosen ones elevated. She sees the prospects of violence everywhere and feels little forgiveness.

2. *We saw Juan Andrea Doria's galleys.* Prince Andrea Doria of Genoa had brought the young Philip, when he too was a prince, on his first overseas journey from Barcelona to Genoa in 1548. Doria was the head of one of the four great families of Genoa, he was an ally of Philip's father Charles and, most important, he had at his command the most powerful fleet in the western Mediterranean. Close relations between Genoa and Castile went back to the fourteenth century. More recently the Genoese Christopher Columbus had been supported by Ferdinand and Isabella in his voyages of discovery. Juan (properly Gian) Andrea Doria was the nephew of Andrea Doria and remained loyal to Philip. Philip's daughter Catalina married the Duke of Savoy, whose court was in Genoa, in 1585, cementing the friendship of the two states still further. Being a Mediterranean power, the Genoese fleet comprised mainly low-floating galleys, but a handful of Genoese ocean-going galleons were used in the Spanish Armada – against the wishes of the Genoese. Juan Andrea Doria was famous enough in Spain to be known to Lucrecia.

3. *Upon the first was the prince Don Carlos.* On 8 July 1545 Philip, then prince of Spain, had been blessed by the birth of a son, Carlos, to his teenage wife María of Portugal. Four days later María died – Philip was a widow and a father at eighteen years of age. Twenty-three years later, on 24 July 1568, Don Carlos, heir to the greatest empire the world had ever seen, died a miserable and tormented death from a combination of starvation and self-induced illness. Philip's grief at the death was heightened by his own part in the tragedy of his son. His mental torment was surely further increased by the rumours that he had had Don Carlos murdered. The story of Don Carlos lowered Philip's reputation at the time. Later the tragic prince became the subject of poems and plays; two hundred years after his death, he was turned into a hero by the Romantic movement. But even without artistic

embellishment this was an extraordinary tale, a private family tragedy played on the greatest public stage.

Carlos seems to have had an unexceptional childhood. After his mother's death he had no immediate family to care for him in infancy. But this was not unusual at the time – death of women in childbirth was terrifyingly frequent. His father was absent for two long periods of several years of his childhood. When Carlos was fifteen his father married Isabel de Valois, his third wife. Carlos and Isabel were virtually the same age and became great friends and companions. It was later rumoured that Don Carlos and Isabel de Valois were lovers and that this was the reason his father turned against him. This, together with Carlos's supposed political liberalism, became the centrepiece of Schiller's 1785 play *Don Carlos* – both are inventive products of the playwright's need for dramatic conflict. By the early 1560s, having survived the perils of infant morbidity and childhood disease, Carlos, a lively and physically active character, was at the beginnings of manhood with the world at his feet.

In this new era of centralised states with their all-powerful princes, male heirs to the throne became desirable to the point of obsession. Infant mortality made succession extremely uncertain, so a king with a son who lived to maturity would have achieved one of the great goals of his life. So Philip had done well – or got lucky. He had a son even before he became king, and had seen this boy grow into an apparently healthy young man. But the appearance was not a reflection of reality. When Philip was away in England in 1554 he received reports that his son was backward in learning. Then as the years went on Carlos's behaviour became erratic. His temper was ferocious and easily roused, though he generally showed an even and agreeable face to the world. As he approached maturity and became integrated into court life, stories of his eccentricities began to circulate. These tales were picked up by those assiduous gossips, the foreign ambassadors, and relayed back to their masters – the character of the heir to the Spanish empire was of over-riding importance. Obnoxious cruelty to horses and servants as an adolescent could not be hushed up but were within bounds of a prince's licence. Once the prince was mature and introduced to the affairs of state, this boyish petulance became a danger. Don Carlos, it rapidly became clear, was not well in his mind.

The situation for Philip was agonising. He persevered with his son's education and continued to nurture him as a potential heir to his throne, while at the same time the foreign ambassadors wrote home advising their masters not to involve their families in a marriage with such a dangerous young man. Philip was well aware of the difficulties, writing to the Duke of Alba in 1564, when Carlos was nineteen, that his son was very slow in developing his intelligence, personality and judgement. Over the next three years, when Philip might have desperately hoped that a late flowering would have turned this strange youth into a suitable man, Carlos's behaviour did not improve. As it became clear to him that he was being passed over for military appointments (he expected to lead the army to the Netherlands in April 1567 and was furious that the Duke of Alba was sent instead) Carlos took to issuing threats against his perceived rivals – including his father the king. The situation became intolerable and Philip may have been relieved that his hand was finally forced.

In the latter half of 1567 Carlos began accumulating money and lobbying for support for some kind of expedition. His confused plan was to sail to Italy with the possible purpose of raising an army and establishing his right to some portion of his father's empire. Ironically it was Don Juan of Austria, Philip's half-brother, who himself caused the monarch some small difficulties, who precipitated the end.

Carlos had asked Don Juan to join him on his expedition. Don Juan realised the gravity of the situation and, on Christmas Day 1567, mounted a horse in Madrid and rode to the Escorial at San Lorenzo to inform the king. Twenty-five days later, back at the royal palace in Madrid, Philip took matters in hand. On the night of 18 January 1568 he entered the bedchamber of his only son. The king was helmeted, armoured and escorted by four guards. As the noise of the men removing weapons from his reach woke the sleeping prince, he looked sleepily at his armoured father and asked, 'Has Your Majesty come to kill me?'

Philip later wrote to the Pope:

> . . . since, for my sins, it has been God's will that the prince should have such great and numerous defects, partly mental, partly due to his physical condition, utterly lacking as he is in the qualifications necessary for ruling, I saw the grave risks that would arise were he to be given the succession and the obvious dangers that would accrue; and therefore, after long and careful consideration, and having tried every alternative in vain, it

was clear that there was little or no prospect of his condition's improving in time to prevent the evils which could reasonably be foreseen. (quoted in Parker, 1995)

No, Philip had not come to kill his son, but his life as a prince was over. He was now to spend the rest of his existence locked in the tower of Arévalo Castle. But before his accommodation could be made ready Carlos managed to bring about his own death. He first tried to swallow poison and objects that would damage his health and then took to covering his bed in ice to induce sickness. Carlos's persistence tragically worked and he died on 24 July 1568 aged twenty-three. Philip's grief was compounded when his young wife Isabel de Valois died in childbirth ten weeks later on 3 October – she was just twenty-two.

Carlos's madness has not been subjected to scrupulous diagnosis but historians have made certain assumptions. The most universal of these is that Don Carlos inherited his madness or at least his disposition to it. Geoffrey Parker (1995) writes: 'It seems clear that Carlos shared the mental abnormalities displayed by several of his relatives. His great-grandmother Joanna the Mad had been a whimpering lunatic locked up in Tordesillas castle from 1506 until her death in 1555, whipped and beaten into submission by her keepers (with the express approval of her son, Charles V).'

Before that Joanna's grandmother Isabella had been imprisoned in Arévalo, where she died insane in 1496. It was also widely thought that Carlos's cousin Sebastian, the young king of Portugal who led his nation's army on an unnecessary expedition into North Africa and died with most of them at the battle of Alcázar-el-Kebir, was to some degree mentally disturbed. Parker is explicit about the family connections:

Don Carlos, like his cousin, the unbalanced Sebastian of Portugal (also tragically abandoned by his parents), had a double dose of Joanna the Mad's inheritance, thanks to the inbreeding of the royal families of early modern Europe: instead of eight great-grandparents he had only four, and instead of sixteen great-great-grandparents he had only six!

We are supposed to conclude from this that Carlos's illness had a genetic cause. A recessive gene carried by members of the Habsburg family had the chance to be expressed whenever two carriers of the gene married and had children. In-breeding meant that this happened with greater frequency than normal – if the Habsburgs had stopped marrying each other their recessive madness gene would probably never have been expressed.

Before we get carried away with family madness we should consider some other factors. Madness or mental disturbance happens in almost all families at some time or another. When it happens to members of a family that is ruling half the nations of Europe it is both more visible and more dangerous. Don Carlos undoubtedly showed serious signs of mental disturbance, but the reason we know about this and the reason he was incarcerated were because of his position as heir to the Spanish throne. Had he been from an ordinary family he might well have been left to witter out his life in peace and obscurity.

There is another factor to consider in assessing the reasons for the state of Carlos's mind. In 1562, at the age of seventeen, he fell down some steps and seriously, though possibly temporarily, injured his brain. He was blind for a time and seemed likely to die from his injuries. The great doctor Vesalius was called. He is said to have carried out a trepanning operation – that is cutting a hole in the patient's skull with a drill or saw – but a detailed report by another of the surgeons present shows that an attempt to do this did not succeed. Carlos's behaviour before this accident was abnormal so we cannot blame this for all aspects of his mental disturbance. It is certainly possible though that the aftereffects of the accident and the treatment affected his mental faculties.

4. 'if *he had not done so much evil in Flanders and France, Spain would be at peace.'* This outright and severe criticism of Alba's methods puts Lucrecia and her supporters firmly in the 'peace faction' of the court, allying them with the disgraced Antonio Pérez and with the Mendoza family.

A touching and incongruous light is thrown on Alba's character by the following: the principal nursemaid to Prince Don Carlos after his accident, sitting beside his bed through night after night, was none other than the fearsome duke, scourge of the Netherlands and of all who advocated conciliation in place of strife.

The Ordinary Man came to me. I saw that he carried a cross in his hand. He took the cross to the palace and placed it on its highest tower.

I said to him, 'Why do you place the cross here?'

He replied, 'Because death comes from here.'

I saw that a river of blood[1] was coming from the stables and encircling the palace. In it there were snakes and vermin and many crows with bloodied beaks cawing fearfully. From this river three men emerged who proceeded to sack the royal court and palace and to cut the throats of a vast number of children and old people.

I was full of pity and began to cry out but the Ordinary Man said to me, 'Do not weep and be sad. A sorrowful face must not be shown before the deeds of God.'

Then I said to the Ordinary Man, 'Juan has told me that many Moors are to rise up from Medina del Campo to make war just as the Armada is leaving.'[2]

He replied, 'I know not of that. The Lion Man will give you a better account but I will tell you that if these people are to rebel it will be after the king is dead, for when they see that the enemy is upon Navarre, they will rise up in support.'

This said, the Ordinary Man took me to Toledo where I saw that all the people were gathered together, shouting, and that many of them were dying of thirst. We entered the city and went to the Holy Church. At the base of the tomb of Santa Leocadia a spring had gushed forth and I saw that the whole of the tomb was covered in blood. The Ordinary Man explained that this was a sign that the city was to prevail. Then he placed me in the chapel of San Eugenio. I saw that the saint was very incensed, not like a man who was angry but rather like one who,

seeing that nobody wanted to go out and do battle but rather
shouted in confusion and lacked courage, attempted to motivate
the citizens. In the chapel of Our Lady of the Tabernacle I saw
that many lances had appeared. With this, and what they had
seen of San Eugenio, the clergy decided to go out and do battle.
They went out to fight but the enemy were so numerous that
most of them were killed.

As we were watching this battle the Ordinary Man took me
to the Alcázar where I found Fray Lucas dressed in a white alb.
He was voicing great lamentations at the foot of a crucifix and
praying that the people be given strength for they were so
discouraged.

The Ordinary Man said to me, 'Approach Fray Lucas and tell
him not to weep so much because of the things that God does.'

When I did this Fray Lucas responded, 'I do not weep because
of the anger of God but for the travails of His people.[3] In the
Holy Scriptures we are commanded to feel for those near to us.'

Then the Ordinary Man took me to the seashore where I found
the two companions in deep mourning. I asked, 'Why are you
both so anguished?'

They replied, 'We have reason enough. It would be better if
you could warn Fray Lucas and Don Alonso not to allow those
of the household of Quiroga or the canons of Toledo to go out
into that battle that you have seen.'

And the Ordinary Man said, 'This is because, being over-
compliant with their master, they are all like him,[4] and with one
bad man many good ones are also made bad if they are in his
company – just as when a bad man attends a sermon God does
not allow him to benefit from the holy words which are said to
the others.'

The two companions said to me, 'When you see Don Alonso
you will tell him to arm Piedrola's nephews. They are to go out
into the second battle. We already have these things before our

eyes. Previously we saw what was to happen – it was
prophesied from the mouths of saints – now it is coming to
pass. Console yourselves that you are to prevail once you are left
without the king.

And with that I awoke.

1. *a river of blood.* Lucrecia is being shown terrible things which are all the more frightening for being so realistic. The Spanish people are being butchered in the streets and the holy city of Toledo is in danger of falling. The siege of Toledo is depicted in particularly realistic fashion with Lucrecia hurrying from one place to another within the city seeing men preparing to go out and defend the walls or praying for salvation or crying in lamentation. While these dreadful events take place in the present in dreamland, it is assumed that they are commentaries on the future of the waking world. Are these actual events predicted to occur in the 'real' world or are these visions some sort of guidance about what is to come?

   This becomes a little clearer later in the dream when Lucrecia is told 'Previously we saw what was to happen . . . now it is coming to pass.' She is also given instructions about what to do when these things begin to happen. These instructions are more and more specific and relate directly to the events which are taking place in the dreamworld. The clear implication is that the sack of Madrid and the siege of Toledo which have been prophesied in earlier dreams are now at hand and that Lucrecia must get her followers to prepare by telling them exactly what their role should be. The events she is seeing in her dreams will soon be happening in her real world. The days of observing are drawing to a close and preparations must begin for the final catastrophe.

2. *'many Moors are to rise up from Medina del Campo to make war just as the Armada is leaving.'* Lucrecia's fears of a Moorish rising are based on recent Spanish experience. Her paranoia may read to us like xenophobic fantasy but this was not a peaceful time for Europe's citizens. And Spain, great power though she was, felt vulnerable, particularly along her long and difficult-to-defend coastline. Spain's position as

both a Mediterranean and Atlantic power, a position she shared only with France, gave her great strategic advantages and great defensive difficulties. Spain's future problems, however, were to come from her external enemies and her own mismanagement rather than from internal dissenters.

The Spanish *moriscos* did not rise against their fellow citizens opportunistically, as Lucrecia implies they might. They rebelled against the authority of the Spanish state when it oppressed them.

3. *'I do not weep because of the anger of God but for the travails of His people.'*
A neat and sophisticated illustration of a central theological problem, given by a young woman who had no formal education and professed herself ignorant and illiterate.

If we believe that God is responsible for everything – this is what the Christian religion demands – then we both worship Him and weep because of His actions. We are told to praise God and to feel compassion for those who suffer. Fray Lucas Allende answers this paradox by telling us that he weeps for the suffering of God's people.

4. *'This is because, being over-compliant with their master, they are all like him'.*
This explicit criticism of Cardinal Quiroga, the Inquisitor-General, seems unwarranted and extremely unwise. We can only assume that Lucrecia and her mentors either did not intend that Quiroga should ever see these passages, or that they had some deeper plan. Quiroga, despite his fearsome title, was less intolerant of religious curiosities than many of his colleagues. He was inclined to leave Lucrecia unmolested when others called for her arrest.

*The Ordinary Man came and said to me, 'I have a desire that the
things that are enclosed in the breasts of my companions should
be revealed to you.'*

*He took me to the window from where I saw an army of
Moors in their customary dress. Each one carried an arquebus.
A thousand men went ahead of the army and just behind these
there were about three hundred with loaded arquebuses which
they passed to those in front so that they could shoot. Others
carried barrels of gunpowder. While all this was happening I
heard them saying, 'We have the court passes cut off so that
people cannot get to Toledo.' And I saw that they were killing
our people.*

*We went to the seashore, where the Old Man asked me,
'What is it that Juan has said to you?'*

*I answered, 'That I should ask you if it is now time to go to
Toledo.'*

*He replied, 'Tell him to follow his own thinking. He is already
getting enough advice.'*

*Then he asked me if I knew how the king was. I answered
that I certainly knew he had been ill. The Old Man told the
Ordinary Man to take me to the palace. There I found His
Majesty in bed, lying on his back, at his side a silver spittoon
and at his feet the saw that the Ordinary Man had carried in
earlier visions. I saw the infanta wearing a white vasquiña[1]
looking very thoughtful at His Majesty's side. The two were
alone but then the prince entered the room, wearing a red cap.
The king put his hand to his side and said, 'Oh, it hurts me
here.'[2]*

*The Ordinary Man said to me, 'If pain is pressing upon him
rather strongly it will be due to the words of Beaumont.'*

136

Then I saw that the king's bedhead had become an artichoke.[3]
Many men were entering, bearing tribute, and were pulling off
the leaves of the artichoke and breaking them into pieces which
they threw on to the floor. And when only the heart of the
artichoke remained upright, they pulled it out by the root, all
this being done so secretly that the king was not aware of it.

When I had seen all of this the Ordinary Man took me out to
the palace grounds. I saw that these were now all covered with
grass and many domestic animals and birds grazed there. The
Ordinary Man raising his eyes to heaven said, 'Blessed be he who
sustains them, for the master used to put out his grey on a patch
of waste ground and gave pasture to the stock, and now that he
has sold it[4] *God has allowed the palaces to revert to grass.'*

And with that I awoke.

1. *vasquiña.* A *vasquiña* or *basquiña* is an outer garment worn over a skirt.

2. *The king put his hand to his side and said, 'Oh, it hurts me here.'* Philip was not a physically robust man but neither was he feeble. He loved to hunt and, contrary to his image, he was not a recluse. He loved his gardens and he loved to travel around Spain, marvelling in his letters home at the variety of the natural world of the peninsula. But he had long periods of sickness principally brought on by that curse of the age, gout. This, modern medicine advises, is 'a disease of the purine metabolism, characterised by attacks of arthritis and raised serum uric acid. The big toe is the joint most commonly affected. There is often a familial history' (Critchley, 1978). Diet is also thought to be a factor.

    Philip survived the childhood illnesses that carried away most of the people born in his time – though he was sick enough at five for his mother Isabel to fear for his life. Philip II's most recent English-language biographer, Henry Kamen, has taken particular note of the king's health and diet. They show a physically active young man gradually reduced to an invalid:

His [Philip's] kitchen accounts for January 1544 reveal a daily diet based on a lot of meat ('for stewing, roasting and soup'), backed up by bread, chicken and eggs. fish, consumed in the coastal areas of Spain rather than inland, never featured. Twice a week lettuce and endives were bought. Once a week the royal table had fruit (melon, oranges) . . . From 1550 wine, which he had drunk occasionally before, was a regular item with meals. (Kamen, 1997a)

Letters home from the Venetian ambassador in 1561 commented on the king's health and diet:

'He suffers from stomach and digestive orders and for that reason has begun recently on the advice of his doctors to make frequent outings . . . [he] eats excessively of certain foods, above all sweets and pastries . . . His habit is to partake only of highly nutritious food, and he abstains from fish, fruit and similar foods, which have a tendency to produce ill humours.' (quoted in Kamen, 1997a)

Gout first seriously struck the king in 1563 when he was thirty-six years old. It is hard to know exactly what his food intake was, though Kamen is surely right to say that his steward would not have put food in front of him which he did not like. So we can guess that his diet was mainly meat washed down with a little wine and occasionally accompanied by fruit. The king had a quite modern view of health. Doctors were not to be trusted and often did more harm than good, as did the multitude of herbal remedies on offer. The best thing was to take plenty of exercise, get out in the countryside and generally look after oneself and – an unfortunately circular prescription – take a bit of care with one's health.

At Monzón in 1585 there was an epidemic of some kind which killed several hundred people including some members of the king's retinue. In October Philip became ill with fever and gout, but recovered by December. By 1586 he was having 'periodic attacks of gout' and by 1587 poor health became a constant feature of his life. The impression of the king being almost permanently ill perhaps started around this time as his hair went white and his body became that of an old man. Lucrecia's visions of Philip as a sick man in the winter of 1587–8 reflected general opinion in Spain that the king was becoming unfit to lead the country.

Philip wrote in July 1587, 'This gout is so persistent that it will not let me go. It will not let me walk without help, and for five or six days now has not let me walk at all. It has been worst in this hand, not letting me write or do anything. Nor has my eyesight been very good' (quoted in Kamen, 1997a).

The sickness and pain are thought by some historians to have contributed to his ill-judgement in the Enterprise of England. Henry Kamen is explicit: 'The decisions concerning the Armada . . . were made by an ailing king. The gout had affected him in his hands and feet through the spring and summer of 1587 . . . the pain would not go away. It prevented him thinking clearly about anything else.'

His condition was to gradually worsen and then decline sharply in May 1595. He was practically immobile and in constant pain. By early 1596 the gout deprived him of the use of his right arm. He also began to suffer from dropsy, an unpleasant condition causing swelling in the legs and lower body. He could only move by means of a wheelchair. He was then sixty-nine years old. For the last three years of his life Philip was a virtual invalid, eventually dying of infections associated with his gout and dropsy.

This litany of disease gives a picture of a sickly man dragging his wretched body through an immobile, enclosed and increasingly miserable existence. We should remember though that Philip lived most of his life as an active king, mentally and physically involved in the life of his country. It is his final years that have been his legacy to history – a sick man tied to his desk at the centre of a decaying empire.

Philip's reputation has suffered in comparison to Elizabeth of England's. Her personal vitality in the late 1580s was often contrasted (and has been ever since) with his infirmity. This can be read as a metaphorical comment on the sheer brio of the English state, but it is also true that monarchs lived both as political entities and as symbols. Philip's sickliness was more apparent because his country was in difficulty and he can be seen as both a cause and a symptom of Spain's problems.

3. *I saw that the king's bedhead had become an artichoke.* The men bring taxes and tributes to Philip, while they secretly rob him of his country's assets. Through this inventive metaphor the king is again seen as a hopeless defender of the people's interests.

4. *'now that he has sold it'*. In the cities, towns and villages of Castile there were common lands set aside for use by landless peasants. They were allocated according to long-held tradition and no rent was charged. In the 1580s the king, being desperate for money, decided to sell off these lands to the highest bidder. This process, known as disentailment, benefited the wealthy and made the poor even worse off, as they now had to pay rent to use land which they had always regarded as somehow their own, or at any rate held in common. In a dream of a week later, a man says to Lucrecia that 'he [the king] has taken away our lands'. Disentailment not only disadvantaged the poor, it further damaged the economies of the already benighted villages and towns of Castile.

The crown could not raise taxes from those with no money, so it procured money by selling the rights of the poor to the wealthy. This was not the way to win affection from the people.

I dreamed that I heard a voice which said to me, 'Come to the window and look out.'[1]

I did so and saw that there was so much blood on the ground that it rose to the height of one vara and in it were many dead bodies. Among them I saw one alive but very bloodied and he said to me, 'I am the son of him of Córdoba; I am he who saw that he was a traitor. Last May I received the first letter and the first gift that we were given which was of 15,000 ducats. These were shared between three and it is necessary that you should know these two, since you know me.'

Having said that, these people passed by and I saw some men approaching beating a deer.

I asked, 'Why do you do it harm?'

They answered me, 'The king of these creatures has worked against us; he has taken away our lands and now many women are sick because of the poverty he has plunged us into.'

Then I saw from the window, that three tall men were coming from Toledo. The one in the middle carried a cloak of black damask across his arm and I heard him say, 'With this I entered and with this I leave.'

I saw that these men were beating at the blood in order to stop its progress into Toledo. They continued to do this all the way to Madrid where they caused it to flow into a stream.

At this time I saw that a number of Moors came, bringing many loaded animals. I asked them where they were going and they said, 'To Granada for from there we cannot be ejected no matter how many may come, for the Turk is to send us much aid.' And as these people passed I saw many French and English coming. And with them, crowned as king was ——[2] who has one eye clouded so that it does not see (but I was unable to determine which of the two it was).

Now the three men from Toledo brought men with them and attacked all these enemies and killed a great many of them, taking the crown from the one who wore it. The followers of the man who had the damask garment on his arm said to him, 'Put on the crown that you have won.'[3]

He replied, 'You would have me put such a bloodied crown on my head?'

And breaking it in two he cast it away.

They returned to Toledo where there was much disagreement for some wished to elevate as king the man with the damask garment and others another. As they argued I heard one voice say, 'I choose that man as king' (indicating the one with the garment) and saw that many raised him up as king and many said no. Three times I heard a voice say this: 'You shall be cursed if you do not do it.'

But there were many who disagreed and one of Quiroga's chaplains said, 'It is not good that that man should be king nor would he govern well.'

As he said this a burning thorn bush came down from heaven and burned those who spoke in this way and so the man with the garment was made king.

As this was done I saw that all the merchants opened up their shops which had been shut and the plaza was well provided and supplied.

I asked, 'How is Cristóbal de Allende to die?'[4] *[The man with me] answered, 'Putting himself so much among his enemies that he will be dead. Tell him to go by the pathways so that his people shall not fail to support him and that he must guard himself and if he comes out of this good things shall befall him afterwards.'*

As I listened to this the Ordinary Man came to me and asked me what I had seen.

I told him all that I have recounted and he said, 'I wish to show you an astrological vision.'

I saw a star which meant the king, and it was as open as a pomegranate and had as many grains as they do.

The Ordinary Man said to me, 'If they fail to understand the meaning of that, the Lion Man will say what it is.'

And there came to me a morisco dressed in green, who said to me, 'Are you not going? See, they are saddling up for you.'

And with that I awoke.[5]

1. *I dreamed that I heard a voice which said to me, 'Come to the window and look out.'* Lucrecia continues to live with her parents and brothers and sisters. Any prospect of marriage has been both increased and postponed by her dream career – she is coming to the attention of more people but she must, for the time being, remain an unmarried innocent. No longer working at the royal palace, she helps her mother to run the household and make a little money – Richard Kagan tells us that the two of them would occasionally buy bolts of cloth in the market and then go about the neighbourhood selling pieces door to door.

Family finances are a little easier since Don Alonso de Mendoza has been giving them alms. Lucrecia's mother Ana welcomes this and her daughter's growing notoriety while her father Alonso begins to resent the undermining of his own position as family provider. He also foresees the dangers that the circulation of her dreams might bring to his daughter and the possible harm to his family's reputation. Alonso de Léon spends a lot of time away from Madrid and so is increasingly marginalised as Ana, Mendoza and Allende become the chief influences in Lucrecia's life. But Lucrecia does not just tell her dreams to the priests. She naturally talks to her friends, neighbours and to anyone who shows any interest in the strange visions that fill her nights. We know about some of these acquaintances because they were to give testimony at her trial, but there must have been many others that spoke to Lucrecia or to someone who had talked to her, or to her mother, or to her sisters, or to her friends.

For the time being an uneasy but fruitful equilibrium prevailed. Lucrecia told Fray Lucas de Allende her dreams, Don Alonso de Mendoza gave the family money, Lucrecia's father carried on with his work, his daughter was the centre of mild interest and attention. But this tranquil state could not last.

While Lucrecia chatted happily to her neighbours about her dreams, Allende and, in particular, Mendoza were intent on more influential circulation. Mendoza's finished versions of Lucrecia's accounts were passed among certain circles. Madrid, city of the court, ante-chamber to the palace, began to know of this young woman and her dreams.

The words of dreamers were, we have seen, met with tolerance, interest or indifference in Spain, where the tradition of religious prophecy was respected. But Lucrecia's visions were political, they were circulated among disaffected courtiers and, perhaps most important, they came at the time of that notorious Spanish phenomenon, the *desengaño*. This disillusionment of the Spanish people with their long-ruling king is traditionally estimated by historians to have begun immediately after the defeat of the Armada. The modern view is that a loss of confidence in the country and in the court set in somewhat earlier. The Antonio Pérez affair was one factor in the dissatisfaction with the king and his advisers, and was cleverly used by Pérez's friends and supporters as a focus for the general disillusionment. But while the Pérez affair may have been cleverly manipulated to the king's disadvantage, other events harmed him more directly.

Philip had suffered difficulties and tragedies throughout his reign but managed to recover his authority by a succession of military and political victories – Lepanto in 1571, the annexation of Portugal in 1580, the recapture of the southern states of Flanders in the early 1580s. There was the vast promise of the New World of the Americas and, in 1569, the claiming of the Philippines for the Spanish crown. But the euphoria of these achievements was not sustained. Spanish conquests ground to a halt, leaving the people of Castile to wonder what all this had gained them.

Much has been made of the effect of the English raids on Spanish ports and shipping in the Caribbean and then on mainland Spain itself. Although these raids took only a tiny fraction of the wealth coming from the Americas, they shook the confidence of the merchants who organised the trade and engendered a feeling that Spain, the most powerful country in the world, was unable to defend its own people.

Lucrecia's dream transcripts are a clear indication that the English navy bulked large in the Spanish sense of frustration and impotence. The real crisis for Philip and his people though, and the reason for their disillusionment with their king, was economic.

Although the supplies of silver from Mexico and Peru were seemingly inexhaustible, the Spanish people never felt the benefit of this treasure. There were, in hindsight, understandable reasons for this. The first concerned Spain's military strength. Spanish armies were the best in the world. They were also distributed all over Europe and across the globe. But this was at a time when warfare had become astonishingly expensive, even for the wealthiest nations.

> The new technique of war, involving the use of masses of professional infantry and artillery . . . was making it . . . a highly capitalised industry . . .The centralized States which were rising in the age of the Renaissance were everywhere faced with a desperate financial situation. It sprang from the combination of modern administrative and military methods with medieval systems of finance. (Tawney, 1937).

Spanish power was based on military conquest which was financed by the silver of the Americas. But there was never enough money for all these armies and so Philip borrowed and raised taxes and still went bankrupt. As if this was not bad enough for the Spanish people, the flood of bullion from America had a hugely inflationary effect on prices in Spain. The prices of everyday goods went beyond the reach of ordinary people and the higher cost of manufacturing killed off the export trade of Spanish industry. A change was happening in Europe in which real power was to lie, not in armies and fleets, but in the economic muscle that powered them. The economic transformation of Europe in the sixteenth century has been written about many times. Perhaps the key point for our purposes is that the rise of commerce, with its links to the Reformation and to the excitement of the New World, was both based on, and helped to bring about, a change in thinking about the future.

As the trade with the Levant, dominated by Venice, and now cut off by the newly assertive Ottomans, gave way to connections to the Americas and the Baltic, the wealthy towns of southern Germany turned away from the routes over the Alps and towards the Rhine and the north for their supplies. The Netherlands were ideally placed for trade with England, the Baltic, the Americas and, via the Rhine, with the interior of Europe. As well as their geographical advantage, the liberal constitution and policy of the Netherlands meant that everyone felt welcome. Antwerp became the centre of a network of trading centres – Lyons, London, Seville, Frankfurt, Strasbourg, Venice and others – where both goods and money were traded. Capital flowed into and through these cities helping to finance trade, manufacturing and expeditions.

The increasing sophistication of the products of manufacture, in particular textiles, increased the amount of value added to them. This value was added at a number of stages and at each stage someone, a merchant or financier, was taking a risk: he was buying something without the certain knowledge that he could sell it. This risk was rewarded by profit. A whole new class of people thereby became wealthy, sometimes very wealthy indeed. Then another level of sophistication was added since the merchants who spent every day at the markets, haggling, inspecting goods, making contacts and so on, sometimes wanted to share their risks. They would ask someone with money to advance enough to buy a shipment, guaranteeing that they would be paid out of the profits. These money men need be only indirectly connected with the trade in which they invested. From this arose a system of banks and financiers international in their outlook. As well as generating a vast and virtuous circle of goods and money this process had another great difference from what had gone before. No one invests unless they expect a return at a later date. The new system of financial capitalism depended utterly on faith in the future.

In all of this Spain was a marginal player. Spanish goods became up to three times as expensive as those available from elsewhere. Her wool merchants preferred to sell direct to the Dutch than to Castilian weavers, and the Spanish textile industry was hung out to dry. Instead of receiving benefit from their good fortune the Spanish people were taxed even more to pay for the exponential costs of their armies. The populations of the old artisan towns of Castile dropped alarmingly as people emigrated to the Americas (in the half-century from 1570 Burgos lost two-thirds of its households and Toledo half) and on top of that came several years of bad harvests.

By the 1580s much of this was already coming to pass. Through it all the Spanish people struggled, perhaps only dimly aware of the forces that were transforming the rest of Europe but only too aware that their plight was getting worse. Many, it seems, blamed the king and this upwelling of discontent put Lucrecia in danger. While a strong and popular regime could afford to tolerate malign prophets, a weak and resented one could not.

Lucrecia, too, was firmly outside this new Europe. She had no faith in the future of the secular world, only a certainty that its destruction was about to happen.

2. *And with them, crowned as king was —— who has one eye clouded.* In the transcript the name of the man who is crowned as king is left blank. It may be that Lucrecia named him but Mendoza chose not to.

3. *'Put on the crown that you have won.'* The prophecies of Lucrecia and of many who came before envisage a new world emerging from the destruction of the old, and reigned over by a half-king, half-God – the reincarnation of the David to whom God had promised, 'I have exalted one chosen out of the people. I have chosen David my servant; with my holy oil have I anointed him: With whom my hand established: mine arm shall also strengthen him' (Psalm 89: 19–21). And further, 'His seed also will I make to endure for ever, and his throne as the days of heaven' (Psalm 89: 29).

David replies by pointing out to the Lord that he has treated his people harshly and asks, 'How long Lord? wilt thou hide thyself for ever? shall thy wrath burn like fire? . . . Lord, where are thy former lovingkindnesses, which thou swarest unto David in thy truth?'(Psalm 89: 49)

The answer of the Christian Church to this reproach is that there will be an end and a new beginning in which the Lord's former loving kindnesses will come to pass again. Lucrecia envisions Piedrola the soldier-prophet (the man with the damask garment) as the new David in this and other visions. He is reluctant to be crowned, but is anointed by God in the form of a burning bush from heaven. The new world order is mustered into practice by the shopkeepers opening up – life returning to a greater normality.

4. *'How is Cristóbal de Allende to die?'* Cristóbal is brother to Fray Lucas de Allende. As we shall see in the next chapter, he is becoming involved in Lucrecia's story in a way that reunites her with Spain's mythic past.

5. *And there came to me a morisco dressed in green, who said to me, 'Are you not going? See, they are saddling up for you.' And with that I awoke.* This is one of the few constructed endings to a dream. There is a sudden turning of the focus of the dream from the events on display to Lucrecia herself. Not only does the *morisco* come to Lucrecia, 'they' too are doing something for her. It is like being in a room watching a film when quite unexpectedly the whole crowd turns to look at you. Lucrecia is being told that it is time for her to leave this dream.

The Ordinary Man came to me carrying a mirror in his hand. I asked him what it was for. He answered, 'You are the mirror[1] in which all these people are seen so that you can give warning and all that has been lost may be regained. Look what people you see in this mirror.'

I looked into the mirror and saw a great many armed people and said to him, 'If I am this mirror how is it that I see so many people?'

He answered, 'You do not understand that? Don't you see that they are to see themselves in you?'

I asked him who the people were and he said, 'Look at the place from which they come.'

I looked and saw that nearly five hundred men were coming out of the Sopeña.[2]

He said to me, 'Take notice of the three who place themselves at the front.'

I saw that their helmets were not covering their faces and I recognised Cristóbal de Allende and Fray Lucas. Between these two rode the pastor who is called Miguel and they trembled just to see him. He bore no arms and wore a pastor's habit but carried a sling in his hand. Then I saw that Fray Diego, Juan López and Trijueque all uncovered their faces.

He asked 'Will these men be afraid?'

I answered, 'No, even though fear is natural to men of flesh and blood, they will do their deeds.'

Looking at these people I saw that they were setting themselves in formation. Crossing the Rio Tajo by a drawbridge, they organised themselves into squadrons headed by Cristóbal and Trijueque and proceeded to the gate of Toledo.[3] There they killed numberless enemies and turning at the second gate they raised the siege of the city, putting the enemy to flight. Many of the enemy were dead and many tents were empty, but only seven of the pastor's company were hurt in this battle.

Fray Lucas turned and called upon the Navarro to bless them. He asked if the wounds were deep and Fray Lucas responded, 'Look so that you may know.'

At this point I heard a voice say, 'Let Navarro also bless one of the enemy who is wounded.' This he did and healed him and this man then requested Holy Baptism. Fray Lucas went and baptised him and then took him back to the Sopeña for treatment. Fray Lucas gave thanks to God that already the Church was being restored and I saw that they took the convert into the Sopeña.

At the sound Ursula Beltrán came out, much agitated, and said, 'It is enough that I have to attend to the people that are inside without having foreigners brought in.'

Fray Lucas answered that the man was now a Christian and Ursula Beltrán, hearing this, embraced him lovingly.[4] Then I saw Fray Lucas return to the battle with his companion.

When he arrived Pastor Miguel said to him, 'Let Toledo be opened up, I wish to enter there.'

Cristóbal replied, 'It is not safe to do so until the siege has been raised.'

And so it was done. fighting all the way, they reached the third gate where the siege had just been raised leaving the enemy heavily injured. I saw that the pastor's company bore away to the Sopeña the spoils that they had taken from the enemy. The pastor and his men then entered Toledo and from a house near the Inquisition came many shots from arquebuses. But the pastor just laughed, and using his slingshot, killed many people, for he made no missed shots.

In Toledo I saw that they had elevated a man to be king and as a result communities and factions had formed. Then the news that Pastor Miguel was in the land came to the ears of the

*Infanta Doña Isabel. She sent to summon the pastor, but he
replied, 'It is more necessary for me to subdue the land and clear
out of it those who are breaking the commandments of God.'*[5]
And he went about the city causing great destruction.

*I saw Fray Diego by the side of Fray Lucas and these two
monks wore short capes over their armour and their lances were
of the style of pilgrims' staffs.*

*When I had seen all this the Ordinary Man closed up the mirror
in which he had shown it to me and said, 'On another night I
shall show you whether the pastor has achieved victory.'*

*He took me to the seashore where the two companions were.
When I arrived the Old Man addressed me as 'mirror' and then
the Lion Man called me 'star'.*

I asked, 'How is it that you now give me these names?'

*They answered, 'Don't you think that you deserve them? You
will give light to people with your words and will guide them by
the way revealed to you. Both you and he who has said many
masses will see each other in such distant lands that when you
reach twenty-seven years of age*[6] *and come down again through
the land you have left for lost, you will find it in flower and full
of trees.'*

And with that I awoke.

1. *'You are the mirror . . .'* Lucrecia assumes, like everyone else, that when
   she looks in the mirror she will see herself. Instead she sees this vision.
   She has become that which she sees. The enigmatic explanation of the
   Ordinary Man indicates that the reverse is also true: 'Don't you see
   that they are to see themselves in you?'

2. *I looked and saw that nearly five hundred men were coming out of the Sopeña.*
   Lucrecia dreams of her supporters emerging from a cave hideout to

defeat the besiegers of Toledo. In these dreams the place is called *la Sopeña* which literally means 'the Undercliff'. The initial capital indicates that this was a particular place – a cave in the banks of the Rio Tajo.

In her vision Lucrecia is reimagining one of the great legends of Spanish history. The overarching historical myth of the Christian Spanish people of Lucrecia's time was the *Reconquista* – the winning back of the peninsula from its Arab conquerors. And the central legend of the *Reconquista* was the story of Pelayo, a mythic king who was said to have struck the first blow against the Arab forces after hiding out in a secret cave.

Arab armies arrived in Spain in 711, just eighty years after the death of the prophet Muhammad. The growth of the Arab empire had been rapid, as was the conquest of Spain – in a sense this was to be Christian Spain's first apocalypse. The Arab armies, with the aid of Berber forces from North Africa, defeated the recently crowned Roderic, king of the Visigoths, and by 715 had almost the whole peninsula under their control. They were to rule most of Spain for the next seven hundred years. But the Arabs did not quite conquer the whole of Spain. Though they pushed rapidly north, they were to meet resistance in the province of Asturia. A Christian kingdom was established on the otherwise Islamic peninsula and from here the *Reconquista* was to begin.

Contrary to earlier assumptions it is now thought that the Arab campaign was so fast and overwhelming that the Christian Visigoth armies did not even have the chance to retreat into the mountainous regions of the north. The only people living there were indigenous Asturians, among whom was a nobleman called Pelagius or Pelayo. When the Arab armies arrived Pelagius and a band of followers took to the mountains and lived in caves waiting for their chance to strike against the occupiers. In 718 or thereabouts Pelagius led his followers out of their mountain hideaway and attacked Arab and Berber forces at a place called Covadonga. Pelagius won the day and even managed to kill the regional Arab governor. Arab forces were expelled from Asturias and never returned.

The battle at Covadonga does not rate a mention in many of the chronicles written later and so may have been quite a small affair (it evidently was to the Arab chroniclers) but it acquired legendary status and we should not entirely degrade its historic importance. The establishment of an independent Christian kingdom on the peninsula was an interesting complication. Although the rolling back of the Arab dominions was to be a centuries-long process, the battle of Covadonga was long considered by Christian Spaniards to mark its beginning.

There is no doubt that Lucrecia was familiar with the legend of Pelayo in all its glory. The wooden cross that the nobleman carried into battle was encased in gold and gems and the chronicles told that the Virgin Mary appeared to the troops at the time of the battle. Most of all though, there was the story of Pelayo in his cave, riding out to defeat Spain's enemies in battle.

Lucrecia's vision was not simply a dreamed evocation of the past for her and her patrons. She and they took very seriously the warning that Spain would be destroyed and that a small band of survivors would again emerge from caves to reconquer. These were not merely the fantasies of an impressionable young woman, they became the beliefs of a band of senior churchmen and courtiers. The events in Lucrecia's dreamworld now erupted into real life, not as symbols or warnings but as instructions to act. Lucrecia's visions of the cave and its band of warrior-saviours was not to be decoded – it was to be recreated. The real world must be made to imitate the dreamworld; and in this way the dreamworld would be brought into being. Thus was born the cult of Lucrecia.

It was in February 1588, shortly after the dreams in which she describes the Sopeña, that preparations were begun in earnest. Fray Lucas de Allende's brother, Cristóbal, owned a piece of land alongside the Rio Tajo some 35 miles south of Madrid. At this point the river has cut a series of cliffs in the rock and in the cliffs are a series of caves. Richard Kagan reports that

In March or April 1588 the caves were reportedly enlarged and stocked with stores of wheat, oil, and wine, even some firearms. Mendoza's correspondence confirms the purchase of these and other provisions, along with shipments of various church ornaments intended to furnish a small chapel that was reportedly designed by Juan de Herrera, the royal architect. Permission of the papal nuncio to have mass said in this chapel was also secured. (1990)

As well as provisioning the cave throughout the summer of 1588 Lucrecia and her supporters (she visited the caves at least once) were to act on other visions. From time to time she dreamed of an army wearing white crosses. In response Guillén de Casaos established an organisation called the Holy Cross of the Restoration, whose members wore a black scapular bearing a white cross beneath their garments. He even proposed travelling to Rome to petition the Pope to allow the group to establish themselves as a new religious order. The group was to become more important as Lucrecia's fame spread – principally in the wake of the Armada's disastrous defeat, which she predicted. Some of the members of this group appear in Lucrecia's dreams, including Domingo López Navarro, Juan de Trijueque, Diego de Vitores, Cristóbal de Allende, as well as Alonso de Mendoza, Fray Lucas de Allende and Guillén de Casaos. Others who supported the group included Hernando de Toledo, the Dukes of Medinaceli, Medina Sidonia and Nájera, and the Duchess of Feria (an English Catholic, Lady Jane Dormer). All of these important courtiers were anxious about the fall of Spain and, it seems, willing to play their part in the re-enactment of its founding myth.

3. *Crossing the Rio Tajo by a drawbridge, they . . . proceeded to the gate of Toledo.* The Sopeña that Lucrecia's patrons and supporters intended to occupy was near a town called Villarrubia, and so about 30 miles from Toledo itself. In Lucrecia's visions the consistent theme is that all of Spain will be lost except Toledo, the spiritual centre of Spanish Catholicism. The historic precedent which inspired the legend on which this vision was built took place in the far north of Spain and was ignored by the chroniclers of Toledo – that city itself fell to the Moors quite easily. Lucrecia has drawn the history of her nation towards its centre. The relief of the siege is led by the figure of Pastor Miguel, a priest who is also a soldier and therefore a combination of secular and spiritual authority. Miguel is the first name of Piedrola. The same person is later called Navarro reflecting Piedrola's home province.

4. *the man was now a Christian and Ursula Beltrán, hearing this, embraced him lovingly.* The short tale of Ursula Beltrán's love for the convert is at odds with Lucrecia's general fears of Moorish uprisings. (Beltrán was a real-life neighbour of Lucrecia and a family friend.) All the Moors in Spain had been forced to convert to Christianity or face expulsion in 1492. The fact that many continued Islamic practices and sham Christian liturgies does not alter the curiosity of this tale where apparent conversion is seen as a desirable end.

5. '*It is more necessary for me to subdue the land and clear out of it those who are breaking the commandments of God.*' Not only has the country been overrun by its enemies, the people have themselves behaved badly. This combination of external and internal evil is necessary to bring about and to justify the complete catastrophe that must happen in order for everything to begin again.

6. '*when you reach twenty-seven years of age.*' The two companions are now respectful to Lucrecia. They call her 'mirror' and 'star'. She is for the first time offered a vision of a beautiful future for herself. The land which she will believe lost will later be found 'in flower and full of trees'.

The Ordinary Man came and said to me, 'Tell Fray Lucas that by raising the siege of Toledo you will cut off three heads. One will be that of the Marquis of Carpio, another that of Juan González de Taida, but the other, being so great, I shall not name until it is necessary, when they shall be displayed in Madrid at the palace, for there they committed the crime of treason. Go along now to the seashore for the Old Man wishes to tell you a message that you are to give to Fray Lucas.'

At the seashore, where the two companions were, the Old Man said to me, 'Tell Fray Lucas he should think himself fortunate to have in his grasp things which many saints failed to understand. Now they are to discover what is in unknown books where the pages are joined together,[1] and they will see that you have the truth of testimony in your hands.'

The Lion Man asked me, 'What is it that Don Alonso wrote to you last night?'

I replied, 'He wished me to ask you the meaning of the palm tree which sprang up between the walls of Toledo which had in its branches many little dogs with their tongues hanging out.'

He responded, 'I have already told Fray Lucas that the palm signifies the prophets, and the one which is between the walls signifies the one who is hidden in Toledo[2] and is to grow and become so worthy that he will grasp the whole world and become lord of it. The little dogs[3] which it had hanging from its branches are his friends and here you will be able to understand what I told you in another dream: that the Pastor Miguel had dogs and their howling represents the outcry you are to make against your enemies. Having their tongues sticking out represents the desire they have to see themselves in a world where truth is to be valued.

'This I would not tell you if it were not for the sake of Don
Alonso; if I did not love him so much as I do I would not have
declared to him and to Fray Lucas all that has been written. It
seems to me that it has saddened him that I say to you that you
are to go with him who has said many masses; indeed since he
took the habit, few days have passed when he has not said Mass.
Tell him that if he should fall into any grave fault or fail to do
his duty, then I should also show of him what I have shown you
of Quiroga.'

I said to him, 'Don Alonso asks you whether you can give
him licence to place his brothers in Toledo.'

The Old Man replied, 'It pleases me well to see the humility
of Don Alonso who, while knowing these things, asks for
licence. Tell him to bring them by the end of March for from
then on until October there will not be one hour of calm.'

Then the Lion Man said to me, 'See how God shows us some
small mercy for he warns you as he warned the patriarchs of
olden times. The rescue of this man that I told you of must be
carried out at the same time as you hand over the papers to the
king, for if not they will give him poison so that he appears to
die at the same moment as the king. And if he dies then the
children of this king will come to inherit, but if you get him out
then not even the two children that the king has will live. For it
is written that the house of Austria is not to inherit[4] because
God wants to make a new world and to make great again the
lineage of the past.'[5]

As he spoke I heard again the same drum that I have heard these
past nights in England. I asked him, 'Why do I hear this drum
each night but see nothing?'

The Lion Man answered, 'This is so that you may know that
it is sounded among you and understand how quickly the affair
progresses. I shall show you a vision.'[6]

He showed me a knight with a naked sword in his mouth, one

foot in the stirrup and the other on the ground. His horse had a handful of green grass in its mouth and the man was saying, 'Because there is no manger. This is for you to understand that you shall lack food because your enemies are approaching very fast, as time will tell.'

The Old Man said to me, 'That man that you saw, the one that my companion brought out from under the earth, is this one that Philip has shut away. And since Philip is there above him you will have a hard task indeed to get him out. But do it you must, with the papers in hand. Tell Don Alonso that he must collect as much as he can and to be so secret that not even his friends are aware lest they throw him out of the house. To all of you in your Sopeña, the Holy Spirit will come to give succour and aid. In the month of April you will come to know the bad news about the Marquis of Santa Cruz[7] and then you will be able to gather quickly.'

And with this I awoke.

1. '*Now they are to discover what is in unknown books where the pages are joined together . . .*' We take the 'they' in this comment to be Fray Lucas and Don Alonso de Mendoza. The books where the pages are joined together ('sino junten unas hojas con otras') could refer to uncut pages. Pages that remain uncut are unread – an echo of the apocalyptic tradition where the existence of a divine message is made known with the injunction that the message itself will only be revealed at the Day of Judgment.

2. '*the one who is hidden in Toledo*'. Piedrola was being held in the Inquisition prison in Toledo at this time. The remainder of this dream concerns the importance of freeing the soldier-prophet. Later in the dream Lucrecia is told '. . . since Philip is there above him you will have a hard task indeed to get him out. But do it you must . . .'

Lucrecia even hears of a plot to poison Piedrola in the event of

Philip's death – an effective way of preventing him from succeeding to the throne.

After Piedrola's arrest in the previous November Alonso de Mendoza had worked hard to get him freed, writing to officials of the Church in Rome as well as lobbying in Madrid. Piedrola had become a kind of symbol to his supporters (who included Mendoza and others who subsequently supported Lucrecia). They believed that he was unjustly imprisoned and that his criticisms of the king were valid. It is known that Piedrola advocated a negotiated end to the war with the Dutch and this placed him in alliance with Antonio Pérez and the Mendoza faction.

3. *little dogs.* Small dogs are not usually the stuff of noble protest but Lucrecia presses them neatly into service. Their generally unwelcome racket is turned to righteous outcry, their slavering tongues to longing after truth.

4. '*not even the two children that the king has will live. For it is written that the house of Austria is not to inherit'.* At this time Philip actually had three children alive. The heir to the throne, Philip (Felipe) was ten years old; Isabel, unmarried and still living at court, was twenty-two; and Catalina, recently married to the Duke of Savoy, was twenty-one and living at her husband's court in Genoa. The two children mentioned are presumably Isabel and Philip.

The next sentence revives an occasionally heard theme among Philip's subjects – his non-Spanish forebears. 'The house of Austria' is of course a telling description of the Habsburg dynasty, used to highlight their foreign and even usurping origins. For many Spaniards the true monarchs of Spain were the successors of the kings of the Asturias, of Léon, of Pamplona and the Counts of Barcelona – the leaders who preserved Christianity in Spain during the period of Arab rule and who led the *Reconquista*. The culmination of this succession of princes was the union of Ferdinand and Isabella – the Catholic monarchs who not only drove the last Arab kingdom from Spain and united its two great rival territories but won back the province of Navarre which had been separated from the rest of Spain since the twelfth century. Had Ferdinand and Isabella had a son who survived into adulthood, the history of Spain and of Europe might have been significantly different.

In 1496 Ferdinand arranged a marriage for his daughter Joanna which was, as John Lynch (1991) writes, 'to prove the most decisive, for it not only gave Spain her future dynasty but began her tragic association with northern and central Europe'. There is little doubt that the sight of Spanish troops laying waste the city of Antwerp, the dynamo of European prosperity, would not have been even a bad dream had Joanna of Spain not been placed in marriage with the Archduke Philip, son of the Habsburg Emperor Maximilian some seventy years before.

At the time of the marriage any such consequence would have seemed fanciful. Joanna was not then even heir to the newly united Spanish throne and the union was merely a way of Spain gaining a little friendship and influence with the other royal houses of Europe. Remembering how Joanna's mother Isabella resisted her own father's wish to marry her off in the same way, and the beneficial consequences of Isabella's marriage to her fellow Spaniard, we might wonder if these international matches often produced truly desirable results and whether marriages within countries are, despite the problems of aristocratic rivalry they foster, more inclined to strengthen the country, its monarchy and the relation between the two. An *alter*-Philip, descended only through Spanish forebears would almost certainly have ruled a less troublesome realm.

Within four years of her marriage Joanna produced what her parents could not – a healthy male heir. The future Charles, king of Spain, was born in 1500, the same year that his mother Joanna became, through the deaths of her older siblings, heir apparent to the Spanish throne. (Her younger sister is known to English readers as Catherine of Aragón, the wife of Arthur, eldest son of Henry VII, and then of Arthur's brother who became Henry VIII.)

Though depicted as from the 'House of Austria', Charles was born in Ghent and brought up in the Burgundian court in Brussels. His bizarre inheritance was a manifestation of the mingled blood of his forebears. His father Archduke Philip had died when Charles was six and bequeathed him dominion over the group of states known as the Low Countries (including Holland, Zeeland, Flanders, Brabant, Luxembourg, Hainault and Artois). He also inherited the eastern part of present-day France known as Franche-Comté and a strong claim to the Duchy of Burgundy and was made formal ruler of all this at the age of fifteen.

When Ferdinand, king of Aragón, died in 1516 (Isabella of Castile predeceased her husband by twelve years) the teenaged Charles became claimant to the Spanish throne because his mother Joanna (Ferdinand's daughter) was by now mad enough to be declared unfit to govern. We should remember though that there was not at this stage, nor had there been since Roderic in the early eighth century, a king or queen of the whole of Spain. Isabella had been queen of Castile and Ferdinand king of Aragón. Charles was able to make a claim on both thrones through his maternal grandparents and to unite them in his person. Ironically the first man who could call himself king of Spain for eight centuries was a foreigner.

The crown of Aragón also now included Sicily, Sardinia, the kingdom of Naples and parts of North Africa, and the realm of Castile included the new discoveries of the Americas. On the death of his paternal grandfather Maximilian in 1519 Charles also inherited the Habsburg heartlands of Austria, the Tyrol and southern Germany. By the age of twenty he had, by the simple fact of being born and surviving for long enough, accumulated the greatest empire the world had yet seen. Most of this was passed on to his son, Philip II. Philip was at least born and brought up a Spaniard but his inherited ties to other parts of Europe made the description of his dynasty as 'the House of Austria' a telling one.

5. 'because God wants to make a new world and to make great again the lineage of the past.' This notion of a usurping dynasty enabled Spaniards to experience the longing for a 'true' ruler. We are once again in the territory of the new David, a once and future king.

6. 'I shall show you a vision.' The Lion Man no sooner explains one element of a vision than he declares that another will be revealed. It is taken for granted that the things that Lucrecia is to learn must be revealed to her in this way – by metaphor and allusion. In this case the vision of the knight explains itself.

7. 'In the month of April you will come to know the bad news about the Marquis of Santa Cruz'. The Armada was the great event and the great failure of the later years of Philip's reign. It was also the central national event of Lucrecia's dream career. The Spanish people invested much hope in this enormous undertaking, though it held many fears too. Though their armies were still the best on earth, this sea-borne venture

was, in scale and ambition, beyond any previous conception. Their faith in their king to bring off such a task was, at best, qualified.

Don Alvaro de Bazan, Marquis of Santa Cruz, Captain-General for the Ocean Seas, was inevitably made 'Commander by Sea for the Enterprise of England'. There was no other choice. Santa Cruz had served heroically at Lepanto. More crucially, when Philip half inherited, half conquered the kingdom of Portugal, Santa Cruz had used Portuguese galleons to defeat French ships used by his rival. These battles took place off the Azores in Atlantic waters, whereas Lepanto had been a Mediterranean affair. With the acquisition of Portugal in 1580 Spain became not just an Atlantic trading nation but an Atlantic fighting power. She now had the ships, the expertise and, in Santa Cruz, the admiral, to consider dominating the mid-Atlantic as she dominated the western Mediterranean.

Garrett Mattingly tells us that the Spanish were under the impression that, in the battles off the Azores, they had beaten English as well as French ships, and that in the euphoria of victory Santa Cruz 'offered to take on the whole English navy at a word from his king' (1959).

The word he got may have surprised him. Philip asked for an estimate of what the Marquis would need to defeat the English at sea and prepare the way for an invasion. His reply rather belied his earlier bravado. No doubt he felt confident in the abilities of his fleet but the force he required to do the job was staggering:

> One hundred and fifty great ships, including all the galleons available, and the rest, merchantmen as large and as heavily armed as possible, forty *urcas* for stores and provisions (large freighters, one might say), and some three hundred and twenty auxiliary craft of all kinds, dispatch boats, picket boats, fast armed cruisers for scouting and pursuit (zabras and fregatas), a total of five hundred and ten sail, besides forty galleys and six galleasses, the whole to be manned by thirty thousand mariners and to carry sixty-four thousand soldiers, a force greater than Europe had ever seen at sea. (Mattingly, 1959)

To keep this Armada supplied for an eight-month campaign would cost the king, Santa Cruz estimated, four million ducats. It was a ludicrous sum and in any case an impossible fleet to assemble. At the same time Philip's commander in the Netherlands, the Duke of Parma, came up with another scheme. Send him 30,000 infantry and 4,000 cavalry and the wherewithal to build 800 barges, send a fleet to distract the English navy, and he could slip across the Channel and take the English land defences by surprise. This too was unfeasible – how much surprise would remain when 800 barges and an entire army were drawn up along the Flemish coast (in a country full of spies sympathetic to the English)? Philip suspected that the suggestion was actually a ruse by Parma to get some more troops sent up to the Netherlands from Italy and Castile.

In the end Philip devised a plan which took a little from each of his two commanders. A fleet considerably smaller than Santa Cruz's estimate would sail from Lisbon. This would be large enough to take on the English navy and would carry a force of Spanish infantry. Meanwhile reinforcements would be sent to Parma and barges built, though not in the quantities the general requested. The Armada would sail up the Channel and rendezvous with Parma off the Flemish coast. It would then escort Parma's troops in their barges across the Channel, where they would land together with the troops conveyed from Lisbon. Once in England the formidable qualities of the battle-hardened Spanish infantry and the brilliant military skills of the Duke of Parma would do the rest.

Such an invasion plan may seem fanciful now, but the Spanish had good reason to believe that the English defences and armies were not a great obstacle. Martin and Parker's 1988 book *The Spanish Armada* gives a sobering picture of the unpreparedness of English land forces and fortifications. In a final chapter entitled 'If the Armada had Landed' they show that only the small castle of Upnor overlooking Chatham docks had the angular bastions necessary to withstand the modern siege guns that Parma carried. The cities of Canterbury, Rochester and even London had only medieval walls, which would be blown away by decent artillery. In addition the English troops were inexperienced, unreliable and badly equipped.

Even though the Spanish were guilty of some self-delusion in their expectation that the English Catholics would rise to join them, a partial occupation of southern England would have allowed Philip to insist on English withdrawal from the Netherlands and on return of the crucially strategic port of Flushing. Once they crushed the Dutch rebellion, the Spanish could then turn to gaining dominance in France and Germany. Seen from this perspective, the 'Enterprise of England' looks less foolhardy and more inevitable.

Within five weeks of the execution of Mary Queen of Scots in February 1587, Philip emerged from a period of quiet contemplation into furious activity. The Armada was to be built, assembled, supplied and manned with all haste. Santa Cruz must be ready to sail before the end of spring. The logistics proved impossible – even without Drake's interference it would have been virtually unattainable. In any case the Marquis found himself having to use his ships for other skirmishes. In September 1587 he returned to Lisbon from a voyage to the Azores, which were under threat from the English, to find messages from the king that he must sail for England as soon as his support ships arrived from Naples. But there were more delays. His fighting ships needed repair. In December 1587 Philip said Santa Cruz must now sail with whatever ships were ready while the element of surprise was with them. Then news came of English squadrons massing in the Channel and the king agreed to a delay to allow a bigger fleet to be assembled. Their earlier relation was reversed: Philip was now impatient and the marquis tentative and, in Philip's eyes, pessimistic. The admiral had some justification; as Mattingly points out: 'To be sure of beating the English he had wanted at least fifty galleons. He had thirteen, and one of those so old and rotten that he doubted whether he could get her to sea.' In addition, instead of his fearsome fleet of five hundred, he had 'four galleasses and a motley collection of sixty or seventy other ships, hired or commandeered in every sea from the Baltic to the Adriatic, some of them leaky or cranky, many of them slow, clumsy sailers, and the best of them . . . undermanned and absurdly undergunned' (Mattingly, 1959).

Nevertheless, by late January 1588, by throwing everything he could at the task of equipping and manning his second-rate fleet, the admiral was within sight of a sailing date. And then on 9 February 1588, exactly one week after Lucrecia dreamed this dream, and one week before he was due to sail, the Marquis of Santa Cruz died. Lucrecia's prophecy had come true (though two months early) and Spain was left to mount the most ambitious naval military adventure ever seen without her greatest admiral.

The Dragon and the Monastery | Chapter 24
10 FEBRUARY 1588

The Ordinary Man came to me and said, 'Come out if you wish to see buried all that have died in Spain.' I went to the window and saw a dragon[1] passing through Madrid, so broad in body and belly that it seemed to occupy all of the street in front of my house. I do not know whether this body was raised above the ground or resting upon the street itself for I could see no legs to support it. I saw that its body was very black and covered with shells but with no wings. Its head was the size of a ram, its horns like those of a deer, each one with seven points and its eyes very black. A very red tongue protruded from its long mouth from which came black smoke as from a place where a great fire burns but with no flame. Its head faced west and its tail to the east. This was so long that it was coiled upon itself many times and the tip seemed to reach the sky.

This dragon made its dragging progress through the streets of Madrid and as it went it scooped up with its horns all the many dead bodies that it found there, tossing them backwards. I saw that some of these came to rest on its back or in the folds of its body and were swept off into heaps by its tail. But those that did not come to rest I saw disappear with great splendour into the high heavens. And all of this was like the threshing of wheat for bread, when the chaff is left to one side and the grain to the other, a thing I have seen for myself.

The dragon, having heaped up those that were collected by its tail, climbed laboriously upon them like a hen upon some eggs or a clutch of chicks. And, just as a hen seems to broaden itself, so the dragon extended itself out to cover all of them. Raising its head to the sky and waving its tail it roared, sounding like a host of bulls or lions. As it roared I could see that the bodies beneath it were being consumed and a great pool of black and stinking

water formed. At the edges of this pool many ugly weeds sprang
up, offensive to the eye.

The dragon did likewise in many parts of the city and in all of
these pools I heard from beneath the water cries and howls such
as frogs make in ponds. Among the bodies there were some
Moors and these the dragon did not collect up with its tail, but
devils, with the appearance usually given to them in paintings,
came and carried them away.

I saw that as the dragon arrived near the Merce monastery
the holy image of the Blessed Virgin of the Remedies emerged
through the door at the foot of the church but I could not see
who carried it. The dragon, which was near to me and to the
holy image, seeing it and hearing my voice, plunged its head into
the earth, hiding the whole of it.

The Ordinary Man at my side said, 'The Virgin of Atocha
and all the holy images and devotional Christ figures in Madrid
are destined to reappear in lands and places that are now in
infidel hands.' As he said this I saw the monastery sink into the
ground, leaving not even the memory that there had been a
building on the site.

From there the Ordinary Man took me to the seashore where I
found only the Old Man. He said to me, 'Do you know whether
Fray Lucas has come?'

I answered, 'They tell me that he is to come on Wednesday
night.'

In response he gave a great sigh and I asked him why he did
so.

He said, 'Because of the great trials that you are all facing. But
console yourselves, for once you have come through these times
you will see Spain in possession of greater relics than she has had
since the creation of the world and she will be very close to Rome.'

When he had spoken the Lion Man arrived and said to me,
'Tell Don Alonso that I have been busy, that we must not waste

time but get to work and banish the unbelieving from our side.'
(This he said making a gesture with his arms as though he had
something he wished to be rid of.) 'I understand from Don
Guillén² that this will be advantageous and pleasing to you all.
Tell Don Alonso also that he should do what he had in mind when
he came from Toledo and that then he should go to his house and
give no more information to anybody than he has given already.
And when I see you with him for the third time, which will be
before March, I shall tell you things which will please him. I do
not command him to go away but to lock away these papers of
mine. For one day the name of Esdras will be much spoken in the
streets,³ and he fasted much for the things he has written down.
It seems to me that they have not been taken note of but one day
Don Alonso will become more than he is now.'⁴

And with that I awoke.

1. *I . . . saw a dragon.* Lucrecia's visions have sometimes shown others predicting the end of the world, sometimes shown how she and her patrons must act at the end, and sometimes shown the end taking place.

A creature called a dragon appears in the Revelation of St John the Divine:

> And there appeared a great wonder in heaven: and behold a great red dragon, having seven heads and ten horns, and seven crowns upon his heads. And his tail drew the third part of the stars of heaven, and did cast them to the earth. (Revelation 12: 3, 4)

> And there was war in heaven: Michael and his angels fought against the dragon; and the dragon fought and his angels, And prevailed not; neither was their place found any more in heaven. And the great dragon was cast out, that old serpent, called the Devil, and Satan, which deceiveth the whole world: he was cast out into the earth, and his angels were cast out with him. (Rev. 12: 7–9)

In this end-game the Devil, in the form of a dragon, is cast from Heaven but now stalks the earth. In Lucrecia's vision he comes to the world beneath her window. The dragon in Lucrecia's dream is precisely described. It is, in Lucrecia's vision, the instrument by which God chooses those who are to survive into the new creation.

In Revelation the beast stalks the ravaged earth while the 144,000 chosen ones stand in glory on the mount of Sion. But the beast does not destroy the earth. It simply requires that each person worship the beast or be killed. John then sees angels sent forth from Heaven to 'reap' all who worship the beast and these are effectively destroyed by the wrath of God. Lucrecia's vision differs from St John the Divine's in its particulars, but the overall message is equivalent.

The small differences from the Scriptures are less important than understanding the scale of the Bible's effect on Lucrecia and her fellow believers' view of the world. These effects remain central to our own culture. The Bible became not only the spiritual touchstone of European life but its cultural and literary foundation. But as well as that, the Bible also became central to our idea of what a book should be. That was no accident but a natural consequence of the sense that the Bible answered the human need for there to be meaning in history and meaning in human existence. As Robert Carroll and Stephen Prickett affirm in their Introduction to the 1997 Oxford edition of the Authorized Version:

> Because the Bible takes it for granted that there is a meaning to the whole cycle of human existence and that every event, however trivial it may seem, has a figurative, typological, or, as we would now say, symbolic relation to the whole, we have learned in other areas of our existence to look for narrative, with a pattern of hidden meaning, rather than a mere chronicle of events. This expectation runs very deep in Western society, affecting not merely fiction but biography, history, and, of course, science – that distinctive product of a belief in a rational and stable universe where every part has its meaning in relation to the grand 'story' of the whole.

A book is not, cannot be, a collection of disconnected pieces of writing. The mere co-existence of pieces within a book makes them connected. There is a presumption that a book is, at some level, internally coherent. This runs so strong that incoherence is seen as a paradoxical way of acknowledging the validity of the presumption. It is impossible for any part of a book to be insignificant as even this is automatically imbued with meaning. The Bible tells the story of the world. It has a beginning, an origin, and therefore must have an end, a resolution. The Book of Revelation is the counterpoint to the Book of Genesis and brings the collection of books that comprise the Bible full circle. In this the Bible foreshadows the culture it brings into being. As Carroll and Prickett maintain, we have transferred to books our desire for coherence in the world. Each book is a world of and in itself.

2. *Don Guillén.* From this comment it appears that the Lion Man has somehow been able to speak directly to Don Guillén de Casaos, a friend of Lucrecia's family and one of her closest supporters. This is confirmed in the dream of 5 March.

3. *'For one day the name of Esdras will be much spoken in the streets'.* Esdras is the author of two scriptural books which are placed within the Apocrypha or Deutero-Canon, and of the Old Testament Book of Ezra. Originally used in fifteenth-century Germany to describe books which should only be available to certain readers (Gk *apokruphos* = hidden), the term Apocrypha then became adapted to describe those which were of doubtful authorship or origin and which therefore should be excluded from the canon. These were the same books and the same word was used to describe them, but the word had now taken on a different meaning. In the same way that 'apocalypse' has come to signify a catastrophic ending rather than a revelation, so 'apocrypha' has come to mean something of doubtful origin.

Don Alonso de Mendoza thought Lucrecia's visions strikingly similar to those in the second book of Esdras (known as 2 Esdras). There is some resemblance in the visions themselves but it is possible that Mendoza saw other parallels. In one vision Esdras is told to write down the whole history of the world, dictating it to five men who are 'ready to write swiftly':

> The Highest gave understanding unto the five men, and they wrote the wonderful visions of the night that were told, which they knew not: and they sat forty days, and they wrote in the day, and at night they ate bread. As for me, I spake in the day, and I held not my tongue by night. (2 Esdras 14: 42–3)

Esdras, as the Lion Man says, 'Fasted much for these things he has written down'.

Mendoza likes to see Lucrecia as a new Esdras, dictating her visions to her faithful scribes, who have been given understanding by 'the Highest'.

4. *'It seems to me that they have not been taken note of but one day Don Alonso will become more than he is now.'* The Lion Man predicts a great future for Don Alonso de Mendoza. We need to remember that it is Don Alonso who is making the fair copies of these dream transcripts. The temptation to imply that his talents were under-used may have been strong. On the other hand Don Alonso may have had no need to flatter himself; Lucrecia might have done this deliberately. If so it would have been a clever way of encouraging him to believe still more in her visions. It is also possible, of course, that this is a faithful record of the dream and of the Lion Man's words.

The Ordinary Man came and took me to the seashore. The two companions were there and the Lion Man said to me, 'What did Don Alonso say?'

I replied, 'He asks whether you think he should provide armour for me so that I may go out and fight.'

He said, 'It will not be necessary. It will be enough that you carry the cross before you.'[1]

Then the two companions disappeared, leaving me with the Ordinary Man, who took me to England. There the country was in a state of rejoicing over the illness of the Marquis of Santa Cruz.[2] I saw that Drake had just received a letter from Juan González de Taida in which he gave information on the appointment of a captain-general of the Armada and said that if the Marquis did not sail with it the English would more easily defeat the Armada.[3] Taida had also heard forecasts in Spain that England would be conquered in the second battle, as the Armada was to be disposed with great care to await the arrival of the prince of Parma.

I saw that Drake also received a letter from the Great Turk. In this the Turk said, knowing that it would be well received, that his men had gained ground in Poland and that Maximilian was in difficulties, warned as he had been that he, his people and all his goods were destined to serve Turkey. Now the Turk was secretly preparing troops to be ready by July and he expected to be in Spain by December.

The Ordinary Man returned me to the two companions and the Lion Man said to me, 'Within six years you will have done well to have the Pope a prisoner in your power for he will want to set the prince of Parma upon the throne of Spain.[4] This prince knows, from many sources, that your king is to die this year and therefore if he fights, it is to win for his own sake. He has planned things well for himself. While the king lives he will conquer other kingdoms for at the moment the troops are docile whereas afterwards they would refuse to obey him. Tell Don Alonso and Fray Lucas that they should give their own opinion on this so that they cannot say afterwards that I warned them too late.'

Then he told the Ordinary Man to take me to Madrid and he did so, saying as we went, 'In the fifth year Don Alonso and Fray Lucas will be in Toledo and will reside there. But none of you shall dwell there except under the rule of the king who is to come, and he will dwell between Toledo and Segovia.'

He told me to direct my eyes towards Valencia and Seville. I saw all of the people fleeing towards Madrid and crying out in loud voices. Behind them came a great fire, so great that it seemed that the entire world and all of the people were burning up. Before these people could reach the walls of Toledo and Madrid they were put to the knife.

The Ordinary Man took me then to Medina del Campo and to Antequera and I saw that most of the moriscos had rebelled and were awaiting the arrival of the Great Turk's troops in July. He took me down through part of the Sopeña where I saw men working. A morisco came by on his way to hunt and looked inside the rock and asked the workers there whose property it was. They told him, Cristóbal de Allende, and took him to look at it.

The Ordinary Man said to me, 'With these three kings in Spain the Antichrist will come, for in Philip's time so many troubles are to come to an end and this last generation will come. For God will not renew the world more than three times and this will be the last.'[5]

And with that I awoke.

1. *'It will be enough that you carry the cross before you.'* Now Lucrecia sees herself as Pelayo, the mythic warrior, emerging from the cave to turn back the enemies of Spain. But these fantasies have consequences in the real world. The Sopeña is to be stocked with supplies, weapons are to be gathered, men and women are to be notified of the time to leave their homes and take shelter. And, when the time comes, her followers will obey the instructions of her dreams and ride out, to take on the enemies of Spain in battle. All of this is to happen soon.

2. *There the country was in a state of rejoicing over the illness of the Marquis of Santa Cruz.* The Marquis of Santa Cruz died in Lisbon on 9 February 1588. In view of her words, it is likely that, at the time of this dream, Lucrecia did not know of his death though news of his sickness had undoubtedly reached Madrid. On 2 February the Old Man had told Lucrecia in a dream that she would come to hear some bad news about Santa Cruz in April. This bad news came to pass two months early. Santa Cruz was probably dangerously ill by 2 February 1588 but Lucrecia was probably unaware of this when she dreamed of his forthcoming demise.

3. *if the Marquis did not sail with it the English would more easily defeat the Armada.* Philip, presumably knowing of Santa Cruz's illness, already had a successor in mind – Don Alonso de Guzmán el Bueno, Duke of Medina Sidonia. Lucrecia would not have known his identity yet but she guessed in her dream that a name had been written in before the Marquis's death.

    Any idea that the Armada under Santa Cruz would have succeeded was a product of wishful thinking reinforced by Medina Sidonia's self-deprecation. Here it appears that Lucrecia is expressing this belief before the first ship left harbour but she is merely qualifying her pessimism. Even if Santa Cruz leads the Armada, she is saying, it will be defeated; if he does not, then that will happen more easily. There is no doubt of the outcome, only its attenuation.

4. *he will want to set the prince of Parma upon the throne of Spain.* The prince (by now the Duke) of Parma's family connections are an illustration of the elaborate links between Europe's ruling dynasties.

    The secular name of Pope Paul III (ruled 1534–49) had been Alessandro Farnese. He had a son (illegitimate, of course) named Pier

Luigi. Pope Paul wished to create a dynastic seat so, in 1545, invested his son Pier Luigi as Duke of the city of Parma. In 1547 Pier Luigi, first Duke of Parma, died, leaving his son Ottavio to inherit the duchy. Now cross the continent . . .

In 1522 the Emperor Charles V fathered an illegitimate daughter, Margaret, by a Flemish woman of low status. The emperor's offspring was thought a match for the duke of a small city, so Margaret married Ottavio and became Duchess of Parma, and the Farneses became attached to the Habsburgs.

In 1545 Margaret of Parma gave birth to Alessandro, named after his grandfather. Her father Charles abdicated then died and her half-brother Philip succeeded to most of his realm. But Philip was a Spanish king and did not choose to hold court in the Netherlands. Instead, in 1559, he appointed Margaret of Parma as his Governor-General which began a long association of the Farneses with the Netherlands. As a youth Alessandro spent time with his mother in the Netherlands and at Philip's court in Madrid. In 1560, when Philip confirmed the new peace with France by marrying Isabel de Valois, the new couple were welcomed to the carnival at Toledo by, as Kagan describes them, 'the three young gallants of the court: Don Carlos, Don Juan of Austria and Alessandro Farnese'.

These three youths (Philip's son, his half-brother and his half-sister's son) were brought up in each other's company. The young prince of Parma was, *de facto*, a member of the king's immediate family. He was also a soldier and in 1577 went to the Netherlands at the time of an acute crisis for Spain. In October of the following year Don Juan of Austria, the latest of a string of governors-general, died aged only thirty-one. He had already chosen as his successor Alessandro Farnese, prince of Parma. Philip agreed. It was, as Kamen (1997a) writes, 'possibly the most fortunate [appointment] of his reign'.

Alessandro Farnese, aged thirty-one at the time of his appointment, quickly showed himself to be the most brilliant soldier of his time. Moreover he quickly demonstrated that he possessed the political skills that had been so sorely lacking in his predecessors. When he took command of the king's forces in the Netherlands only the most southerly of the States-General were under the control of his forces. He quickly ensured the support of these southern Catholic provinces, establishing a stable base before gradually advancing north, taking the cities of Ypres, Bruges and Ghent in 1584, Brussels in March 1585 and retaking the prize of Antwerp in November 1585. Philip managed to keep the funds flowing for this military effort, which involved an army of 60,000.

It was not just Parma's victories that were so impressive, but the manner of them. Parma's troops, unlike Alba's and unlike the rudderless army of 1576, showed magnanimity to the defeated garrisons. This showed military and political intelligence. Parma had no wish to conquer the Netherlands; he simply wanted to bring it under the governorship of the appointee of its rightful monarch. Many of the towns were taken without a siege, or even a shot being fired against them. As Parker (1985) says, 'Thanks to his grasp of geography and strategy he was able to force the reduction of powerful towns which his troops could not even see, by means of distant blockades.'

Here, for once, was a foreign general using the watery geography of the Netherlands to his own advantage. His master-stroke was the blockading of the Schelde waterway which cut off the main manufacturing towns of Flanders and Brabant from the sea. He then worked his way up the coast capturing the Flemish ports – only Ostend remained in rebel hands – and then inland along the Schelde itself. Brussels fell in the spring of 1585 and Parma then took Antwerp, one of the best-defended towns in Europe, without firing a shot.

This in itself shows how Parma's behaviour had changed the attitudes of the townspeople of Antwerp towards the Spanish – many of them must have been present when their city was sacked by Spanish troops on the rampage just nine years earlier. They would not have risked surrender if they had not trusted Parma's ability to restrain his forces. The main reason for their capitulation though was Parma's great bridge across the Schelde which cut Antwerp off from the sea. This 2,400 feet construction was supported by piles sunk 75 feet into the soggy Dutch soil. It was one of the wonders of the age and was brilliantly successful.

By 1585 Farnese, now Duke of Parma since his father's death, had control of 95 per cent of the southern provinces – only the ports of Ostend and Sluys still held out. He was in control of the area roughly corresponding to present-day Belgium. The great question of Parma's career is, why did this great sweep of victories not continue? Why did Parma and his brilliant, tough and professional army not push northwards across the great rivers and take the northern provinces for the king? The reason, it seems, was English intervention. And even though this was botched and ostensibly ineffectual, and even though the English and Dutch squabbled like cats in a bag, the English expedition to the Netherlands did enough to save both countries from Parma's seemingly invincible war machine.

By 1585 Parma's successes had made England understandably nervous – 60,000 Spanish troops within a few hours' sailing time of the English coast were as welcome as snow in August to Elizabeth and her Council. The death of William of Orange and the apparent crumbling of all resistance to Spain was deeply troubling to Elizabeth. In 1584 she had expelled the Spanish ambassador to London (Bernadino de Mendoza, Alonso de Mendoza's brother) after a plot to assassinate her was clearly shown to have Spanish involvement. In August 1585 the English could no longer distance themselves from the Netherlands conflict; the Treaty of Nonsuch was signed with the Dutch rebels. By December 1585 the Earl of Leicester was at Flushing with 8,000 English soldiers.

Though Leicester was recalled to London within five months, his mission an apparent failure, English involvement galvanised the Dutch rebels and gave them the determination to fight on. This was enough to slow Parma for the time being, and to allow another factor to interfere with the Duke's conquests. The English expedition of 1585 served to enrage the king of Spain – here were foreign troops operating on *his* territory. This made him determined to act against England as quickly as possible. He immediately began to draw up plans for an invasion of England and to tell Parma to prepare his troops.

This combination of events proved fortunate for the English and for the Dutch. For all of Parma's successes he had not gained the biggest prize of all. Although he controlled the southern shore and the lower reaches of the Schelde and the small seaports to the south, Dutch boats and English ships controlled the coastline and the sea. Moreover, Dutch and English troops held the great strategic jewel of the port of Flushing sitting on top of the entrance to the Schelde and Parma's only feasible large-scale access to the sea. Parma might have taken Flushing if he had been given enough time, as he might have taken the still-obdurate port of Ostend (supplied from the sea by Dutch boats) but Philip had decided on a different strategy – strike at the English and the Dutch will cave in. It was a logical choice and a fateful one. Parma, the greatest strategist in Europe, was stopped from doing what he did best.

English intervention had stiffened Dutch resistance and made Philip impatient to invade this troublesome enemy. The English failure in the Netherlands may have turned out to be her greatest success.

In early 1588, when Lucrecia dreamed her dream this night, Alessandro Farnese, Duke of Parma, nephew to the king, was at the height of his power, abilities and prestige. The débâcle of the Armada, for which Parma took a share of the blame, had yet to happen. The whole world was in awe and fear of his armies. No wonder Lucrecia attached ambition to his achievement. It is unlikely that Parma had designs on the Spanish throne but Lucrecia's thoughts were not, we can safely assume, unique. Parma was Italian and his success, though welcome to the Spanish, was also viewed with suspicion. We should recall that Parma's mother was Philip's half-sister: he had Habsburg blood in his veins.

5. *'For God will not renew the world more than three times and this will be the last.'* The world was made at the Creation and renewed at the end of the great deluge (Noah's flood). It was renewed again by Christ's mission. The third renewal, the Ordinary Man asserts, will be the last.

The Ordinary Man came to me saying, 'Why do you not do your work? How is it that, knowing what the angel and I say to you, you show yourselves to be such cowards in the face of such a minor thing?'[1]

I answered him that I feared no one and asked, 'How do I know who you are?'[2]

He said to me, 'Alas for those who know the truth and deny it, as they do, for fear of a man. They know that there is a light on high where all are to be judged and it is there that all the fearful thoughts you have all harboured will be known. Follow me, even though I am angered to see what little courage you have.'

I went out with him and we came to the palace. There we saw the king in one of the rooms, his ears covered but his eyes open looking at the forests. By his side was Don Guillén and with him a veiled person. I also saw Fray Lucas and with him Don Alonso and I stood before him with a naked sword in my hand.[3]

We each spoke in order according to our seniority in age so that the covered man was first, then Don Guillén, then Fray Lucas, then Don Alonso.

Finally I, moving the sword from side to side, said in a loud voice, 'Make way for me. There was a time when you thought to say it was the Devil who showed me these things. I do not ask for justice from that judge who must judge us all.'

That vision then disappeared and I turned to the Ordinary Man and asked him to take me to where the two companions were.[4]

He answered me, 'I do not mean to until you have spoken to the priest. Remember Jonas the prophet and not your mother, and do not think about what people may say but, with the greatest prudence that you can, work your way free of the claws

*of the lions and go into hiding because you have said enough for
a woman. Leave the world and go to that place you have been
thinking of.'*

And with this I awoke.

1. *'How is it that . . . you show yourselves to be such cowards in the face of such
   a minor thing?'* In early February 1588 Fray Diego de Chaves, the royal
   confessor, became concerned about reports of a woman whose dreams
   were alleged to prophesy the destruction of Spain. At other times this
   might have passed without any need for action but these were anxious
   times for the king and his close circle of advisers. Chaves was close to
   Philip and concerned for his protection. He was also a Dominican with
   a reputation for disapproval of unorthodox religious practice (he had
   launched the attack on Piedrola which saw that prophet end up in
   prison, and had urged the arrest for murder of Antonio Pérez).

   Chaves asked Juan Baptista Neroni, who carried the title Vicar of
   Madrid, to investigate. Neroni walked around the parish of San
   Sebastián and found many people willing to talk about Lucrecia. This
   is no surprise – she never made any secret of the content of her dreams
   and frequently told her friends and neighbours about the strange and
   portentous things she had seen. When her neighbours repeated these
   to Neroni he was horrified – the loss of the Armada, the death of the
   king, the outbreak of a new *communidades* revolt like the one that
   nearly toppled his father; this was overt sedition.

   On 13 February Neroni ordered Lucrecia's arrest on the grounds
   that she was fomenting scandal and unrest among the people. Lucrecia
   was taken to his house for questioning. Records were kept of the interrogation and, even at this first encounter with the church authorities,
   Lucrecia demonstrated her skill in handling interrogations. At her first
   session she said that if the dreams were from the Devil then would
   Neroni please pray with her to 'Our Lord to remove them, and if they
   were from God, then she did not deserve them'.

   Lucrecia continued in this vein – contrite without admitting any
   guilt. Seeing that more questioning would get him nowhere, Neroni
   asked Fray Chaves and Fray Juan de Orellana to give their theological

opinion of the dreams. They disapproved, though another expert, Fray Luis de León, was more conciliatory (though as a friend of Mendoza he had annoyed the priest by commenting that the dreams were interesting but not from God).

These men were well versed in theological doctrine, but there was little objective knowledge that could be brought to bear. The most widely known guide to visions had been written by Jean Gerson, a French scholar of the early fifteenth century. His treatise *De distinctione verarum visionum a falsis* ('On the distinction between true visions and false') became the standard guidance for the Church. But when it came to Lucrecia's case Gerson's rules were not to prove definitive. The judges' verdicts were unsurprisingly neatly in accordance with their previously declared views on visionaries and dreamers. Richard Kagan quotes part of Chaves's and Orellana's report:

'The dreams of Lucrecia are not from God, nor from ignorance, nor from her own sense of vanity and wish to be esteemed. They do not even come from the devil, who might have pretended to use this little woman to upset Spain and to disrupt plans for the holy armada against England . . . She herself confesses that she does not believe in the dreams and has told the same to her accomplices . . . This evil dreamer does not want these things to be told to the king, our lord, to whom it would matter if these things were from God. Rather she tells them to the common people in order to stir them up.' (1990)

This belittles Lucrecia without saying what the sources of the dreams might be.

In the mean time Mendoza, infuriated, got busy. He wrote to both the papal nuncio in Madrid and to Quiroga, the Inquisitor-General. Mendoza asserted that it was pointless to question Lucrecia directly about her dreams as 'Prophecy belongs to the spirit not the will'. The Church should devote its time to studying the content of her dreams not their author. Quiroga was sympathetic and ordered Lucrecia's release. Before being sent home Lucrecia was put through an experience deliberately designed to intimidate her.

She was taken into a room in the official house of Juan Baptista Neroni. There was another man in the room as well as Neroni. He was Pedro de Valle, a secretary of the Holy Office, the Inquisition. Neroni said to Valle, 'Here is the prophet – look at her.'

Lucrecia answered, 'I am not so good as to merit such a great name; anyhow, I have never claimed to be a prophet.'

Pedro de Valle then stepped forward and placed his hands on her head. He said to her, 'I have undone many prophets with these hands.'

Neroni told her to keep her dreams to herself and sent her home.

Lucrecia's release was on a condition, proposed by Quiroga, that she be confined in a convent where her dreams could be studied by theologians. This condition was never fulfilled, for the simple reason that Lucrecia's mother would not allow her daughter to leave home. Mendoza suggested Lucrecia come to a convent in Toledo and this time her father objected. Behind this stalemate there was a fundamental conflict within the de Léon household about what should happen next.

Alonso Franco de Léon had been away in Valladolid when his daughter was arrested. An Inquisition file records that, on his return, he made this astonishing threat to Lucrecia: 'Daughter, in my family nobody has ever believed in superstitions because dreams are only dreams, and if you believe in them I will give the order to have you killed.'

Somehow, from this high pitch of fury, Lucrecia's father was persuaded by his wife and Mendoza to let the transcriptions proceed. The exchange at the beginning of this dream implies that Lucrecia and her supporters were wary of continuing. The Ordinary Man is scathing in the face of their weakness, but there is not much sign that they hesitated before pressing on with their work. Mendoza, having secured her release may have felt a false confidence in his own powers which rubbed off on to Lucrecia, otherwise she would surely have been scared off by Neroni and de Valle. Perhaps we underestimate the degree of cynicism people had towards their church authorities and overestimate the seriousness with which such threats would be treated. At any rate Lucrecia went back to dictating her dreams and Mendoza and Lucas to transcribing them. The arrest had the effect of considerably increasing Lucrecia's notoriety within the court and outside. Her recognition and condemnation by such powerful men had given her a considerable leap in status.

2. *I answered him that I feared no one and asked, 'How do I know who you are?'*
Lucrecia shows her own understanding of the entanglement that awaits her. What does it mean if you do not know God or His messenger

when you see him? How does a religion based on faith deal with the possibility of error – that a true believer might honestly believe that a phenomenon is Godly when it is not?

Lucrecia's question combines a rhetorical figure of speech with an earnest request for an answer. 'How do I know who you are?' means 'Why should I have any certainty about your identity?' but it also means 'Tell me the things that will give me certainty about your identity.'

The Ordinary Man's answer is elliptical but unequivocal. Lucrecia knows the truth, he implies, and must not deny it. It is a great thing to be told that you know the truth but, of all that you know, what is the truth?

3. *I stood before him with a naked sword in my hand.* The king is alone with Lucrecia and her three closest supporters and a 'covered man' – probably Piedrola. Lucrecia is direct in her words to the king. He has accused her of being a messenger of the Devil. Menacing him with her sword, she makes her Job-like statement, 'I do not ask for justice from that judge who must judge us all.'

4. *I turned to the Ordinary Man and asked him to take me to where the two companions were.* Now Lucrecia is not simply taken to different places by the Ordinary Man. She begins to see him as her escort and is confident enough to ask to be taken to the seashore. It may be that she is eager to see the companions because she does not like being scolded by the Ordinary Man and seeks further understanding. She is also anxious about his identity and perhaps about theirs too. He does not comply with her request.

There came to me a man. He came in the way that the Ordinary Man usually comes but he had his face covered with a black veil. He went to stand by the wall of my room opposite to where I have my bed. And in all of the room there was only a faint glow which seemed to be the light of the moon entering through a hole in the roof. In this faint glow I saw the man without discerning more about him than that he was a bulky man.

Remaining there by the wall, I heard him call my name three times saying, 'Lucrecia, Lucrecia, Lucrecia.'

And while he called me I was dreaming a dream of the following form.[1]

I dreamed that I saw Juan López[2] *with a constable's rod of office and he said to me, 'We are going to see a fiesta that is happening in this town of Our Lady of Peace.' And he tried to persuade me to go through the mud.*

I said to him, 'I do not wish to go this way. There are dry streets in Madrid by which we can go to the fiesta.'

I watched and saw that he and a cousin of mine walked through the mud in the middle of the street, but my cousin no sooner put his feet in the mud than he jumped out again and went into the house of Cuellar the accountant (for all this was happening in the Calle de Barrionuevo).

Juan López continued through the current of mud in the street while I walked on the dry parts at the side. We continued in this way down the street until, just before the Calle de Concepción Jerónima he pushed me into a house that I know and had heard to be the Inquisition's prison.

There, in a church, I found three images of Our Lady. One of these had San Ildefonso at her right side and at her left a prophetess – I call her this for on her back was a sign which said

'Prophet'. Our Lady had her arms about the shoulders of these two persons (as though embracing them) and covered them with a robe of white taffeta which was about her shoulders and around theirs.

While I was saying a prayer to this image, Juan López entered, saying that now I should finish. At that moment I noticed there was a woman in the church. A youth entered and threw a hatful of bunches of grapes to her, at which she called two old women who were also there and gave them some. These old women gave me a couple of pieces of bread with a few very over-ripe grapes. I ate the bread but do not remember eating the grapes and then left the church and found the streets hung with damasks and other coloured things.

It was at this time that I heard my name called three times. I woke up and being properly awake was quite perturbed to hear myself being addressed in that way. Thinking it must be my host's wife, I said, 'God save me, who calls my name?'

The man who stood by the wall[3] (and whose eyes I could now see were open) responded, 'I am the Ordinary Man.'

As he said this I closed my eyes and returned to a peaceful sleep and he continued to speak: 'Moved by pity for Fray Lucas I come to tell you to give no more advice. If the church officials, when they call you to account, say that I am the Devil, do not worry. I am taking pity on your youth. Why have you become involved in giving advice to people? I also wish to warn Don Guillén not to show any papers to anyone. Rather you should both ingratiate yourselves with them. I would not warn you about this if I did not care so much for you.'

I asked him, 'Why do you wear this black veil in front of your face? It troubles me much.'

He answered, 'You cause me anger by being surprised by so many things.'

I said, 'How is it that the Ordinary Man has never said this to me? If you are really he, how is it that you come with this new attitude?'

He answered me, 'I have always deceived you and now, because your childishness annoys me, I undeceive you.'

At this point it occurred to me to say the Verbum Caro. As I began to speak I saw the man move back slowly to the bedroom door, so I said, 'If you had spoken the truth when you said you were the Ordinary Man you would not be frightened by the words that I say.'

He answered me, 'I wish to go for you do not appreciate the good advice that I give you. And when I am gone, if some man should come who looks like me, do not believe him. He will be the Devil.'

Now I gave a great sigh and said, 'Oh prophet, how is it that you do not come to my aid since you promised that you would when you helped me to descend from the tower?'

The man said, 'Why do you call on the prophet? Do you want him to aid you with his witchcraft?'

As he spoke I saw the prophet come riding, armoured, on a white horse. He had a lance at his shoulder and a sword and a cross in his hand and he cried out in a loud voice, 'Conquer him and you will be worthy to receive the cross and arms and a horse.'

Then the Devil began to cry out saying, 'Prophet, do not reveal who I am. Since I did not conquer you, nor can I, let me do my work and do not come to warn her.'

Rising up in his stirrups, the prophet raised the cross on high and said, 'Back, Satan, on behalf of God I command you.'

The evil spirit said, 'I shall do all the evil that I can among the friends that you have so that they may turn against you.'

The prophet said to him, 'I say to you on behalf of God, tell me why you troubled Juan López and the beatas.'

He answered, but without looking at the prophet, 'I will tell you, so that you may see how cunning I am. Realising that he *gave money to Cristóbal de Allende, I placed the temptation of greed before him. I suggested to him that since he was alone in the business, he should consider handing over less money, for the affair might not succeed and then the money would be lost, for it would take a great deal of effort to win the day. And in the same way I approached the beatas who are vessels containing little strength. I put before them the idea that they would lack their daily sustenance because of having given the money. I said that they should not go where they had been told, for no notice would be taken of them and that if they were brought there by force everything would have to begin again. I said that if they heeded this advice their money would be returned and nothing would happen. And so, to all three I made a case that they would be serving God.'*

When he had said this I heard the prophet address himself to the Devil, 'Tell me no more. I do not wish to hear you defame these people.'

The Devil went away, howling, and the prophet said to me, 'Have courage. Do not be like those you have heard of.'

I said, 'Do you know if I am to see the Ordinary Man tonight?'

He answered, 'You will not. Tell Don Alonso that he must look to see that there are no ill-judged words in the papers that he is to give the cardinal,[4] *for they would be like poison for those dogs who are so anxious to be on your trail.'*

And with that I awoke.

---

1. *And while he called me I was dreaming a dream of the following form.* Lucrecia is having a dream within a dream. This phenomenon is familiar to many dreamers. The sensation of apparently waking from one dream, only to be within another in which you are the dreamer of the first dream, is a fairly common experience. Lucrecia emphasises the effect

by saying that, when the veiled man wakes her by calling her name, 'I woke up and being *properly awake* . . .' though of course she is not.

This is not a simple dream-within-a-dream. The outer dream, which concerns the veiled man, though related to us first, actually occurs at the end of the inner dream. But this does not work in any logical way since Lucrecia describes the entry of the man into her room but later implies that she first knows the man is there when he wakes her from her other dream. Things are further confused by her apparently going back to sleep while the veiled man speaks to her. The latter part of the dream is then not so much the outer dream as a return to the inner level of dream. All this confusion may not matter very much, beyond showing us the mind's relentless ability to make some kind of narrative meaning out of the most bewildering material.

2. *I dreamed that I saw Juan López.* An unusual appearance by some of Lucrecia's friends, family, neighbours. This part of the dream has a chaotic sense of images being strung into a journey. The Calle de Concepción Jerónima is close to Lucrecia's house, between the Calle de San Sebastián and the Plaza Mayor.

3. *The man who stood by the wall* . . . We know that Lucrecia knows that something is not right here. And the man who stands by the wall also knows that she knows. He tells her that she must not listen to others when they say that he is the Devil. Then he says, 'when I am gone, if some man should come who looks like me, do not believe him. He will be the Devil.' This is all supposed to convince Lucrecia that this man is not the Devil, but the effect is entirely the opposite. Lucrecia has clearly identified him and does not even feel the need to openly declare this – she simply describes him in the next sentence as 'the Devil'.

For the past three months, Lucrecia has been given advice, support and warning by a variety of men, both in her dreams and in her waking life. Although Mendoza and Allende have stuck by her she has been told by Neroni and Chaves that her dreams are evil and intended to foment unrest among the people. She is perhaps feeling isolated, and if so her meeting with the Devil is a vivid expression of a sense of confusion and abandonment. This is made explicit in her cry for help from the prophet, who is a thinly disguised Piedrola, who had promised always to come to her aid in her dream of the night of 4 December 1587.

Lucrecia has been told by some that her dreams are the work of the Devil. If this is true then the Ordinary Man is the agent of the Devil. In a sense this dream is an argument against that and in favour of the divine origins of her dreams since, by attempting to imitate the Ordinary Man, the Devil shows that he is not in league with him.

The initial appearance of this veiled figure is the stuff of nightmares. He is seen in the faint glow of moonlight standing against the wall of Lucrecia's bedroom, his face half covered; a ghoulish frightening figure repeatedly calling her name. But once he engages Lucrecia in conversation he begins to lose his potency. First he says he is the Ordinary Man, which Lucrecia does not believe. She is then able to fend him off by the recitation of a simple prayer, the *Verbum Caro*. And when the prophet Piedrola arrives in stirringly dramatic fashion on a white horse, the Devil admits that he is outgunned.

More demeaning though than all these defeats is his boast of victory. For the past three months Lucrecia has been presented with visions of terrifying bloodshed, torment and death. She has seen people being murdered in such numbers as to make rivers of blood, she has seen Spain's enemies combining to conquer her people, she has heard the dying cry out the end of the world. And in the midst of all this terror and destruction we are told by this bragging Devil that he has 'placed the temptation of greed' before Cristóbal de Allende and then persuaded some holy women that they should not be giving money to Lucrecia's supporters. This, claims the Devil, will show the prophet how cunning he is. In fact it shows him to be a petty meddler.

There seems no ulterior reason for Lucrecia gratuitously to denigrate the Devil in this particular way. This is likely to be her real idea of what he is like and what he is up to – trickery and cunning, rather than wanton destruction. He plays this role often enough in the Bible – tormenting Job and tempting Christ – for the image to have stuck to him. In this way of perceiving him, he is like a minor Greek god, coming to earth to meddle, to disturb and to spread a little wickedness. In this he serves the minimum requirements of one form of Christian theodicy – God is good, but there is evil in the world because Satan interferes. But his marginalisation from the mainstream of history risks making him a comical figure – cunning, playful, persistent, but rather stupid and easily discovered and faced down by the alert believer.

There is a disturbing outcome to this personalising and caricaturing of the Devil. We may believe that God and the Devil are engaged in a mighty struggle for men's souls and for dominion over the earth. If we look closer we see that this is a one-sided struggle. Satan is, once in a while, given a chance to commit some improper deed. But this is always with the permission of God. God instructs Satan, He casts him out, He allows him, He banishes him, He gives him the prospect of return. God rules the Heaven and the earth. God decides who will go to Heaven and who He will send to join His distaff son in hell. It is God who will destroy the world and make it anew. It is God who will sit in judgment. It is God not Satan who, in Lucrecia's visions, orders the people of Spain to be butchered in the streets. It is God whom we must fear.

4. '*Tell Don Alonso that he must look to see that there are no ill-judged words in the papers that he is to give the cardinal*'. It is likely that, as a condition of Cardinal Quiroga engineering Lucrecia's release from Neroni and Chaves, he asked to see some of her dream transcripts. There seems to be a contradiction in the instructions given by the men in Lucrecia's dreams. They want her to tell others what she has seen but they warn her and her patrons not to give the authorities reason to proceed against her. It is a dilemma from which she cannot and will not escape.

*The Ordinary Man came to me and took me out of my house,
saying, 'Let us hurry for the companions are eagerly awaiting
us.'*

*As we arrived at the seashore the Old Man said to me, 'It
would be well for your people to begin to retreat now.'*[1]

*I asked him to where, and he answered, 'Wherever you may
wish.'*

*Then the Lion Man called me and said, 'Days have passed
since I promised to point out to you those who would join forces
with you and now it is time to speak. Tell Fray Lucas that if he
bears in mind what I told him he will not nominate Juan López
nor many others, for prayers are needed more than defensive
arms. But tell him that while he is in Toledo he should prepare
some papers to give to the dogs*[2] *for by means of such sops they
will accept your words. Your people will then be able to gain great
honour. The people will come to bring you out in procession but
you will not wish this, for time will not permit. Now you must
look to the heavens to see what may descend from there.'*

*I looked, and from the south an angel descended. His arms
and legs were bare and his body clothed and from his chest
emerged a burning axe. In his mouth he held a naked sword and
in his hands a bow with many arrows, and a dragon coiled itself
about his legs. This angel set himself upon a high hill that had
also descended from the heavens and settled upon the earth.*

*As he settled there the Lion Man asked him to speak and he
began in a loud voice, 'I am the messenger of the Father, the Son
and the Holy Spirit, these three persons having but one will.
Thus Jesus sends me to punish the priests, and would have done
so earlier if not for the love of his Mother the Holy Virgin Mary
who has always interceded for them. This she did out of regard*

for San Ildefonso, for whose sake she descended from Heaven, but her son has conceded only that Toledo will be spared for it was there that she set her sacred feet.'

When he had said this I saw that the angel seemed as full of anger as a person possibly could be. He began to load and shoot his bow, firing so many arrows and so fast that the air was filled with them and the sun was covered over. He showered abroad the fire that he bore in his chest and uncoiled the dragon from about his legs and launched it into the air.

The Old Man spoke to the angel and said, 'Tell me what is the meaning of this great justice that you visit on the priests?'

The angel, turning to him, and still very angry, said, 'Don't you see that your Holy Body is to be shaken within five years? Wind your robe about your arm and draw this sword' (indicating the one he carried in his mouth). The Old Man did so and, once he had it in his hand, asked the angel, 'What am I to do with it?'

He answered, 'You must wound the high priests.'

Then the Old Man threw the sword into the air saying, 'Do your work.'

And when this was done the angel explained the reasons for the actions, saying, 'I have fired arrows because the hearts of the priests have launched arrows at the poor. I have emitted fire from my breast because they have burned with the sins of the flesh, and I have loosed the dragon because they have followed its example in the sin of gluttony.'

Turning then to the Old Man he said, 'And the sword is because they have never followed your example.'[3]

This said and done, the angel disappeared, leaving much blood upon the earth round about the hill where he had stood. Then the Lion Man said to me, 'Wait, you will now see the king's angel descend.' And, raising my eyes, I saw another angel descend from the heavens upon a cloud of blood and fire which settled upon the earth. The cloud contained a mass of loathsome creatures: toads, serpents, lizards, vipers and such-like. This angel had the face of a lion, the chest and arms of a man, the legs of a bear and the feet of a goat.[4]

He spoke in a great voice, 'I am the angel of God who, by the sentence of the Trinity, am come to punish Philip, and not him alone but all of his monarchy. I do not come to do so with sword and lance (for his enemies will have charge of that manner of punishment) but with the lash of God, which will be very painful and more so for Philip in particular. For he has punished the just without reason or justice and has always tried to favour the bad (in whose likeness I appear). This is why I come.'

Then this angel disappeared and the Old Man said to me, 'You are to tell these things to the one to whom I reveal many mysteries, and tell him to remember the word of God to St Peter on the subject of the ewe.'

Then the Lion Man called me and said, 'Tell Don Alonso to look at his paper. It is important.'

With that I awoke, crying out with a pain in my back that I had had when I went to bed, and with this I was so far from remembering anything of this that it was as if I had not dreamed anything at all.

Commending myself to God and sitting upon the bed I placed my hand upon my brow and, by closing my eyes, recovered the vision[5] which began to re-present itself to me as though I were seeing it again, for which I gave Him what thanks I could.

1. 'It would be well for your people to begin to retreat now.' The world is quickening to its finish. In this dream time is beating. It is full of urgent phrases: 'begin to retreat now', 'it is time to speak', 'time will not permit'. How will it all end?

2. *'he should prepare some papers to give to the dogs'.* The Lion Man assumes control and gives instructions. The companions are now advising Don Alonso de Mendoza to publish material that will convince the people of Lucrecia's message, and instructing Lucrecia to retreat to her refuge, presumably the Sopeña. He suggests that the people will rush to honour Lucrecia. If Mendoza and Allende and her other supporters believe literally in these dream messsages they must be anxious that their preparations for a sanctuary will be too late. Now they know for certain that Toledo is to be saved.

3. *'And the sword is because they have never followed your example.'* A shocking act: the Old Man has thrown away the angel's sword. But now he is commended and the priests condemned – they too should have refused to do harm to others.

4. *the face of a lion, the chest and arms of a man, the legs of a bear and the feet of a goat.* This piecing together of one body from many is clearly intended to increase the fear induced by the angel's appearance: after all, the sight of a bear, or a goat or even a lion would not be so frightful. The angel later says that he has come in the likeness of the bad; since these animals of themselves are not evil, it is the incongruous combination which itself is malign; a perversion of God's creations. To us there is a comical aspect to such an assemblage and a sense that the creature has been pieced together in too much of a hurry. To Lucrecia the sight of the angel was astonishing, awesome and holy – such terrifying visions paradoxically embodied the concept of the sublime.

5. *I placed my hand upon my brow and, by closing my eyes, recovered the vision.* Almost everything that Lucrecia tells us in these transcripts is reportage from the world of her dreams. We all know that dreams are difficult to remember, difficult to relate and impossible to recreate. What we have of Lucrecia's dreams is a construction – marvellous, gaudy, bloody, poetic and rebuilt. In this short passage we step into Lucrecia's other world for a moment. It is a tranquil interval which we might wish her to hold on to for a little longer; sitting on her bed, her hand on her brow, the teeming scenes of the night temporarily lost to her bodily pain. Then the vision returns, 'as though I were seeing it again'.

All that we have just read came close to slipping away for ever, and was recovered in this moment of reflection.

The Fishermen Come to Madrid | Chapter 29

5 MARCH 1588

The Ordinary Man came to me together with the two companions. The Old Man wore a white robe about his shoulders.

I turned to look at the Ordinary Man and said to him, 'Baptist, regard what Martin of Our Lady[1] has said to me. He wishes you to grant what he asked of you.'

Placing his hand upon my face, he answered me, 'Who told you my name?'

I made no answer but turned to the Lion Man and asked, 'How is it that these past nights I have not gone to where you are?'[2]

He answered, 'The nights without rest are those of the Ordinary Man and if you come to where we are the visions would be even longer than his.'

And the Old Man said, 'We come to break words. This is the second occasion that we have come to see you and we come only to help you in the way that Piedrola does. You should bear in mind his words to you when you were descending from the castle.'

The Lion Man said, 'This is not the time to discuss that for she wishes to ask me I know not what.'

So I said to him, 'What have you told Don Guillén about me?'[3]

He answered, 'I do not waste words answering questions which are of no importance. I have already explained Don Guillén's thinking to you. You are the only one who sees, they merely hear and I simply come to tell you to take as true indeed the things that the Ordinary Man has shown you. Don Alonso and Fray Lucas should remember the flask that broke in my hands and keep in mind that, if they do not make it known,

194

those in Aragón will allow passage to all your enemies to take revenge on Philip.'[4]

I said, 'They remark how the flesh and the blood touch my feelings.'[5]

He answered, 'If they did not you would be as one who is dead.'

The Ordinary Man then said, 'Do you remember when I came to you bearing a handful of bulrushes as commanded by the Old Man? And I was insistent that Fray Lucas should explain it? Take comfort, the bulrushes represent your enemies and while they are fresh you have much work to do – but later they will be dry and will turn white. Do you not remember when you saw the nose of a dead and shrouded man all eaten away? Philip's senses will be eaten away.'

Having said this the Ordinary Man fell silent and the Old Man said to me, 'What did they understand by my bare legs?'

I said, 'Sir, they said nothing to me.'

He said, 'Naked is my house and since it touches God so closely, it pleases Him to have the churches pay by removing the evildoers from among the good.'

Then the Lion Man came to me and, raising his hand and holding it in the air above my head, he began to speak in a tongue that I did not understand[6] *and the Ordinary Man answered in the same language. This lasted a long while and when they had finished the Old Man came to me and, with his hand raised in the same way, spoke Latin words which I did understand for I have heard them spoken by priests at Mass. He spoke for some time and was answered in the same fashion by the Ordinary Man.*

Once finished, the Old Man said to me, 'Tell them I carry it upon my shoulder.'

And with that I awoke.

1. *Martin of Our Lady.* Brother Martin was another transcriber of Lucrecia's dreams. A friend to Sor María del Visitacion, he appears in the dream of 17 March.

2. *'How is it that these past nights I have not gone to where you are?'* It is highly unusual for the two companions to leave the seashore. The Old Man later says that this is only the second time they have come to see her. The reason for this visit is that she needs help. But she is, in her neediness, highly suspicious of those that offer help. In her recent meeting with the Devil none of these three were on hand; instead she called on Piedrola to help her. Her attitude to the three has changed from compliant to combative.

   Tired of what has become to her a charade, she openly calls the Ordinary Man 'Baptist'. She is suspicious of why the two companions have appeared in her room rather than at the seashore, as if these two might be impostors. She has not been taken to the seashore for some time and is offered only a lame reason for this.

   Having bluntly named the Ordinary Man she then rudely demands of the Lion Man – a normally intimidating figure – 'What have you told Don Guillén about me?'

   It is not simply that Lucrecia suspects that these men are impersonating the men that she normally sees but that she has become suspicious of the men, and their displacement from their normal habitat feeds this suspicion. The change of routine has unnerved her.

   Though her dreams are being recorded and transmitted by her supporters, firm in the belief that they are divine and important, Lucrecia is clearly troubled by the possibility that she is being somehow used by the figures in her dream in ways that she cannot quite fathom. What seemed straightforward has become complex. She is no longer content to act as the interlocutor between the dream and woken worlds, allowing others to show, to interpret, to explain. Perhaps her growing importance in both worlds has given her the confidence to challenge those who come to instruct her. Her arrest and growing notoriety are opening her mind to possibilities of fame and disaster.

3. *'What have you told Don Guillén about me?'* We have been told before that the Lion Man is communicating with Don Guillén de Casaos. Are we now to take from this that the Lion Man has been appearing to Don Guillén in dreams or visions? From his reply it may be that he has

spoken to him, though even this would be an extraordinary event – two dreamers summoning up the same figure.

We should allow for the possibility of Lucrecia using her dreams to establish her superiority over Don Guillén. The Lion Man says to her, 'You are the only one who sees, they merely hear.'

4. *'those in Aragón will allow passage to all your enemies to take revenge on Philip.'* We have seen that Aragón remained an autonomous province within Spain and that this was to cause Philip problems when Antonio Pérez fled there in 1590. The Lion Man's message shows that 'your', i.e. Spain's, enemies are also the enemies of Philip. This is a central theme of Lucrecia's dreams – that Spain will have to be conquered and its king removed before better times can come to the Spanish people.

5. *'They remark how the flesh and the blood touch my feelings.'* For the first time we learn of Lucrecia's own reactions to the events she is describing. The scenes which read so matter-of-factly in her account are disturbing to her as well as her audience. A dreamer's response is more private than the content of a dream.

6. *he began to speak in a tongue that I did not understand.* The last passage of the dream is related by a woman who has already told us that she is affected by the visions she sees. Lucrecia does not tell us she is frightened or even worried or moved by the performance of the three men in the last part of this dream. But this odd ritual performed in a strange language seems intended either to intimidate or to sanctify.

*The Ordinary Man came to me and said, 'Do you wish to go
where the two companions are? Do not think that I would ask
you in this way except that I see you are indisposed.'[1]*

*I arose to go with him and as we went through the streets I
saw many stone statues. The Ordinary Man said, 'What do you
think these statues are meant to be? Many of them are cursed
and since this is the year in which the wrath of God comes to
all, go close up to the most damaged ones.'*

*Going towards the palace we came upon a wolf with hands
and feet broken off. The Ordinary Man said, 'This one came out
from beneath the arches of the bridge just like the unbelievers,
as I have told you many times.'*

*He then took me to the seashore where the two companions
were.*

*The Old Man said to me, 'Do you remember the rainbow that
you saw in the sky? Then know that it signals floods and winds
which will stir up the waters of the sea.'*

*This said, the Old Man disappeared and we saw him no more
in that place that night. Then the Lion Man called me and said,
'Are you not all aware that very soon all the hordes of Algiers
will enter via Valencia? That will be during those months when
the gardens open up their flowers for your delight. Also if the
Armada is detained upon the water[2] in April all of its people
will die of the plague and will leave those ships for Don
Antonio's troops. And if these forces set forth in April, as I have
foretold, the foreign prisoner that they carry has the means to
destroy its captains and make off with some of the galleys to the
Portuguese islands.'[3]*

*Then he went on, 'Did you tell Don Alonso what you heard
the Great Turk say?'*

I said, 'Yes' and asked him, 'What is the dispute that the Ordinary Man said had taken place?'

He said to me, 'Was it not between Don Alonso and Fray Lucas? And there was also one in the palace. Remember, I have warned you to take care of yourselves and to retreat by degrees to that place that I mentioned so that you may make all necessary provision.'

Then he told me to look towards the sky where I saw three figures of Christ crucified, two bishops and the apostle St Peter (whose facial characteristics seemed to me to be like those of the Old Fisherman whom I usually saw in the place where we were). I also saw a pope dressed in the Franciscan habit who was being stripped of his honours by the bishops. And as they did this I noticed that the crucified figures sweated blood.

I asked the Lion Man at my side, 'Why do they sweat so?'

He replied, 'Because they have been helpless here on earth and have drunk once more of the chalice that he drank in the garden and these are the three who performed miracles on earth. God is to keep them hidden away until peace comes to Spain. Because this pope brought harm to the holy bodies that he had in his power, St Peter now passes judgment on him, and his degradation is not on earth but on high.'

When he had said this the vision disappeared, leaving the heavens very bloodstained and the earth suffering many tremors. From the caves of the earth emerged many lions and tigers, roaring, who went to refresh themselves in the waters of the sea. And now the Lion Man said, 'The time has passed when mercy could be shown to the world.'[4]

I watched as these lions and tigers dug up the earth with their claws and disappeared beneath it.

And with that I awoke.

1. *'Do not think that I would ask you in this way . . .'* The Ordinary Man seeks Lucrecia's consent but spoils the effect by claiming he only does this because she is unwell. This relationship continues to change and Lucrecia captures this alteration in her account.

   If we take the transcripts to be an accurate record of what Lucrecia told her scribes, then we have either to marvel at Lucrecia's capacity for memorising or admire her ability to reconstruct. We do not know whether Lucrecia was reporting the exact words of dialogues which she dreamed, or whether the details of what she described were the product of an almost total recall of what she saw. Remarkable as this would be, the alternative is in a way even more astonishing. If Lucrecia was giving her impression of what was said and of what she saw, knowingly filling spaces just beyond her memory, and conveying the sense and mood of her visions by adding in the detail, then this shows great inventive power.

2. *'if the Armada is detained upon the water'.* In March 1588 the ships of the Armada sit in Lisbon harbour, the planks swell, the supplies rot, the men go bad through disease and idleness. It will be after April before all the preparations are complete. Medina Sidonia has inherited a shambolic fleet and crew. He has imposed some kind of order on it all, and is so pleased at the efficiency of the operation that he begins to feel the thing can be won. By the last week of May everything in Lisbon harbour will be ready:

   > Twenty-four Portuguese and Spanish galleons;
   > Four Neapolitan galleasses (a half galleon to half galley craft);
   > Forty heavily-armed large merchant ships from Biscay,
   >   Andalusia, Barcelona, Venice, Genoa, Sicily and Ragusa;
   > Thirty-four light frigates and zabras;
   > Twenty-three freighters as supply carriers;
   > Four Portuguese galleys.

   The invincible Armada was eventually to leave Lisbon on 30 May 1588. The weather was extremely fractious, battering then becalming the fleet, which consequently took twenty days to make it up the western coast of the peninsula. On Sunday, 19 June the leading ships of the fleet put in to La Coruña, short of water and still waiting for supply ships from the northern ports to muster. That night a southwesterly gale blew apart the remainder of the fleet, which then had to be reassembled. The experience at least gave Medina Sidonia some idea of the problems he faced – principally that the food and water supplies were inadequate. He took a month to repair and resupply the fleet before eventually (Philip by this time tearing his hair out with impatience) on 21 July, the Armada set sail for England.

Once unleashed, the fate of the Armada was entrusted to God by Philip, but was, in the end (notwithstanding the elements), at the mercy of the actions of several thousand men and at least one woman. We tend to study these great events as a sequence of smaller events, slightly separated in time, so that we can understand them more clearly. But the effect at the time was of occurrences crowding in on top of one another so that the consequence of one action could not be seen or known about before another must be undertaken.

Both the English and Spanish fleets were to be surprised by the other – this would be the first modern naval battle and no one would quite know how to fight it. Once both fleets were barrelling up the narrowing Channel a number of things might have happened; what did happen was perhaps the least interesting though, for England, the most satisfactory. Out of all the possible occurrences one thing that could not have happened was the successful ferrying of the Spanish army of the Netherlands across to England as the centre of an invasion force. Among all the contingencies of history, the utter impossibility of the central object of the enterprise remains a puzzle – how could such a strategy have been devised and followed?

The Enterprise of England, planned for so many years, was to be settled in just eight days. On 30 July 1588, in sight of the Lizard, England's most southerly point, Medina Sidonia held a council of war and sent a message to his king: the Armada will go no further than the Isle of Wight until the time and place of meeting with Parma's troops has been arranged. In any case his captains know that thay cannot go beyond the Straits of Dover.

On 6 August, after four battles with the English fleet – each, writes Mattingly, 'in ships engaged and shot expended, easily the greatest that had ever been fought at sea' (1959) – Medina Sidonia brought his slightly battered but still intact fleet to anchor in the shelter of the cliffs outside the port of Calais. At this time, he still had 'no firm word about when Parma would be ready to embark, or how and where they would meet'.

Calais was a French port and therefore ostensibly neutral. The

Spanish might have expected a warmish welcome; the English might have suspected that the French would resupply the Armada with provisions and shot (both fleets had used prodigious amounts of cannon balls during the previous week). The governor of Calais merely sent a message to Medina Sidonia advising him that his present anchorage was not safe and that he should think about moving very soon (we can imagine how much annoyance that caused in the duke's council) and enclosing a gift of fruit. Officers from the Armada were allowed ashore to buy fresh food but nothing more.

At this time both Gravelines and Dunkirk, just up the coast from Calais, were part of the Netherlands States-General and controlled by Parma. On the night of 6 August he was within thirty miles of the Armada but still Medina Sidonia had no word from him. The Captain-General of the Armada was stuck. He had survived the Channel and reached the Straits of Dover but could go no further. A meeting at sea was the only possibility and this would have to be pre-arranged. Once he sailed out of Calais Roads there was nowhere for him to go – prevailing winds would push and pin him in the friendless North Sea – and yet he could not stay where he was.

The Duke of Parma had written to Philip as early as January, informing the king that the only vessels available to him were cattle barges which could be used to transport troops only if the weather were completely calm and, more importantly, if they were impregnably protected by an Armada of fighting ships. In April Parma wrote again to Philip that if the Armada were delayed a few months he might have a chance of capturing the deep-water port at Flushing. This would enable the deep-draught Spanish galleons to sail into the Westerschelde port, organise themselves into a tight defence around the troop-carrying barges, wait for decent weather and then sail for England. Philip refused to delay further and crucially seems not to have informed the commander of his Armada of the parlous state of Parma's naval strength.

Medina Sidonia's orders from Philip were to rendezvous at sea. This might be off the coast of Flanders or off the 'Cape of Margate'. Not unnaturally the Captain-General of the Armada assumed from this order that Parma had a degree of control over Dutch coastal waters and enough armed escort boats to see his troops out into the Channel. All he needed was protection from the big ships of the English sea-going navy, and this Medina Sidonia was ready to give.

So when the duke found himself anchored under the cliffs at Calais, vulnerable to attack, he wrote to Parma,

I am anchored here, two leagues from Calais with the enemy's fleet on my flank. They can cannonade me whenever they like, and I shall be unable to do them much harm in return. If you can send me forty or fifty flyboats of your fleet I can, with their help, defend myself here until you are ready to come out.

Now, finally, the dismal, exhausting, demoralising, disillusioning truth began to make itself apparent. Parma now knew, and Medina Sidonia surely began to understand, that there would be no rendezvous. Within 30 miles of each other but separated by unpassable waters, they had forced the issue to its point of failure. They had done their utmost and, in doing so, had demonstrated that this thing could not be done this way. Parma would have counted himself lucky to have been able to send four or five flyboats, never mind forty, along the coast to Calais. And here was the nub. The Spanish galleons drew too much water to get within a few miles of the Flanders coast. The English warships were shallower drawers and could get between them and the shore, thereby cutting off any boats coming out from harbour. As well as that, it was the Dutch flyboats that controlled the coast. Parma had long ago realised the futility of taking on the past masters of the shoals, canals, tidal races, mudbanks and longshore winds of this soggy frontier. He knew that a deep-water harbour was the only chance of getting army and navy together. Medina Sidonia had wisely stopped at a place where rock met water – the last such place for 200 miles to the east and north. Now he nervously waited.

The English were nervous too. Parma's army was within 30 miles of the Armada, which they had failed to kill off or even damage substantially in its track up the Channel. The Spanish master plan appeared to be working. Knowing nothing of Medina Sidonia's urgent messages to Parma for help, the English knew only that they must act quickly. The fireships probably saved Medina Sidonia from realising the full extent of Parma's unreadiness.

At around midnight of 7 August 1588 on a gathering south to southwesterly and a flooding tide the English sent burning ships in to the tight-packed anchorage of the Armada. The first two were well dealt with by courageous and skilful seamanship: ropes were secured and they were towed away to safety. But the wind was strengthening and the English had packed the ships' guns with shot. They began to go off as the second wave reached the line of pinnaces and in the confusion six blazing ships danced through the line and into the heart of the Armada. The rest is history.

How was the impossible plan constructed? First and most crucially, Philip had for at least six months listened to his various military commanders telling him to delay the Armada. There always seemed to be a new reason for not sailing – supplies, ships, men not ready, weather not right, English on alert. Now, when everything else was right, Parma pleaded a few more months to take Flushing. Philip was having no more – the Armada must sail. Secondly, although Parma had stressed to Philip that his naval position was weak he is likely not to have wanted this to be widely known. He certainly did not tell Medina Sidonia directly until it was much too late to matter. Whether he wanted to keep the English and Dutch guessing is not clear. Medina Sidonia took the blame for the failure, though many in Spain believed Parma was at fault for not making himself ready – there was a widespread feeling that he was against the whole plan, so simply ensured that it failed. Many others blamed Philip, and the country became, as we have seen, further disillusioned with its ailing monarch.

The Armada would fail, as Lucrecia predicted and the defeat was, for her and her supporters, both a vindication and a danger.

3. *the Portuguese islands.* The Azores. The Don Antonio mentioned earlier in this paragraph is the pretender to the Portuguese throne, defeated by Spanish forces under Santa Cruz off the Azores in 1582.

4. *'The time has passed when mercy could be shown to the world.'* Christ took away our sins and declared God to be merciful. But we have not responded well. We have sinned without repentance and those who declare themselves servants of God are being judged most harshly for their hypocrisy. The era of the loving God is to be replaced by the earlier fearsome deity: jealous, angry, vengeful.

*The Ordinary Man came to me and said, 'It is many days now
since I warned your people about what is to befall them; already
you can count in hours and not in months. May God preserve
you against the setting of sails[1] which would then lead to your
being set upon in your houses. I should not wish to see you in
such difficulties, for you would find yourself the object of much
cruelty. And if that happens I would not wish to hear you cry
out in anger against me for I would make myself deaf to those
who had been deaf to my advice.*

*'Nor would I wish to see you you running to each other
without my being able to help you, for at that time many bulls
will enter Madrid, not in ones but all together, and you will have
made little provision to enclose them. Then the bullfighters,
having no goads, will have to submit their bodies to the horns of
the bulls. The Toledo bridge will be brought down and the waters
will rise so as to cut you off.'*

*Having said this he took me from my house through one of the
streets of Madrid (I do not know which) and said to me, 'How
well built is this street against the day when all will rise up.
Everything is done at the cost of the blood of Christ and the
angels of the Lord will destroy many monasteries where the
body of Christ has been celebrated, because they do not please
Him.'*

*This said, he took me to the palace where I found the king to
be much distressed by news that had come to him that some
ships of the Armada, I know not how many, had been lost.[2]
Then a gentleman of one of the military orders entered (I do not
remember which order,[3] only that the frills of his shirt were
small and flat and that he was a man of good body with a lean*

face and greying hair and the aspect of a good Christian).

He said to the king, 'Will Your Highness be pleased to hear a vision that has been recounted to me by Fray Lucas?'

The king replied, 'You do not please me. It would be better to send for Fray Lucas and hear them all.'

At this point the Ordinary Man said to me, 'It would be well for us to wait and see what colour Fray Lucas's face takes on.'

And so we drew to one side and saw Fray Lucas enter with his companion.⁴ We heard the king say to him, 'Does your companion know of these things?'

Fray Lucas said, 'We are as one in confession.'

And the king said, 'Let the companion go outside, I say.' And commanding that all should go, the king said to Fray Lucas, 'You have done ill to impart this to the Duke of Nájera, for he is my enemy.'⁵

Fray Lucas answered, 'Your Majesty does worse in not giving ears to the gifts of the Holy Spirit, for ears you have, and you should give them where you are well served and not try to stop them up with earth to the detriment of our honour. I well know that Your Majesty is ill-informed but if you will care to hear me, I shall say to you no more than one word.'

The king said, 'It was to speak with you that I called for you.'

Fray Lucas responded, 'Your Majesty should take a carriage and go to Toledo to put your soul in order as best you can.'

Then the king took Fray Lucas by the hand and, pressing it very hard, said, 'What is your feeling about me?'

He answered, 'That Your Majesty is lacking in faith and that those who seek your favour have lionised you; and if Your Majesty desires to be more certain of this I can show you papers.'

The king said, 'And how shall I be able to believe those?'

Fray Lucas responded, 'By other things which are already proven, for the prophets gave no testimony other than what was evident in these things, and by the habit of St Francis which has

*given me to understand the little regard in which you are held in
the Kingdom of Heaven. This, at times, has made me very sad,
for from that hour when Your Majesty closed his ears to
Piedrola, the king's name was expunged from Heaven.'*

*Saying this, Fray Lucas put his hand in his sleeve and
withdrew a bundle of papers which he gave into the king's
hands. And as the king began to unfold it a great quantity of
blood ran from them.*

*Fray Lucas said, 'Without losing any respect for Your
Majesty, I say that you are not worthy to read these things.'*[6]

*And he took them in his hands and rolled them up as before.
And with that I awoke.*

1. *the setting of sails.* The battle between the Armada and the English navy
was imminent, though the sails that are to be set could be either
Spanish or English. The Spanish remained aware of their vulnerability
to sporadic coastal raids, though Lucrecia's visions of Spain's enemies
coming as far inland as Madrid did not come close to materialising in
her lifetime.

2. *I found the king to be much distressed by news that had come to him that some
ships of the Armada, I know not how many, had been lost.* Now Lucrecia
is reporting to us from the future; to her intended audience, these
events are yet to come. The assertion that the Armada would lose some
ships was not a difficult prediction to make. But in December 1587
Lucrecia had told Allende, 'Once the sun was down I saw the defeated
fleet of the Marquis of Santa Cruz fleeing toward the north, having
lost many of its ships and men.'

On 26 August 1588 she would dream of the Ordinary Man telling
her that it was wrong to assume that the Armada sailed under the
protection of the cross. This was a dire warning and a snub to Philip,
who believed that the Armada's fate was in God's hands.

In this vision Philip hears of the loss of some ships. Once his ships
sailed from La Coruña in May 1588 Philip could do nothing but sit and

wait for news. What did he expect, what did he dare to hope – to be told that Parma had made his bridgehead in Kent, that Canterbury and Rochester had fallen, that Elizabeth was suing for peace? His and his country's wait for news was made worse by the knowledge that many things would already have happened weeks before he would learn about them. As Geoffrey Parker (1995) writes, 'The story of the disaster that followed is well known . . . But it was a long time before all this became known in Spain.'

How and when news of the Armada reached Spain is not easy to say, though some official, though not necessarily accurate, messages can be dated. The Armada entered the English Channel on 30 July 1558 and was driven out of Calais Roads and away to the north and east by 7 to 8 August. On 18 August 1588 news reached Burgos, the wool trading centre of Castile, that the Armada had engaged the English fleet and successfully overcome the attacks to continue its progress. This was a fair reflection of the battles in the Channel. On 7 August, the day before the Armada was scattered at Calais, Bernadino de Mendoza wrote to Philip from Rouen. This letter, which reached Madrid in mid-August, inaccurately declared a Spanish victory. Philip immediately wrote to his daughter that 'my Armada has defeated that of England' but he seemed not to believe it without knowing more. It was not long before more accurate reports arrived and these were only too believable. These reports also arrived in late August and early September. Philip then spent another month waiting to discover the full extent of the defeat and the damage to his fleet. On 20 September Medina Sidonia, commander of the Armada, reached the port of Santander and any doubts about the scale of the disaster were swept away. The king was said to have displayed remarkable strength and calm when he first heard the news, though for several months he appeared deeply shocked. On 13 October Philip wrote to all his bishops requesting that services be held to thank God for not destroying everything.

The passage of time lends a sense of inevitability to the defeat of the Armada and we lose the contemporary feeling of wonder at the size and strength of this extraordinary fleet, and the magnitude and depth of the shock and despair that was felt at its destruction. The defeat was a military and psychological catastrophe for Spain. Her troops were by some distance the best and most feared in the world, her empire the greatest, her wealth unrivalled. All this had counted for nothing. Within months of the Armada's defeat Parma's armies suffered their first setback in the Netherlands and a few years later an English fleet took and held Cadiz for a fortnight almost for fun.

3. *I do not remember which order.* Lucrecia says 'I do not know which' and 'I know not how many' and 'I do not remember which' in her account, as if in response to anticipated questions. It could be that Mendoza had begun to press her on the details of her dreams, so that, in each case, she was heading off his queries.

4. *we drew to one side and saw Fray Lucas enter.* This measured conversation between the king and Fray Lucas is more quietly damning of Philip than all the scenes of Spain's destruction. Though the king begins the conversation by criticising Lucas's actions, this priority is quickly reversed. Fray Lucas assumes control. The position of the king is epitomised in a symbolic moment as Philip, the most powerful man in the world, seizes the hand of the Franciscan friar and asks, 'What is your feeling about me?'

   This, we take it, is no matter of curiosity but a pleading for approval. In reply the king is told that he is held in little regard in Heaven. The humiliation of the ruler of half the world is complete when the friar judges him unfit to read the papers he has brought.

5. *'You have done ill to impart this to the Duke of Nájera'.* This dreamt impulse accurately reflects the later feelings of Philip and his advisers. They were displeased that the dream transcripts were circulated among those whom Philip did not favour, and who had thereby come to resent him.

6. *'Without losing any respect for Your Majesty, I say that he is not worthy to read these things.'* 'These things' may well be the transcripts of Lucrecia's dreams. The circulation of these papers was a dilemma for Lucrecia and her patrons in her waking life and in her dreams. So far as we know, they were not sent to the king or to the state authorities by Alonso de Mendoza, and this was to count against him and Lucrecia at their trial.

As I was beginning to go to sleep, I saw a woman nearby. She had a rather long face, of a pale colour which suited her well, an aquiline nose, large eyes and well-shaped dark brown eyebrows. She was dressed in a very white nun's habit with a black veil over her head.

Coming close to me she took my face between her hands and pressed it hard. With the pain that this caused me I said to her, 'Lady, remove your hands, I am in pain for you are hurting me with those metal nails you have in your palms.'

She said to me, 'I come to martyr the flesh to leave the soul clean.[1] I am the Portuguese nun.[2] Will you know me in future?'

At this point I must have made some movement in my face (since I did not like what she was doing to me) and when she saw this she said, 'Why are you making faces?'

Moving my hand from above downwards as though in disdain, I said to her, 'Because truly I am no friend of the Portuguese.'

Now, looking at her more carefully, I saw that she was covered with a cloak of dark reddish brown like the capes of the monks of the Holy Trinity. I said to her, 'How is it that you wear this cloak when it is not of your order?'

She answered, 'Because the Portuguese cloaks are like this.'

As she said this she raised part of her habit beneath her chin and I saw that her throat was so tightly bound that no creature, however small and thin at birth, could be bound so. Indicating her throat, she said to me, 'Do you not have this?'

I said no, and she went on, 'Neither does Martin who reaches so keenly towards God. It has cost me much time on my knees and a deal of fasting.'

I said to her, 'Lady, since you are a saint, warn the king about these times.'

She responded, 'God does not give to anyone more than he can bear. To me He has given the grace to bear these, His wounds, and to you this other task which you must discharge as best you can. I know full well the bad times that are to come but I cannot warn of them for I am not given the grace to do so.'

I said to her, 'Oh Lady, how my head hurts.'

She replied, 'And mine even more for three years now.'

I spoke to her again: 'Lady, have you seen the Armada?'

She did not answer me but brought her hands together, impaling her fingers like an afflicted person and opening up the wounds even more than they had been. She began to weep tears of blood which fell upon my bed and then she disappeared from me and I saw her no more.

Then the Ordinary Man came and said to me, 'Do you wish to come and see some arrows fired by men of faith?'

I answered yes and he took me to the palace where I found His Majesty seated at a great table[3] where many people were eating. The king asked for a drink and I saw that one of the serving gentlemen, in order to mock him, brought him a pitcher of wine and milk (which I had seen poured into it). As he drank from this, the king began to talk a great deal and in a strange language, as though he were out of his mind, laughing and dropping off to sleep by turns. He was talking about awarding dukedoms, lordships and bishoprics and other offices to whomsoever he pleased.

While the king was doing this I saw a man arrive who was dressed in ordinary black clothes. He was of medium height, his face was covered and he carried in his hand a loaded crossbow, its arrow placed ready. He fired many arrows into the king's body at the side where his heart is, but he received them without giving any sign that they hurt him. Seeing that the king showed

no feeling the man with the crossbow said, 'Oh, what a heart of
diamond!' As he said this the Ordinary Man went to him and
took the crossbow and put it behind his own back.

Trapped, the man stepped to one side and there came behind
him three others dressed in the same way (I saw only that they
too covered their faces and carried crossbows and arrows like the
first). Although they too fired arrows into the king he still
made no sign of feeling anything. They began calling him 'heart
of stone' and other such names to signify his toughness and
insensibility.

The Ordinary Man, who was put out by this, said to me, 'You
take this crossbow and shoot at him and see what effect you
have.'

I shot and saw that the first arrow disappeared in the air
without reaching its mark. Seeing this the Ordinary Man
became incensed and his face changed. In amazement, he asked,
'What is this? Is it to be hidden from me?'

He seemed as if he had been caused great sorrow and told me
to shoot again, and I did so. This time the arrow entered his [the
king's] heart and although he gave no sign of pain, water ran
out of him. Speaking to the Ordinary Man, he said, 'It is too
late now for you to become tender-hearted.'

When this was said the Ordinary Man took me to the seashore
where I found the two companions. Leaving me there, the
Ordinary Man went to the Lion Man in some distress and said,
'What is the meaning of this thing that has happened to the girl
and was kept hidden from me?'

He replied, 'I shall tell you and do not be frightened for you
know quite well that what passed during her interview with the
vicario 4 had to be hidden and kept secret so that it should not
reach Philip's ears. That is the meaning of the disappearance of
the first arrow.'

Then the Ordinary Man disappeared from me and I saw him

no more that night. The Lion Man said to me,[5] *'The man that said that he had a heart of diamond was the prophet. The firing of so many arrows without provoking any sign of feeling means that he spent a great deal of time serving him, to no purpose, though he was well occupied for he was carrying out God's commandment. You were given the crossbow to fire at the time of the prophet's imprisonment, since this was the appropriate time for you to fire it. The other people launched their arrows with the spirit of God and prayer, but he made himself deaf to them for he considered them to be talking nonsense. Thus he did not feel their arrows nor did they gain any advantage.*

'The king gave estates to those who did not deserve them and, like men without the sufficiency or understanding to administer what he gave them, they carried out their task according to the condition in which the donor found himself. Later you will be the one to wound him. Death will take him from among you and you must have pity on him because there has never been a king who has had so much and has done less with it.'

And with that I awoke.

1. *'I come to martyr the flesh to leave the soul clean . . .'* Lucrecia lived with the notion that the flesh was part of the realm of the sacred. We are used to the concept of the disembodied soul but this was an invention of early modern Europe. As Caroline Bynum Walker (1989) writes: 'Control, discipline, even torture of the flesh is, in medieval devotion, not so much the rejection of physicality as the elevation of it – a horrible yet delicious elevation – into a means of access to the divine.'

   And in case we should wonder at the fate of our dead flesh in this world where body and soul are as one, 'Orthodox apocalypticism entailed resurrection of bodies as well as souls.'

   The belief was not that the physical and the spiritual would be reunited at the Day of Judgment, but that they had never been separated.

The woman visiting Lucrecia says that God does not give to anyone more than she can bear – the more pain you are given, the more you can bear and the more worthy you are. The word used here is grace. God gives trials and He gives the grace to bear them.

2. *'I am the Portuguese nun.'* This is Sister María del Visitación, also known as the Nun of Lisbon. Prioress of a Dominican convent, she was famous for her stigmata – open wounds in her side that oozed blood in the shape of a cross. She also experienced visions as well as miraculous levitations and various ecstatic visitations. All of this began in 1575, just a dozen years before Lucrecia's dream career began. Sister María's message became more political with the annexation of Portugal by Spain in 1580. By late 1588 she had become confident enough to say, 'The kingdom of Portugal does not belong to Philip II, but to the Braganza family. If the king of Spain does not restore the throne that he unjustly usurped, then God will punish him severely' (quoted in Kagan, 1990).

Her wounds were not now 'only' a sacred miracle but a symbol of the fate of Portugal under the Spanish.

This was the situation when Lucrecia dreamed this dream but this open political dissidence could not be tolerated for long. In December 1588 the Inquisition in Lisbon found Sister María guilty of trickery and deceit – her wounds were self-inflicted and her miracles performed by illusion – and sentenced her to life exile in Brazil. Richard Kagan points out that two weeks before the sentence was published Lucrecia had a dream in which she was told that Sister María was a false prophet. 'Evidently, advance information about the Inquisition's findings had reached Madrid, and Lucrecia, aware of the dangers awaiting false visionaries, hoped to avoid Sister María's fate by establishing herself as a seer who spoke only the truth.'

3. *he took me to the palace where I found His Majesty seated at a great table.* In this passage Lucrecia depicts the king's weakness and his cold-heartedness. He becomes hopelessly drunk on wine and milk – a combination of the worldly and the innocent – but has no feeling in his heart.

The oddest part of the vision is the reaction of the Ordinary Man to the disappearance of Lucrecia's first arrow. He realises that something is happening that he has not been told about. This first makes him angry, then he feels saddened. His reaction is that of a man faced with the knowledge that he is not as important as he thought.

He hurries Lucrecia off to find an explanation from the Lion Man. But there is no consolation for him in having to be told the meaning of what he has seen – this merely confirms his lower status.

4. *'you know quite well . . . what passed during her interview with the vicario'*. The reference to Lucrecia's first arrest, which happened the previous month, comes in a conversation between the Lion Man and the Ordinary Man. Juan Blázquez Miguel (1987) quotes a witness as saying:

> Lucrecia declared before the *vicario* in January 1588, she had dreamed that because of the sins that the King, our Lord, had committed in killing his son and the queen, lady Isabel, and in taking land from the peasants and many other things which are a matter of the exercise of justice but of little help to the poor, whose enemy he was, that God wanted to take him and his son. And that nobody of his lineage should remain, and that the *Moriscos* (rising in rebellion and allying themselves with the Turks) and the heretics (French and English, who would enter by way of Navarre) were to destroy Spain and only Toledo was to be left, where the King, our Lord, and the archbishop were to retire and die a natural death . . . And Piedrola was to be chosen king in competition with the prince of Pascoli and the duke of Pastrama . . .

Not only is this an authentic account of what Lucrecia declared before the *vicario*, it is an accurate summary of the political content of her dreams.

5. *The Lion Man said to me.* The Lion Man's interpretation of this dream is unusual in its detail and its overt political content. The original transcript uses mainly pronouns in this section so that it is not always clear who is being referred to at any point in the passage. The translation preserves the spirit of the original but the following may help to clarify the sense.

The Lion Man explains that the man who described the king as having a heart of diamond is the prophet – i.e. Piedrola. The meaning of the arrows and the king's lack of reaction concerns Piedrola's time in the king's service. We can take this to be his period in the king's army or the time he spent trying to warn the king to change his ways. The Lion Man said that neither of these had any beneficial effect on the king, in the same way that the arrows did not hurt him.

The next sentence is important because the Lion Man explicitly states that Lucrecia's role is to take over from Piedrola now that he is imprisoned – this is why she was given the crossbow to fire. Later on he says that Lucrecia will be the one who will wound Philip. The others who fire arrows are also trying to warn Philip and are also ignored by the king.

That same 17 March I slept again and dreamed that I was in the house of a man called Pedro Robles,[1] who keeps a lodging house for archers in my neighbourhood. There, in a bedroom,[2] I came across Parra, a graduate of the university. He was seated on a bench and in the same room I saw the landlord's wife lying on her left side on a bed, with an infant suckling at her left breast. The front of her body was covered from the breast down with a rug, but her back was exposed from her shoulders to her feet.

Seeing me there, the woman said to me, 'We know all about you.'

I asked, 'From whom?'

Her husband replied, 'From a letter that Don Guillén has sent to me in which he gave me an account of all your visions. And with it he sent me a sword and a helmet and said that I must join in the defence against the enemy.'

I said to him, 'How is it that such a bad Christian as Don Guillén has done such a thing? Who brought the letter?'

He replied that it had been Parra, so I turned to him and asked angrily, 'Who ordered you to bring it?'

He answered me, 'Don Guillén, because he had need of people and called upon this man.'

I turned to the said Robles[3] and asked him, 'Since you are a man who knows about these times and even more about what may happen to women, how is it that you have never tried to tell me anything or let anyone know?'

Becoming very anxious, he looked at my left arm which was bare and made to cut it off at the mid-point.

I said to him, 'So that you may know with what justice I speak, I believe that even if it were cut I would not feel it.'

I spoke to Robles again and said, 'Since you are a man who

217

has always ruled his life according to the stars, how is it that you have not given information to the king (you being his servant) of what is to happen this year?'

He replied, 'In order to live a quiet life, for if I had told of these things I know that I would have had the most troublesome fate in the land. Because I am of the house of Burgundy and the king has done so much harm in those lands, I would have been accused of treason. It has been better that you have revealed these things for you cannot be accused of harbouring any claims. And look at all the weapons the king has made me clean so that as many men as possible could go out and defend themselves.'

When this had been said the woman on the bed made a sign to me to be silent and I understood this was so that her husband could go with Parra (who, out of fear at what I had said, had gone into the street). The husband left then and the anger I had felt abated as I saw that my arm was now covered. I went to the woman on the bed and said to her, 'Come, tell me for what cause Don Guillén sent the letter to your husband.'

'Cover me up,' she said, and I pulled up the bedclothes and covered her. Then she asked for something to eat and I saw that they brought her two poached eggs and some bread. 'You know that in the letter that Don Guillén sent to my husband he told him to hide the arms that he had got from the king and this is what he is doing, and already he is cleaning the helmets.'

While saying this, she ate the yolks of the eggs and gave the whites to me and I ate them. Then she said, 'I wish to go to [the place of] the victory.'

We found ourselves there and I saw that all was knocked down save the chapel of the sepulchre. Then I saw my mother arrive and the woman with me went up to her and said, 'Ah Lady, what heavy sins I have.'

My mother said, 'How so? What are they?'

She replied, 'I have worked so that the labour of a certain woman shall go wrong. Come with me and I will show you who.'

She took me to a vegetable garden above Leganitos[4] and there we saw that there was a cabbage set upon a great pile of long hair which was blazing. I saw that with the heat the cabbage was opening up, and she said, 'Just so are the thighs of So-and-so (naming her) opening up.'

Then I said, 'How can it be remedied?' and she answered, 'By throwing on a little water.'

I went to the spring of Leganitos and brought a great pitcher of water and threw it on. Then I saw Don Alonso spurring his mule along and I said to Martin, his servant, 'Whence comes Don Alonso?' and he answered, 'From the convent.'

I asked him how I could get to Piedrola's house and he showed me a road. Leaving my mother and the other woman I found myself on an area of grass, not tall but very thick, and, after much walking, I saw that the vegetable patch had become a garden. And coming towards me, I saw my mother and the other woman (who wore a very white shift and a head-dress of a Turkish style).

Being all together in that garden, I saw a man sitting in a corner on the grass and heard him begin to sing, 'Cherries. Do you want cherries?' He repeated this many times.

I asked him, 'Who are you? Are you my father?'

He answered, 'No, I am the owner of the garden.'

I asked him the way out and he said, 'Over the waterwheel.'

I told my mother and the other woman, 'No one must pass until I have made sure it is safe.'

Going to it I placed a foot upon it and sank into the water. I said, 'There is treason here.'

Then the man said, 'May the Devil protect whoever has taught you so much. Well would I prosper if he were in my garden.'

*I walked around the walls of the garden seeking a way out
and discovered a secret door hidden by a layer of plaster. I kicked
it and as it fell a river was revealed, with a wide meadow at its
bank. I sat down there out of pure tiredness, saying, 'Let those
who are thirsty drink and give thanks to God who has brought
us out into level country free of all the treason and troubles the
world had prepared for us.'*

And with that I awoke.

1. *I slept again and dreamed that I was in the house of a man called Pedro Robles.*
   It is becoming more common for Lucrecia to dream without being
   accompanied by the Ordinary Man. She is increasingly autonomous
   as well as increasingly active in her dreams.

2. *There, in a bedroom.* The scene in the bedroom is quite novel for Lucrecia
   and shows an appreciation of some of the consequences of her dreams.
   In real life Robles runs a boarding house for soldiers. In the dream he
   says that he is sent arms by the king in order to clean them so that
   people can be sent out to defend themselves. Don Guillén de Casaos
   has written to him seeking support for Lucrecia's cause and, according
   to Robles's wife, telling him to hide the king's weapons. Robles is being
   courted by both the king and Casaos. This is a clear indication that
   Lucrecia and her supporters will not be fighting for the king in the
   battle to come.

   Robles becomes angry when Lucrecia asks him why he has not
   warned her about what is to happen to her. He is known to Lucrecia
   as an astrologer and his answer implies that he too knows that terrible
   things are to happen to Spain and to Philip but that he cannot tell
   anyone what they are.

3. *I turned to the said Robles.* In Zambrano et al. this name is transcribed here
   as Rojas but the conversations in the bedroom only really make sense
   if we take Rojas and Robles to be the same man. We have therefore
   decided that this is the original intention and have replaced 'Rojas'
   with 'Robles'.

4. *She took me to a vegetable garden above Leganitos . . .* The remainder of this dream has hallucinatory qualities which will be recognised by all dreamers: the melting of one scene into another, the shifting in and out of characters, the entirely self-centred viewpoint, the slight sense of paranoia and the escape. These make the flow of the narrative less important than the evocation of atmosphere.

The last part of this dream, from 'Leaving my mother and the other woman' onwards contains themes familiar to dreamers:

Lucrecia leaves her mother and the other woman, but later sees them coming towards her. She meets a man in the garden and bizarrely asks him if he is her father. She wishes to leave and take the others with her out of the garden, but there is no way out that is safe. Lucrecia kicks a hidden door out of the wall (forcing herself from one state to another by apparently invisible means) and sees a captivating vision of a 'level country', of a river with a wide meadow at its bank. Finally she comes to rest 'out of pure tiredness' – a paradoxical yet familiar desire in the middle of sleep.

Is this the end that Lucrecia desires – to emerge out of vengeance and destruction into the tranquillity of the level country?

Having been awake all night with a severe fever, I went to sleep at six o'clock in the morning and dreamed that a man whom I did not know entered and told me that Don Diego de Córdoba was in my house. I said to the man, 'What does he want of me?'

He answered, 'To tell you that Fray Lucas is with the king.'

'What does Fray Lucas want? That I should go and teach him how to speak? I do not wish anyone to come in here.'

Having said this I woke and in a little while slept again.

Then I dreamed that the king was sitting in a chair at my bedside[1] and I heard him say, 'Lady, Fray Lucas told me that you were lying indisposed in bed and therefore I am come to see you.'

I replied, 'In his fear of you Fray Lucas thought to excuse me by saying I was indisposed but your nails can no longer hurt me.'

Philip answered me, 'Look! I am the king.'

And I said, 'I would take greater pleasure from a visit from Piedrola.'

Thinking that I did not yet recognise him, he said again, 'Do you not see that I am the king?'

And I answered, 'For this year.'[2]

He said to me, 'I have come to ask what will happen to my son, for he is ill.'

I answered, 'Bear in mind that he is like the son of David and give thanks to God that He does not take him – in time your counsel could harm him.'

Lowering my eyes to look at his feet, I saw that they were naked and asked, 'In what did Your Majesty come?'

He replied, 'In a litter.'

And I said to him, 'Be sure to return on foot.'

He said, 'I want nothing from you except that you do not
expose me.'

I answered, 'Alas, Philip, if only you knew whose hand holds
the tambourine!'

I intended to give him a message but I awoke to the noise of
Fray Lucas and my mother entering my room.

1. *the king was sitting in a chair at my bedside.* Lucrecia is sick in the waking
world and in her dream. She clearly does not want any visitors. She
lost her respect for the king some time ago and now has another
chance to show her disdain.

For his part, the king is gracious enough to be concerned not for
himself but for his son – with good reason. His fourth wife Anna of
Austria had borne him five children, four of whom died before the age
of seven. Philip, the only surviving son (the king had two surviving
daughters from his previous marriage to Isabel de Valois) was now ten
years old. Philip was well used to family deaths – his mother, his father,
his sister, his four wives, five of his children. He must have feared for
his son every time he became ill.

2. *'Do you not see that I am the king?' And I answered, 'For this year.'* Lucrecia's
predictions of Philip's death did not immediately come true, neither
did the invasion and destruction of Spain come to pass in the way she
envisioned. Nevertheless this year was, in hindsight, the zenith of
Spanish power – after 1588 Spain never held the world in its hands
again. Philip lived another ten years, during which he fought yet
another futile war, this time against the claimant to, and subsequent
occupant of, the French throne, Henry IV. While Spanish troops were
in France, Dutch republican forces took back the north-eastern
provinces of the Netherlands. On the northern frontiers of Mexico
Spanish troops were fought to a standstill by indigenous Indians, and
in 1598 an Indian uprising in Chile took back much of the land
conquered by the Spanish in the preceding decade. English and Dutch
privateers preyed on the Spanish transatlantic trade while joint expeditions against Spanish-American colonies occasionally halted it

altogether. Harvests failed in Castile, leading to depopulation of rural areas and desertion of villages. Manufacturing in the towns was crippled by the inflationary effects of American silver.

But we should be wary of seeing history as a succession of military, political or even economic events or as the story of the rise and decline of nations. It can be argued that Spanish control of Europe and the world was always an illusion; an expensive, destructive illusion that was better ended for all concerned. While some have suggested that, after 1588, Spain slipped back into isolation from Europe, it is plain that the work of Cervantes, Lope de Vega, Velázquez, Suárez, Calderón, Murillo, Quevedo and their contemporaries placed Spain at the centre of European culture. Spain's place in the world did not end in 1588, but it undoubtedly changed.

If Lucrecia's visions of Spain's physical destruction did not come to pass, what about her visions of her own future? We have two stories to resolve: the story of Lucrecia in the waking world and the story of the Lucrecia who appears in her own dreams. Firstly Lucrecia de Léon, citizen of Madrid.

On 19 April 1590 the former royal secretary Antonio Pérez, held in prison on the charge of murdering a fellow courtier Juan de Escobedo in 1578, escaped and fled to Aragón. The escape threw the regime into turmoil. Pérez had maintained that he had acted with the connivance of the king and many at court (including Lucrecia's supporters) thought him misused as a convenient scapegoat by Philip. Pérez's escape was welcomed by half the court and an embarrassing situation became potentially dangerous for the king and his close Council. Previously tolerant of mild dissidence, they now saw possible sedition in every criticism. Dissent of any kind was viewed with suspicion. Within two weeks of the Pérez escape Fray Diego de Chaves, the royal confessor, decided Lucrecia de Léon must be silenced. Juan Ortiz de Salvatierra, an officer of the Inquisition, began investigations and interviewed both Fray Lucas de Allende and Lucrecia.

On 20 May 1590 an officer of the Toledo Inquisition visited Alonso de Mendoza's house and took away hidden papers including transcriptions of Lucrecia's dreams. Three days later the Supreme Council of the Inquisition met to discuss Lucrecia's case and two days after that asked the king to sanction the arrest of Lucrecia and her associates. The king's secretary Mateo Vázquez gained the king's consent and immediately, on the evening of 25 May, ordered the Inquisition to make the arrests. Lucrecia, Allende and Diego de Vitores were arrested in Madrid that night, while Guillén de Casaos and Alonso de Mendoza were seized in Toledo on the following day. All were transferred to the Inquisition prison in Toledo.

There was a set procedure for the 'trials of faith' undertaken by the Inquisition which involved gathering evidence, interviewing the accused, putting charges to the accused and giving them the opportunity to defend themselves. Finally all the evidence, including the various statements of the defendants, would be put before the judges who would decide which crimes they were guilty of, and pass sentence. Interrogation of the accused might involve torture, a widespread practice in the judicial systems of medieval and early modern Europe, though one for which the Spanish Inquisition is particularly notorious. An *auto de fe*, literally 'act of faith', would then be held, either in private or public, at which the conviction would be read and the sentence carried out. The severest punishment was to be burned at the stake, the mildest to do penance. After the first twenty years of the Inquisition, which were marked by extreme savagery, the rate of executions was very low and reserved for unrepentant heretics. Kamen (1997b) writes: 'The proportionately small number of executions is an effective argument against the legend of a bloodthirsty tribunal.'

Despite the Inquisition's fearsome reputation the Toledo prison and interrogation regime was ludicrously lax. The suspects were questioned and all professed ignorance or denied any wrongdoing or blamed each other. Mendoza was the notable exception. He wrote to the Catholic authorities in Rome claiming that he had been arrested for the political offence of protesting against taxes on the clergy. Meanwhile he appealed on legal grounds against the prejudice of several officers of the Inquisition. This unusual tactic threw the normally meticulous Inquisition process off track. The investigation of Mendoza's complaints took an inordinate amount of time, during which the proceedings against the suspects ground to a halt.

In the prison itself Mendoza carried enough weight to live pleasantly and to elicit favours for his fellow accused. Guillén de Casaos gave evidence that 'the warden and his assistant, Miguel de Xea, ate and drank in his [Mendoza's] cell; ordinarily there were many birds and capons, blancmange, cakes and pastries, and other foods; the cell was more like a tavern than anything else, because of the noise at mealtimes during the day, and at night they stayed on drinking, eating and talking until 9 or 10 o'clock' (quoted in Kagan, 1990).

There were also allegations that Lucrecia herself had been in Alonso de Mendoza's cell together with other women and in the company of two of the Inquisition's officials Zárate and Mendoza. There is some evidence that the Inquisitor Lope de Mendoza was captivated by Lucrecia and unwilling to proceed against her. It goes without saying that the prisoners freely communicated with each other and Mendoza did likewise with the outside world.

This general laxity ended with the appointment of a new Inquisitor, Pedro Pacheco, in September 1591. He dismissed the existing officials and arrested the prison warder, his assistant and several of Mendoza's servants. Lucrecia was interrogated on 4 November 1591 about her part in the prison abuses and, when her answers proved unsatisfactory, was tortured for the first time on 7 December 1591. In the torture chamber (a transcript of the session was made and is still preserved) she said that she wished to 'discharge her conscience about everything' and begged not to be tortured again. She said that she knew she had been very bad but was not to blame for dreaming 'those cursed black dreams' and for telling them to Don Alonso de Mendoza.

A new set of inquisitors arrived in December 1591 and now Lucrecia began to show a keen forensic intelligence. She admitted that she dreamed many dreams, but said that she did not want them written down and that the heresies they contained were the fault of the transcribers. Concerning the dreams which criticised the king, she said that she could not remember them well, but that she did not speak of these to anyone except Allende and Mendoza and did not defame the king. For every charge about a specific dream that the new Inquisitor Sotocameño brought Lucrecia had a ready answer – either she could not remember specific passages, or someone else had invented this detail, or she had never believed in the dreams, or she did not understand what she dreamed. At no time did Lucrecia confess her guilt. The procedure of the Inquisition meant that the other suspects were re-examined in the light of what she said before their counter-claims were then put to her. The machinery of the Inquisition process ground slowly on.

In June 1595, five years after her trial had begun, the Supreme Council of the Inquisition began to lose patience and ordered a progress report. They then instructed the Inquisitors to torture Lucrecia again to get to the truth. On 23 June 1595 she was taken back to the torture chamber. Once again she showed her nimble intelligence. First telling the Inquisitors that she invented some of the dreams about the loss of Spain in order to please Allende and Mendoza, she said she also thought these were things the king should know. Accused of lying and on the point of being tortured she said that only a few of the dreams were her own; all of the others were invented by Mendoza, even to the point where he instructed her to memorise them so that she could recite them to others. She was willing to do this because Mendoza told her it would 'offer a lesson to His Majesty, to help the Republic, and to stop the king from appointing to office people who did not merit it'.

This was enough, it seems, to save her from torture. Days later she confused her interrogators again by saying that she did not invent the dreams about, for example, the loss of the Armada, but it was Allende and Mendoza who had interpreted them in a bad light. She also said she forgot many of the dreams once they were written down so could not accurately say what she dreamed and what she invented. She was impossible to pin down.

In July 1595 it was decided that the trial process had lasted long enough. All of the evidence was placed before three judges. One judge believed her guilty of inventing dreams for seditious purposes, possibly in league with the Devil, while another, Juan de Pantoja, took the opposite view: 'she is not to blame nor did she ever want her dreams transcribed, and indeed it had pained her to dream them'. The third judge believed her guilty of at least some of the charges brought against her.

On 20 August 1595, five years and three months after her arrest, Lucrecia de Léon appeared at a private *auto de fe* in a Dominican monastery in Toledo. She was found guilty of blasphemy, falsehood, sacrilege, sedition, making a pact with the Devil, allowing her dreams to be transcribed and encouraging others to prophesy the future. We might expect that such crimes would attract the severest punishment but Lucrecia was probably aware that the condemnation was not unanimous and that she had become a nuisance rather than a threat to the Church and king. Her punishment was one hundred lashes, exile from Madrid and two years' seclusion in a religious house. The sentence may have been lessened in view of Lucrecia's status as a mother – she had given birth to a daughter in prison in 1590. Diego de Vitores was the father.

Fray Lucas de Allende was eventually sentenced in March 1596 to one year's seclusion in a religious house. He was last heard of living in a Franciscan house in the town of Ciudad Real. Don Alonso de Mendoza was, after a protracted series of sentences and appeals, finally sentenced in September 1597 to two years' seclusion in a religious house. This light sentence took account of his already lengthy (seven and a half years') imprisonment. He went to a monastery on the outskirts of Toledo where, thanks to his connections, he lived in some style. He decided to stay after his sentence was served and died there in the autumn of 1603.

Guillén de Casaos died in prison in October 1595 before being sentenced. Diego de Vitores, the scribe who became Lucrecia's lover and the father of her child, was, in view of his time in prison, reprimanded and exiled from Toledo and Madrid for two years. He was last heard of living in his home town of Zamora.

Where, though, did Lucrecia go? The best efforts of historians have not so far managed to track her much beyond the passing of her sentence. There was some difficulty in finding a religious house that would take her, particularly as her father refused to pay the keep for herself and her now five-year-old daughter. After leaving a hospital in Toledo which had temporarily accommodated her, she disappeared from the written record. Her career and her intrusion into history were over.

The Well, the Christ-Child and the City at the End of the World | Chapter 35

THE SECOND DREAM OF 19 MARCH 1588

On 19 March 1588, the date of the dream which concerns us now, Lucrecia's arrest, imprisonment, trial and punishment were still to come. Lucrecia continued to dream and to tell others of her dreams up to and even after her arrest. But the story within her dreams is different from the story of her dreams. In the first few months in which her dreams were recorded Lucrecia saw the imminent destruction of Spain and of her world in firstly symbolic and then increasingly naturalistic visions. Then her dreams began to involve herself and her supporters. They appeared as onlookers, then as participants in the unfolding events. They began to receive instructions, through Lucrecia's visions, on how to act when the crisis came. Lucrecia and her companions, along with most of their contemporaries, believed in the near-imminent end of the world. Her dreams became increasingly urgent in their warnings of when and how this would happen. But how long could this urgency continue? How long could Lucrecia continue to prophesy the end of the world? How could the story within her dreams be brought to an end without the end of the world?

In the last two nights Lucrecia, suffering from a fever, has had an interrupted sleep. She has dreamed of a conversation with the king and of a group of people preparing for the conflict to come. But she has also dreamed of the Nun of Lisbon showing her how God provides the grace to bear the trials that He inflicts, and of an escape to 'a level country' where her troubles are behind her. In the dream with which this book ends, Lucrecia experiences a vision of grace.

After this, although her dreams still show exuberance and variety, she became caught in the necessity of reiteration and the momentum of her visions melted in the light of the world's persistence. In this dream Lucrecia comes to a resolution of the troubles which her dreams have brought her and provides an ending to the story within her dreams.

The Ordinary Man does not appear in this final dream, nor the Old Fisherman, nor the Lion Man, the king, Fray Lucas, nor any person from Lucrecia's waking life. The dream has allusions and echoes of biblical and other sacred stories and its descriptions of the scene at the well and of the journey with the children have an allegorical quality. Above all Lucrecia manages to give the story within the vision a sacred intensity and mythic sweep while also providing the descriptive detail that gives it life. If this is something that Lucrecia does throughout her dreams, on this occasion she surpasses herself. The miraculous event at the well is grounded by the meticulous description of the Christ-child's clothes. And the epic journey is transformed into reality by one momentary action – the shaking out of the little girl's skirts – itself a stroke of genius by the unconscious author. The childlike qualities of the epic are given maturity by the observance of the everyday. The mythic is dissolving into its twin offspring – literature and history.

At the end of the dream we are allowed to share both the immensity of the task that Lucrecia has completed and her mixture of satisfaction and loss as the children walk away from her. Had Lucrecia's visions been preserved for this alone we would have cause to give thanks for this dream-washed woman and her band of scribes. They have bequeathed something precious to a world quite beyond their dreams.

That same day of 19th March, having eaten, I lay down to sleep and dreamed that I was in the countryside on a dark night. I saw many people lying down as though to sleep on the ground and in the middle of them was a well. The light of the moon (although I could not see it) shone on some of them and they woke and said to me, 'Give us a drink for this well has both rope and bucket.'

I began to raise buckets of water and then whistled to them as a herdsman does to his stock when calling them to drink. They got up and came to drink. All were dressed in black and amongst them was an old man who said to me, 'You are to wash the ears of these men with this water.' When he had said this I saw him no more.

I settled my right knee on the ground and, without untying the rope from the bucket, I passed my left arm through the handle and lifted it on to my left knee. Then, as each man came to drink, I dipped my right hand into the water and washed his ears with it. In this way I passed the whole night, giving drink and washing those men.

Then the old man who had been there at the beginning appeared to me again and said, 'A good Rebecca you have been, but this will be the last bucket you will draw and with it you will receive grace.' I set myself to drawing the bucket of water and as I pulled on it the weight of it became so much that I felt my strength failing. It was not even enough to stand on the rope to prevent it slipping back while I worked with my hands, for the bucket again began to descend and it seemed that it would draw me after it. In the end I worked so hard that, with great difficulty, I got the bucket out of the well.

When I had hauled it up I looked at the water that was in it and saw it to be much clearer than before, even though all of it had been very clear. On top of the bucket was a boy child about the size of a two-year-old. He had a most beautiful face and smooth, blond hair down to his ears (like the plaits that I have seen worn by the boys and girls who come from the mountains to sell things at court). He was dressed in a white linen shirt, open at the front, its yoke sewn with black thread and its sleeve openings were wide to show his arms. Over this shirt he wore a garment of silk in that colour they call purple. This was quite short, no longer than the shirt which just came to his knee, and its sleeves (it had sleeves) were no longer than the mid-point of his arm, and quite tight. It too was open in front like the shirt. In his right hand he carried a sphere about the size of an ordinary ball or a sweet lime. It was of a dirty black colour and I saw that on its upper part was set a cross of proportionate size and from its lower half hung many minute chains all twisted about each other.

This small person, dressed and adorned in this way, stood with one foot on each side of the rim of the bucket. His small hands held the sides of his little garments apart and seemed to invite whoever looked at him to cover up his chubby, gleaming little body with them.

Still holding the bucket in my hands, raised above the ground before me, I said to him, 'Child, whose son are you?'

He answered, 'I am a father.'

So saying, he descended from the bucket to the ground. Then the old man came to me with his face covered and took the bucket from my hand and I saw no more of him.

Day began to dawn and some of the men sleeping there began to become visible while others remained obscure. The child said to me, 'Pick me up in your arms.' I answered him, 'Truly I am very tired, you have left me exhausted with your great weight.'

Then he said, 'I weighed even more upon Christopher,' and because he gave signs that it would please him to have me carry him, I bent down to do so. I held him close to my breast and his little stomach was level with my chin and he said to me, 'I also have with me a little girl if you can carry her, for she is very weary. But you are tired too, so you would not be able to.'

Having left the men behind, I was walking towards the east and, glancing down to my left, I saw beside me a little girl of some five years – dark complexioned, with black eyes and eyebrows. She wore widow's weeds and was covered with a shawl and walked, it seemed to me, with much fatigue, holding on to the side of my clothing. Seeing her like this and in an effort to comfort her, I said, 'Where do you want to go to, my love?' and she said, 'I want you to take me to the high city.'

Then the boy child said to me, 'A river lies along the way to the place the girl speaks of and you must seek a place where it can be crossed. I did not wish to give you so much trouble but since she wishes it we must go there.'

I said to her encouragingly, 'Hold on tight, do not get lost, I will take you there.'

While speaking we had walked so far to the east that it seemed to me that we had reached the end of the world. We came up against a rock face which at this point appeared to reach all the way to Heaven.

The boy child said to me, 'We must go this way. It is what the girl wants.'

So I turned to the left as he indicated and climbed some hills and high cliffs. Once at the top, my little boy said to me, 'I have nothing to eat.'

Wishing to give him something, I looked about but there was nothing. Then the child extended his little hand, saying, 'This fruit grows among the jagged peaks and so there is no softer fruit for these troubled times.'

I looked at what he had in his hand and saw that it was a ripe apricot which he then ate. Then we arrived at the river and my boy looked at the girl there on the bank and said to me, 'Look what a great task this girl has given you. But go across, I shall set you on the promised land.'

Entering the river I immediately found myself on the other side with my little boy and girl. And then I came to enter into a city through an eastern gate, a gate through which I had passed on other occasions.

My little boy said to me, 'You are now in Toledo and, until you leave me at a church to which I shall guide you, you must not put me on the ground.'

Then, going up through the streets and turning to the right, I came to a church with steps in front of its door and pillars with capitals. There I set down my little boy, leaving him upon the topmost step. And that same girl who had travelled, clinging to my side, now went to one side of the doorway and,

233

keeping her face turned towards the church, shook all the dust from her little skirts.

My little boy waited until she had done this and when she joined him she placed her right hand on his head and they entered the church together.

And with that I awoke.

Acknowledgements

Lucrecia de Léon first came to my attention through the work of Richard Kagan (see Sources). Professor Kagan was immediately enthusiastic about my own interest in the subject. He has promptly and accurately answered all of my questions and has been immensely encouraging.

I have also received invaluable support from my editors Will Sulkin and Jörg Hensgen. As well as cajoling and encouraging, they have, on more than one occasion, saved this book from the self-indulgence of its author.

This book could not have been written without the meticulous, imaginative and expert work of the translator, Penelope Shortt. Lucrecia de Léon's dreams were originally transcribed as they were spoken with little attempt at punctuation or at clarification of meaning. As well as the difficulties that this presents, Spanish usage has changed in some significant ways since the late sixteenth century. This, together with the never-ending sentences and the extensive use of pronouns, can make the task of deciphering fiendishly difficult. Quite apart from the technical obstacles, any translation of this kind faces the problem of tone. The dream transcripts often have a mythic and sometimes a poetic quality, and they are the record of a speaker from another age. We wanted to preserve something of the 'sound' of a sixteenth-century voice, while avoiding the archness that can come from the literal presentation of an archaic text. Penelope Shortt has overcome these obstacles to produce an English version of the dreams that is both beautiful in itself and true to the original transcripts.

I am also indebted to Martin Toland and to Walter Robinson for their assistance.

I would like to thank all of these people for their support, while acknowledging that any errors are entirely my responsibility.

Sources

The principal sources for information about Lucrecia, her life and her dreams are Richard Kagan's *Lucrecia's Dreams* and *Sueños y procesos de Lucrecia de Léon* by María Zambrano, Edison Sims and Juan Blázquez Miguel. Kagan's book contains a full calendar of Lucrecia's dreams together with the locations of the transcripts within the Archivo Histórico Nacional, while Zambrano et al. has an appendix containing the transcripts of all of the dreams that are in this book, given in the original Castilian. Kagan's book is a very readable account of Lucrecia's life. I am happy to acknowledge my debt to this work.

There are many books in English on the Spanish Golden Age. The modern reader is particularly fortunate that both Geoffrey Parker and Henry Kamen have published such informative books in the last two decades. Both these authors have managed to produce work that is both academically rigorous and highly readable.

The works listed below include all those cited in the text together with books and articles used as sources of information which are not directly quoted.

Barnes, Robin (1988) *Prophecy and Gnosis: Apocalypticism in the Wake of the Lutheran Reformation*, University of California Press, Stanford

Benassar, Bartolomé (1979) *The Spanish Character: Attitudes and Mentalities from the 16 to 19 centuries*, University of California Press, Berkeley

Burns, Jimmy (1994) *Spain: A Literary Companion*, John Murray, London

Bynum Walker, Caroline (1989) 'The Female Body and Religious Practice in the Later Middle Ages', in *Fragments for a History of the Human Body*, Pt 1, Urzone, New York

Calendar of State Papers, England and Spain, vol. XIII, July 1554–November 1558. 1954.

Carroll, Robert and Prickett, Stephen (1997) 'Introduction', in *The Bible: Authorized King James Version with Apocrypha*, Oxford University Press, Oxford

Cervantes, Miguel de (1604) *The Adventures of Don Quixote*, trans. J. M. Cohen, Penguin, Harmondsworth, 1950

Collins, Roger (1989) *The Arab Conquest of Spain, 710–97*, Oxford University Press, Oxford

Collins, Roger (1995) *Early Medieval Spain, Unity in Diversity 400–1000*, 2nd edn, Macmillan Press, Basingstoke

Coplestone, Frederick (1953) *A History of Philosophy*, vol. 3, part 2, *The Revival of Platonism to Suaréz*, Newman Press, Westminster, Maryland

Critchley, Macdonald (ed.) (1978) *Butterworths Medical Dictionary*, 2nd edn, Butterworths, London and Boston

Crow, W. B. (1968) *Precious Stones*, Aquarian, London

Davies, Norman (1997) *Europe: A History*, Pimlico, London

Desfourneaux, Marcelin (1970) *Daily Life in Spain in the Golden Age*, George Allen & Unwin, London

Empson, Jacob (1989) *Sleep and Dreaming*, Faber and Faber, London

Enslin, Morton (1971) 'The Apocalyptic Literature,' in *The Interpreter's Guide to the Bible*, ed. Charles M. Laymon, Collins, London

Freud, Sigmund (1900) *The Interpretation of Dreams*, trans. James Strachey, Penguin Freud Library vol. 4, Penguin, Harmondsworth, 1953

Hamilton, E. J. (1934) *The American Treasure and the Price Revolution in Spain, 1501–1650*, Harvard University Press, Cambridge, Mass.

Hill, David (1993) 'Dreams', in *Oxford Companion to the Bible*, ed. Bruce M. Metzger and Michael D. Coogan, Oxford University Press, Oxford

Homer, *The Odyssey*, trans. E. V. Rieu, Penguin, Harmondsworth, 1946

Hourani, Albert (1991) *History of the Arab Peoples*, Faber and Faber, London

Jung, C. G. (1954) *Against Job*, trans. R. F. C. Hull, Routledge, London, 1954

Kagan, Richard (1990) *Lucrecia's Dreams: Politics and Prophecy in Sixteenth-Century Spain*, University of California Press, Berkeley

Kamen, Henry (1997a) *Philip of Spain*, Yale University Press, New Haven

Kamen, Henry (1997b) *The Spanish Inquisition: An Historical Revision*, Weidenfeld and Nicolson, London

Kermode, Frank (1967) *The Sense of an Ending*, Oxford University Press, New York

Langland, William (*c.* 1362) *Piers Plowman*, Dent, London and Dutton, New York, 1912

Loades, David (1989) *Mary Tudor: A Life*, Blackwell, Oxford

Lynch, John (1991) *Spain 1516–1598: From Nation State to World Empire*, Blackwell, Oxford

Mackay, A. (1977) *Spain in the Middle Ages*, Macmillan Press, Basingstoke.

Marañón, Gregorio (1954) *Antonio Pérez:'Spanish Traitor'*, Hollis and Carter, London

Martin, C. and Parker, G. (1988) *The Spanish Armada*, revised edn., Mandolin, Manchester, 1999

Mattingly, Garrett (1959) *The Defeat of the Spanish Armada*, 2nd edn. Jonathan Cape, London, 1983

Miguel, Juan Blázquez *see* Zambrano et al. (1987)

Milhou, Alain (1983) *Colón y su mentalidad mesiánica en el ambiente franciscanista español*, Casa-Museo de Colón, Valladolid

Motley, John Lothrop (1900) *The Rise of the Dutch Republic*, 5 vols, Harper & Bros, New York and London

O'Malley, C. D. (1964) *Andreas Vesalius of Brussels 1514–1564*, University of California Press, Berkeley

Palley, Julian (1983) *The Ambiguous Mirror: Dreams in Spanish Literature*, Chapel Hill, North Carolina

Parker, Geoffrey (1985) *The Dutch Revolt*, revised edn, Penguin, Harmondsworth

Parker, Geoffrey (1995) *Philip II*, 3rd edn., Open Court, Chicago

Rosenberg, David and Bloom, Harold (1990) *The Book of J*, Faber and Faber, London

Rowse, A.L. (1950) *The England of Elizabeth*, Macmillan, London

Rule, J. and TePaske, J. (eds) (1963)*The Character of Philip II*, Boston

Schiller, J. (1785) *Don Carlos*, ed. H. B. Garland, Harrap, London, 1949

Sigmund, Paul E. (ed.) (1988) *St. Thomas Aquinas on Politics and Ethics*, Norton, New York

Spearing, A. C. (1976) *Medieval Dream Poetry*, Cambridge University Press, Cambridge

Tawney, R. H. (1937) *Religion and the Rise of Capitalism*, revised edn, republished Penguin, Harmondsworth, 1990

Thomas, Hugh (1988) *Madrid, A Traveller's Companion*, Constable, London

Thompson, C. P. (1988) *Strife of Tongues: Fray Luis and the Golden Age of Spain*, Cambridge University Press, Cambridge

Thompson, Thomas L. (1999) *The Bible in History*, Jonathan Cape, London

Trevelyan, Raleigh (1984) *Shades of the Alhambra*, Folio Society, London

Ungerer, Gustav (1974–6) *A Spaniard in Elizabethan England: the Correspondence of Antonio Peréz's Exile*, 2 vols, Tamesis, London

Vranich, S. B. (1976) *Psychoanalytic Review*, 63, no.1: 73–82

Weber, Eugen (1999) *Apocalypses*, Hutchinson, London

Zambrano, María, Simons, Edison and Miguel, Juan Blázquez (1987) *Sueños y procesos de Lucrecia de Léon*, Editorial Tecnos, Madrid

Index

Note: Numbers in italics indicate references in the dreams.